10/23/75

Map 1. Uganda

IDEOLOGY AND POLITICS IN UGANDA

From Obote to Amin

IDEOLOGY AND POLITICS IN UGANDA

≈≈≈≈≈ *From Obote to Amin*

JAMES H. MITTELMAN

Cornell University Press

ITHACA AND LONDON

First published 1975 by Cornell University Press.
Published in the United Kingdom by Cornell University Press Ltd., 2-4 Brook Street, London W1Y 1AA.

International Standard Book Number 0-8014-0946-2
Library of Congress Catalog Card Number 75-14712
Printed in the United States of America by York Composition Company.

In memory of

> *Ida F. Frankel and*
> *Alan W. Mittelman*

Contents

Maps

Tables

Preface

My interest in the role of ideology in politics originated when I was a graduate student in the African Studies Programme at Uganda's Makerere University College. Many of the ideas in this book were developed through conversation with the faculty and students at Makerere in 1967–1968. Two years later I returned to Uganda as an Associate of the Makerere Institute of Social Research and a staff member in the Department of Political Science and Public Administration. Profound changes in government policies had taken place in the interim that made this second visit opportune for a social scientist interested in ideologies of modernization.

Although the early years after independence were marked by restraint at the normative level, after 1969 the Obote regime increasingly relied on ideology as a major agent for initiating social change. The president published a series of documents, known as the Move to the Left, designed to inaugurate socialism in Uganda. But Obote's attempt to launch a modernizing ideology failed miserably and was ultimately superseded by the Amin-led coup of January 1971. These events give rise to the central question of this book: why did ideology fail in Uganda? The purpose is also to draw conclusions regarding theory-building and African politics.

A great deal has been written about the concept of ideology. The premise here is that values play an important role in social change. However, to argue the primacy of ideology would be grossly to exaggerate its impact. With ideology, there is an element of what Marx called "false consciousness." Ideology justifies. An ideology of modernization may guide the implementation of policy, but it also serves the interests of certain socioeconomic formations.

In order to study ideology in low income countries, it is essential to take account of dependency relations. When efforts to introduce new norms and to harmonize norms with changes in the political system are evaluated, the pervasive integration of world market forces and the economies of Third World countries must be kept in mind. The success or failure of a new ideology is often determined by external forces that not only penetrate the economies of these countries but may even have effective veto power over social change. Thus, my examination of a would-be modernizing ideology in Uganda directs attention to the social and economic concentrations linked to, or opposed to, normative values. Nevertheless, the major purpose of this work is not to analyze dependency relations between world market forces and Uganda. Nor is the foremost emphasis on class analysis. Though I firmly believe that prevalent distinctions between political and economic variables are misleading, I make no pretense of delving into all the issues of political economy and capitalist development. My focus on ideology is intended to complement those works that primarily stress dependency and class.

In writing about underdevelopment in Uganda, I have retained the conventional vocabulary: "developing nations," "less developed countries," the "Third World," "low income countries," and "non-Western areas." These familiar terms are used interchangeably to avoid tedious repetition of any single word or phrase. I recognize that such terms are euphemisms that neglect the rise of imperialism and the generation of dependent and subordinate economies by the development of capitalism. When they appear in this text, they will always mean underdeveloped societies; the fundamental reality is that advanced, capitalist societies have played a major role in producing underdevelopment in Africa, Asia, and Latin America. While the discussion often mentions classes and elites, these terms are not interchangeable. "Class" refers to the relationship of members of a group to the means of production, whereas "elite" denotes social status. The relationship between the two is that elites are appendages of a class or classes.

Tribalism and ethnicity are treated in the Introduction, and it should be noted that I follow the names and prefixes of social groups used most frequently by Ugandans themselves in local languages. Thus, "Baganda" refers to the major group occupying Buganda (Uganda's heartland area), "Muganda" to one person, and

"Luganda" to the language; "Ganda" and "kiganda" are adjectival forms used in describing the customs or habits of the Baganda.

A final point of clarification—I fully realize that writing on Uganda in early 1975 presents difficulties. The full effects of Amin's rule are not yet apparent, and a surfeit of rumors circulate. While visiting East Africa in late 1973 and early 1974, I was able to check some of these reports and to gather new data. Ugandans passing through New York and sources at the United Nations have also provided valuable information. However, this book does not attempt a journalistic account of recent events. Reports that cannot be verified are necessarily omitted.

I extend grateful appreciation to many colleagues, students, and organizations who aided my endeavors. The intellectual and financial resources of several institutions contributed greatly to my work. I acknowledge support from the Department of Political Science and Public Administration at Makerere University, Kampala, the Center for International Studies at Cornell University, the Council for Research in the Social Sciences at Columbia University, and the National Science Foundation. Permission for the use of my previously published works, which appear in slightly different form, was provided by *Africa Quarterly, Afro-American Studies,* the Munger Africana Monograph Series, and *Studies in Race and Nations* (University of Denver Center on International Race Relations Monograph Series). I have also drawn on material originally presented in papers delivered to the Universities of East Africa Social Science Conference (Dar es Salaam, 1973), the African Studies Association (Syracuse, 1973; Chicago, 1974), and the Conference on Civilian Control of the Military: Myth and Reality in Developing Countries (Buffalo, 1974). The frontispiece of this book is adapted from a map in Donald Stewart Ferguson, "An Economic Appraisal of Tick-borne Disease Control in Tropical Africa," an unpublished doctoral dissertation, Cornell University, 1971. The Makerere Institute of Social Research gave me permission to use map 3 from *Tribal Maps of East Africa and Zanzibar* (Kampala: East Africa Institute of Social Research, 1960) by J. E. Goldthorpe and F. B. Wilson; map 2 in this book is based on it. Table 5 entitled "Official status of the major languages spoken in Uganda" is reprinted here by permission of the International African Institute and Oxford University Press; it is from the chapter by Clive Criper and Peter Ladefoged, "Linguistic Complexity in Uganda," in W. H. Whiteley, ed., *Language Use and Social Change: Multilingualism with Special Reference to Eastern Africa* (London, 1971), p. 148.

My intellectual debts to students and colleagues are so numerous that I cannot acknowledge all of them individually. A number of colleagues in the Department of Political Science and the Institute of African Studies at Columbia University offered helpful suggestions. For assisting my research, I thank Barbara Korngold, Neville Choonoo, and Cyrus Veeser, whose services were indispensable. I am indebted to Michael Schultheis, who generously shared his materials and insights on recent events in Uganda, and to Godfrey Uzoigwe and Mark Kesselman for their perceptive criticism of individual chapters of this book. Sincere thanks go to Howard Wriggins and Ali Mazrui, who read and commented on the book in its entirety. I am deeply grateful to my good friend and former teacher, Kenneth W. Grundy, for correcting and improving my work; his efforts have provided a lesson in the true meaning of friendship. Above all, I express my appreciation to Linda Yarr for her intellectual independence and social priorities; she was of immeasurable help in writing this book. The influence of friends and colleagues has been so great that these acknowledgments do not do justice to their contributions. All errors of fact or interpretation that remain despite their efforts are entirely my own responsibility.

The point of departure for the analysis that follows is a value judgment. This book treats one aspect of the overriding need to transform the inequitable distribution of power and wealth in the world political economy. As an American writing about the Third World, I am increasingly aware that transformation in underdeveloped areas is inexorably tied to transformation in advanced, capitalist societies.

JAMES H. MITTELMAN

New York City

IDEOLOGY AND POLITICS IN UGANDA

From Obote to Amin

CHAPTER 1

Introduction

The fundamental dilemma of the Third World is dependency. A special case of domination and subordination, dependency's defining characteristic is vulnerability—the inability of a collectivity to determine its response to social forces within the world economic order. This inability limits the structure of political choice. For the subordinated, it restricts or prevents the intervention of a political will.

The major features of dependency include gross inequalities in income distribution, asymmetries in power distribution, and a discriminatory division of labor in the world political economy. These distinguishing features are symptoms of underlying and enduring historical trends. They reflect the impact of metropolitan centers (advanced, industrial nations) upon peripheral (Third World) economies and the replication and extension of this pattern within centers and peripheries. Hence development in the West and underdevelopment in non-Western areas are not distinct processes; nor are they separable historically. Rather, development and underdevelopment are intimately related. The integration of the economies of the industrial nations and the Third World generates underdevelopment.

Remedial measures to oppose external domination necessarily begin with internal policies. Viewed in the context of dependency relations, ideology represents a potentially vital agent for combating the hegemony of those who control foreign capital, together with their local equivalents, over the masses in Africa, Asia, and Latin America. New norms establish a sense of national purpose and engender sustained commitment to a political system. If introduced in conjunction with other measures, a modernizing ideology can be a valuable resource for restructuring a society and mobilizing a population behind developmental goals.

Of all Third World ideologues, Frantz Fanon, the West Indian psychiatrist, is the one usually associated with the call for revolutionary violence. Fanon's reputation rests upon his politico-clinical analysis of the grave injustice perpetrated by colonialism and of the inevitable will to liberation of the colonized. He did not, however, regard racial oppression and colonial domination as the greatest dangers facing Africa; there the greatest peril, according to Fanon, is "the absence of ideology."[1] Similarly, Kwame Nkrumah, perhaps the foremost proponent of African ideology, argued that, as a result of neocolonial balkanization and the absence of unity, African states experience a state of disequilibrium and that the root cause of the disequilibria accompanying social change in modern Africa is a lack of a "steadying ideology."[2]

According to a different view, the introduction of ideology invites political upheaval, and too much ideology hinders realism; it is symbolic, avoiding the hard, knotty problems of development. The most influential expression of the denial of ideology is provided by Félix Houphouët-Boigny. The Ivorian president has consistently shunned ideology and often insisted that the Ivory Coast does not need one. In 1966, for example, Houphouët remarked that Africa was not yet suffering from ideological struggles; yet, referring to the coup that overthrew Nkrumah, he also warned that ideology can cause major political disturbances. Five years later Houphouët further criticized Nkrumah's insistence on an ideological basis for the Convention Peoples Party in Ghana, saying that the former president failed because he saw classes in Africa where none existed.[3] Largely because of its leader's personality and his attempt to attract foreign investment capital, the Ivory Coast has not experienced the populism that marked the effort to introduce modernizing ideologies in Ghana, Guinea, and Mali.

1. Frantz Fanon, *Toward the African Revolution* (New York: Monthly Review Press, 1967), p. 186.
2. Kwame Nkrumah, "African Socialism Revisited," *African Forum,* I, No. 3 (Winter 1966), 7.
3. Félix Houphouët-Boigny, *Réalités Ivoiriennes* (Paris: Centre d'Information et de Documentation Ivoirienne, March 1966), quoted by Kenneth W. Grundy, "The Political Ideology of Kwame Nkrumah," in W. A. E. Skurnik, ed., *African Political Thought: Lumumba, Nkrumah, and Touré* (Denver: University of Denver Monograph Series in World Affairs, 1967–68), V, Nos. 3 and 4, 67; and "Appendix: Houphouet on the Wager," in Jon Woronoff, *West African Wager: Houphouet versus Nkrumah* (Metuchen, N.J.: Scarecrow Press, 1972), p. 328.

But Houphouët's view is not dominant. The dominant pattern is to utilize ideology as one agent to forge modernization. Many of Africa's senior statesmen, whether they accept Fanonist notions of the therapeutic value of revolutionary violence or the Nkrumahist plea for comprehensive pancontinentalism, grasp ideological cudgels in their attempts to build nations and to maintain themselves in power. In recent years the lexicon of African ideology—"négritude," "the African personality," "African socialism," and the "African revolution"—has dotted the pages of international journals and echoed through the chambers of international conferences. The vocabulary of contemporary political discourse is replete with slogans and shorthand terms derived from ideologically inspired experiments in nation-building, for example "consciencism" (Nkrumah), "cultural universalism" (Senghor), "ujamaa" (Nyerere), "Christian humanism" (Kaunda), and "communaucratique" (Touré). Africans and Africanists alike accept a code of communication that was either virtually unknown or had not gained widespread circulation when the onrush to independence began in the late 1950's.

In Uganda, as elsewhere in Africa, members of the governing elite consciously tried to use ideology as a modernizing agent. Following the ending of the British protectorate and the gaining of Commonwealth status in 1962, ideology was articulated in only the most general (and hence least divisive) terms. For leaders intent on forging national unity and stabilizing the political order, the first priority was to prevent fissiparous tendencies erupting in acts of political violence. From late 1962 until the middle of 1966, the pressures of latent parochialism and primordial sentiment were contained. Political violence did not develop into national disruption, and Uganda appeared to be well on the way to realizing national goals of development. In fact, after the first coup in Nigeria, Uganda, with its relative tolerance of dissent, pragmatic bargaining, and multiparty system based on institutionalized pluralism, could have been considered the foremost example of a liberal polity surviving in Africa.[4]

In mid-1966, however, Uganda's neofederal structure collapsed, violence swept the heartland, and Uganda followed the path of

4. G. F. Engholm and Ali A. Mazrui, "Violent Constitutionalism in Uganda," *Government and Opposition*, II, No. 4 (July–October 1967), 585.

many of Africa's other protoliberal polities. The 1966–1971 period
was marked by rapid social change: the traditional kingdoms were
abolished, a unitary government was established, and the president
announced a radical "Move to the Left." But in 1971 Uganda's
course changed at a critical juncture; the would-be socialist president was overthrown, and the army seized power. The Uganda
coup came to represent one of the most decisive issues in inter-
African diplomacy since the days of Kwame Nkrumah.

   In addition to its intrinsic significance, the 1962–1971 experience in Uganda is of special interest to scholars and practitioners
of ideology. Obote's Move to the Left was a calculated attempt to
use ideology as an agent of mobilization, and the military coup of
January 25, 1971, capped a notable failure to employ ideology as
a motivating force for socialist construction in the Third World.
In the effort to decipher the complex events that led to the Move
to the Left, the subsequent decline in the viability of the polity, the
atrophy of political institutions, and the bloodshed and loss of life
after the 1971 coup, the concept of ideology can be employed to
discern the enduring patterns of African politics. Identifying the
linkages between ideology and political violence has strong explanatory power that has heretofore been neglected. The analysis
of modernizing ideology highlights the structure of social cleavage
and points out the limitations under which leaders operate. It also
suggests some major principles that are used—successfully and
unsuccessfully—in determining strategy and tactics for the generation and management of power.

   My premise is that political ideas play a major role in political
action. All too frequently, values and actions are dichotomized or
polarized in social analysis, which obfuscates the impact of values
on behavior.[5] For the most part, the scholarly literature on the
concept of ideology does not include a developmental perspective.
Insofar as this dimension is recognized, the context tends to be
that of the history of Western political systems, that is, those
systems which experienced gradual adjustment and adaptation in
changing relations to the means of production. A developmental
view of the non-Western experience indicates conditions under

---

5. Douglas Ashford, *Ideology and Participation* (Beverly Hills: Sage Publications, 1972), pp. 20, 21, 25, 31, 263–64.

which ideological innovation and diffusion can be dysfunctional and strain (rather than support) new political systems. Accordingly, the developmental perspective has further potential for exploring the realm of political engineering. Unfortunately, political scientists disdain considerations of tactics and strategy, relegating these "mundane" matters to the "policy scientists." Only recently has there been a renaissance of the neglected subject of policy analysis within the discipline of political science.

At a higher level of abstraction, many of the conventional generalizations used to explain issues of social change in Africa are inadequate for my purposes. I do not advance a general theory of development but suggest a mode of analysis in which ideology is viewed as a potentially active agent of social change. This approach rejects the extremities of thought on the concept of ideology, namely, that ideology is pure deception and that ideology is the sole determinant of political behavior. My contention is that there tends to be close correspondence between ideas and socioeconomic interests but that these interests reflect a variety of other factors. Correctly viewed, ideology is neither mere camouflage for economic-class interests nor an unambiguous guide to political behavior. One cannot assume that ideological pronouncements have relevance beyond the rhetorical statements of leaders. But ideology can be a primary tool in the attempt to realize a society's developmental goals.

A study of Uganda's ideology demonstrates the importance of certain considerations that are either largely neglected or treated as areas of only marginal concern to political scientists and suggests that one must not be misled by theory derived exclusively from Western political systems. More specifically, my analysis tries to answer these questions:

1. What does a discussion of ideology in Africa add to the political scientist's knowledge of the concept of ideology in general?

2. What concepts can be developed or refined by reference to ideology in Africa?

3. What impact, if any, does the introduction of an ideology of modernization have on the alignment of social cleavages?

4. What is the relationship between ideology and political violence?

5. Given the Ugandan experience, what propositions can be advanced with regard to instability, coups, and violence in Africa?

As the last question indicates, an examination of ideology necessarily deals with variables other than ideological factors. Analysis of ideology in Uganda requires examination of socialist construction and military intervention in domestic politics. And if these issues are to be taken into account, the inquiry must be extended to some of the reasons for the volatility of African politics. This book, then, tries to explore some of the important variables in one attempt to introduce a modernizing ideology.

For the scholar, analytical issues precede the substantive; I turn first, therefore, to methodological and theoretical considerations. Two of the standard methods of collecting data on ideology are classified as individual-oriented and distributive-oriented. Individual-oriented studies generally employ open-ended questionnaires, general attitudinal and structural tests, and in-depth interviews. One of the most successful is Robert Lane's work on political ideology in the United States.[6] By using extended conversational interviews, Lane provides contextual analysis to place ideological tenets in the framework of general beliefs, opinions, and attitudes. Of fundamental importance is Lane's distinction between the "forensic" ideology of the conscious ideologue and the "latent" ideology of the average citizen. This distinction is valuable in providing a demarcation between elite and mass behavior, and also between conscious ideological intention and residual categories of subjective disposition.[7] The difficulty in working with latent ideology is that it is almost impossible to distinguish between mere values and opinions (which may be salient, intensive, and/or rational) and consciously adopted belief systems. This otherwise valuable approach is limited by its lack of insight into the relationship between attitude, value, opinion, and belief system on the one hand and ideologically inspired behavior on the other.[8]

6. Robert Lane, *Political Ideology: Why the American Common Man Believes What He Does* (New York: The Free Press, 1962).
7. Robert K. Merton, *Social Theory and Social Structure* (New York: The Free Press, 1968), pp. 114–36.
8. Samuel Barnes, "Ideology and the Organization of Conflict: On the Relationship between Political Thought and Behavior" (paper presented to

Distributive-oriented studies focus on ideological documents and pronouncements (for example, constitutions), art forms, and cultural symbols. Methods of measurement include content analysis, large group interviews, and survey research. The main difficulty with this approach is statistical, that is, the sampling problem and procedures for verifying inferences. What population of documents is most representative? Which individuals and subgroups provide accurate indicators of ideology? Should equal weight be given to all informants? Which media and which art forms are reliable as validators?[9]

So far as African political systems are concerned, the choice between these two methods must be influenced by the role of political elites. In Africa politics is highly personalized. The head of state and a governing elite, often in league with foreign interests, control national resources. Normally elites are the initiators, perpetrators, and implementors of ideology. If ideology as formulated by the elites is to make an impact, it must be embraced by the masses. Yet as ideas become further removed from their source, information is lost and the range of political belief narrows.[10] The common man views the world largely in terms of his own lifetime and his immediate surroundings. Empathy and associative sentiment extending beyond traditional solidarity are generally lacking. All too frequently, however, the distinction between tradition and modernity is overdrawn. In fact, tradition and modernity, parochialism and univeralism coexist. Modernization unleashes disruptive

---

the annual meeting of the American Political Science Association, Washington, D.C., 1965), p. 4.

9. Some of the problems of measurement are discussed by William Scott, "Empirical Assessment of Values and Ideologies," *American Sociological Review*, XXIV, No. 3 (June 1959), 300.

10. Philip Converse, "The Nature of Belief Systems in Mass Publics," in David E. Apter, ed., *Ideology and Discontent* (New York: The Free Press, 1964), pp. 211–13. Giovanni Sartori, "Politics, Ideology, and Belief Systems," *American Political Science Review*, LXIII, No. 2 (June 1969), 407, argues that mass belief publics are the dependent variables of elite public belief systems. Aristide R. Zolberg, *Creating Political Order: The Party States of West Africa* (Chicago: Rand McNally, 1966), p. 60, advocates elite-oriented ideological studies on the basis of the consistency of official pronouncements over time and the degree to which leaders from different African countries, often at odds on specific issues, reinforce each other ideologically.

forces of change, but it does not follow that the masses face dislocations and disorientation that cause insurmountable problems. The great majority of the population in a low income country interacts with the overlapping worlds of tradition and modernity. Stress and ambiguity do not necessarily reach intolerable proportions.

But the masses are more aware of local than national political issues, for their political consciousness at the national level may be only rudimentary. Consequently, in studying ideology in Africa, I emphasize the role of the political elite. The common man provides the target for the propagation of an ideology, but the elites represent its source and present concentration. In the absence of widespread political consciousness, public opinion does not select ideology but approves or disapproves what the elites put forward.[11] The term "public opinion" must be used with care. The communications gap in Africa is a major impediment in the elites' attempt to diffuse ideology. Yet, insofar as the means of communication are developed, they are controlled by the political elite and may be used for ideological diffusion.

Consequently, this inquiry focuses on the creative sources of ideology, the hands and mouths of government leaders and the elites who compete for power. This approach, however, does not ignore the role of the masses. When a modernizing ideology is introduced, the nascent proletariat and the peasantry embrace or reject the leaders' attempt to induce political consciousness and thereby determine the ideology's success or failure. Ultimately, a successful ideology must build upon mass support. But the first step in the analysis of ideology is to observe and evaluate elite political behavior and its impact on social structure. The subsequent task is to gauge the behavior of the common man, whether living in the countryside or in squalid urban shantytowns. Of course, it cannot be assumed that the elites in a low income country will attempt to stimulate political consciousness. On the contrary, a privileged elite with deeply entrenched interests may prefer perpetuation of the status quo. But to suppose that leaders in a

11. K. A. B. Jones-Quartey, "Institutions of Public Opinion in a Rapidly Changing West Africa," in H. Passin and K. A. B. Jones-Quartey, eds., *Africa: The Dynamics of Change* (Ibadan: Ibadan University Press, 1963), p. 165.

developing country necessarily constitute a predatory national bourgeoisie would be an error. In certain low income countries, for example, Tanzania, some leaders seem to be well aware of the dangers of embourgeoisement and to be making a concerted effort to remedy the injustices of excessive elitism.

In focusing on national leadership and competing elites, I do not intend to imply that ideological sampling of the Lane variety is without benefit in Africa. Testing for latent ideology, particularly over time, offers valuable insights into the rate and intensity of ideological change. A research design at the most systematic and ambitious level would include both individual-oriented and distributive-oriented analysis in which various strata among the masses, transitional types, and national elites would be tested.

I was unable to fulfill many of my objectives for systematic empirical inquiry in Uganda because of uncertain political conditions in the latter half of the Obote period and after the coup. My original research design, which was to have produced tabular data by empirical measures at several levels, had to be abandoned, but after a period of soul-searching I decided to continue with the project nevertheless. Although I could not get permission from the National Research Council to conduct formal interviews or to do survey work,[12] in over two years in Uganda I was able to gather sufficient data to go well beyond historical narrative or impressionistic interpretation. In addition to secondary material, this book

12. I do not question the prerogative of independent states in Africa to grant or refuse permission for research according to their interpretation of the priorities of national development. Researchers working abroad have an obligation to respect the wishes of the host country. At the same time, however, they have a responsibility to the academic community to maintain a position of intellectual integrity. All too often researchers working in developing countries meet intitial resistance to their proposals, find it easy to secure permission to investigate topics of related but marginal relevance to their genuine interest, and are willing to compromise or even forego their scholarly objectives. The result is an unfortunate tendency among scholars to resort to securing permission for what amounts to research on trivial topics merely to complete theses, fulfill grant obligations, and further publication records. While respecting the host country, the researcher must continue to ask penetrating questions that excite the political imagination. Only then can new intellectual frontiers be realized and explored. Similar thoughts are expressed by a researcher working in another African country, Gary Wasserman, "The Research of Politics; the Politics of Research," *East Africa Journal*, VII, No. 11 (November 1970), 12–14.

draws on a wide range of primary sources—documents, legislation, newspapers of record, and conversations with ministers and civil servants. It relies on observations made in Uganda before, during, and after the period when the most concerted efforts were made to introduce an ideology of modernization; on debates and discussions at Makerere (Uganda's center of learning and only university); on conversations with researchers who succeeded in securing permission to pursue topics relevant to my area of inquiry; and on a number of informal, unstructured interviews. Material gathered from informants in Uganda is incorporated into the text but, for obvious reasons, often without attribution.

There is an appalling lack of information about Uganda's political system. The literature is scanty and episodic; indeed, except for anthropological studies, most of them conducted during the colonial period, Uganda is an underwritten country. Researchers are making a concerted attempt to reconstruct Uganda's history by recovering oral tradition. Historians working in the lacustrine region of East Africa have benefited from a number of well-written traditional histories recorded in vernacular languages: Apolo Kaggwa's *Basekabaka be Buganda*, J. W. Nyakatura's *Abakama*, A. G. Katate and L. Kamugungunu's *Abagabe b'Ankole, Ekitabo I and II*, Sir Tito Winyi's "Abakama ba Bunyoro-Kitara," and P. Bikunya's *Ky'Abakama ba Bunyoro*.[13] Sociologists and political scientists have been latecomers to Uganda. Most of the literature in political science is of the descriptive-historical variety. To date, neither a comprehensive study of national politics since independence nor a scholarly book treating the post-1966 period in a systematic fashion has been published.[14]

13. See the "Introduction" by Godfrey N. Uzoigwe in J. W. Nyakatura, *Anatomy of An African Kingdom: A History of Bunyoro-Kitara*, trans. Teopista Muganwa, ed. Uzoigwe (New York: Doubleday, 1973).

14. The only book yet to attempt a scholarly assessment of the postindependence period is Peter M. Gukiina, *Uganda: A Case Study in African Political Development* (South Bend: University of Notre Dame Press, 1972). This effort is flawed by numerous errors and major emissions, as discussed by Godfrey N. Uzoigwe, "Political Development in Uganda," *The Conch Review of Books*, I, No. 2 (June 1973), 34–43, and in my review article, "The Roots of Ethnic Conflict," *Journal of International Affairs*, XXVII, No. 1 (Spring 1973), 133–37. Two recent books, Grace S. K. Ibingira, *The Forging of an African Nation: The Political and Constitutional Evolution of Uganda from Colonial Rule to Independence, 1894–1962* (New

The pattern of political development in Uganda is representative of much social and political change in Africa. In many ways, Uganda's problems are Africa's: the colonial legacy and the search for dignity; class differentiation and the formation of new lines of social stratification; ethnic fragmentation and the quest for national unity; the modification of traditional behavior and the attempt to integrate the masses into a representative political system; parochial loyalties and the need to create viable institutional norms at the national level. And in many respects Uganda's coup of January 25, 1971, symbolizes the successes and failures of Africa at large.

The case study approach followed here offers the advantage of intensive, in-depth analysis. A case study provides neither the basis for valid generalization nor sufficient grounds for invalidating established maxims. It may contribute to comparative analysis, however, by uncovering relevant variables, suggesting new hypotheses and relationships, and providing evidence that is inconsistent with existing propositions. In the social sciences theory-building proceeds in the context of case studies.[15]

Authors of case studies frequently confess to prejudice either on behalf of their data or in favor of larger theoretical issues. Such apologia are not required here. My point of departure is that the Uganda case has intrinsic significance and that the data have a potentially important role to play in theory-building. With the appearance of yet another new government in Africa focusing attention on contemporary issues, the lessons to be drawn from the recent past must not be allowed to slide into oblivion. I recognize, too, that I have certain biases regarding social forces in Uganda; accordingly, value-free analysis is rejected as an aim of this book. Other scholars who seek objectivity and shun commitment do, in fact, adhere to values that tend to be centrist (for example, stability); but they regard the work of authors with noncentrist views as value-laden. Instead of avoiding value judgments, I consciously

---

York: Viking Press, 1972), and Tarsis B. Kabwegyere, *The Politics of State Formation: The Nature and Effects of Colonialism in Uganda* (Nairobi: East African Literature Bureau, 1974), deal primarily with the preindependence period. Forthcoming is Ali A. Mazrui, *Soldiers and Kinsmen in Uganda: The Making of a Military Ethnocracy* (Beverly Hills: Sage Publications, 1975).

15. Arend Lipjhart, "Comparative Politics and the Comparative Method," *American Political Science Review,* LX, No. 3 (September 1971), 691–93.

advance proposals and prescriptions, on the grounds that it is better for the analyst's values to be explicit than implicit. Insofar as the social scientist gains particular insights from a scholarly discipline, practical suggestions should be one product of his research.

This book does not purport to offer a comprehensive treatment of the Ugandan political system. The intention is, rather, to analyze certain variables and to investigate the relationships among these variables in the Ugandan context. In selecting and correlating variables, the analyst necessarily omits those that he regards as less important or of marginal relevance; in so doing he is "theorizing by omission."[16] Given the vast number of variables involved in social and political analysis, theorizing by omission is unavoidable and should not be regarded as an impediment to scholarly progress (providing, of course, that variables are chosen wisely). By selecting certain variables for analysis, I hope to stimulate scholarly interchange and debate leading to more specific studies. In Uganda dimensions of politics that have been insufficiently studied—class formation, labor unions, legislative behavior, the judicial process, rural development, and foreign policy—are in particular need of exploration.

As the discussion in Chapter 2 indicates, to utilize political science's macro categories of analysis in an empirical investigation is to encounter considerable problems. Therefore, I eschew this cul-de-sac and opt for theoretical parsimony. To attempt to hypothesize about controlled relationships among key variables is better than to run the risk of being overwhelmed by a superabundance of variables.[17]

One element over which the analyst can easily, if not arbitrarily, exercise control is time; this book examines the period from 1962 to 1974, the years from independence to the events following the Amin-led coup. For this inquiry, the major methodological problem lies in operationalizing variables as discrete units of analysis. The scholar may desire neatly segmented variables; however, the complexity of the social and political phenomena to be examined prevents easy categorization. In analyzing ideology, one is dealing

16. William F. Hanreider, *Comparative Foreign Policy: Theoretical Essays* (New York: David McKay, 1971), pp. 10, 11.
17. This point is supported by the discussion in Lipjhart, p. 690.

with propensities. As the discussion in the next chapter suggests, ideology may be seen as a propensity to act in a certain way. While there is a distinction between ideologically inspired and nonideologically inspired behavior, to identify with absolute certainty the cases in which ideology is a major causal element is impossible. Whether a propensity leads to specific manifestations of behavior depends on a variety of factors, among them, structural conditions (particularly socioeconomic interests) that inhibit or facilitate the realization of values and beliefs, the historical events that shape interests, and the intensity with which values and beliefs are held. Recognition of the methodological problems can be a deterrent for analysis, however, and it would be unfortunate if methodological constraints were permitted to dictate legitimate areas of scholarly concern. The alternatives appear to be submissive acceptance of the bifurcation of ideas and action or candid recognition of the methodological limitations with which the analyst views the mix of values and beliefs that influences behavior.

If the role of ideology is to be analyzed, the first step must be to determine whether the appropriate level for discussion is individual beliefs, institutional norms, or cultural values.[18] The extent to which acceptable relations are devised in new societies depends on the psychological dimensions attached to new roles, the principles used to forge working rules for increasingly complex patterns of behavior, and the way in which traditional ritual and myth are employed to communicate new values and modes of behavior. It is doubtful whether there is, or ever has been, a society in which values are perfectly integrated at all three levels. In societies striving to modernize rapidly, leaders attempt to manipulate values for social and political ends. And harsh incongruities are felt among individual beliefs, institutional norms, and cultural values.

To achieve political change by altering values at the individual level may be the most arduous and ambitious option open to low income countries, while the difficulty of using imagery, myth, and legend to structure large-scale activity directed at promoting rapid social and economic change argues against trying to amend values through cultural manipulation. Leaders in developing countries turn

18. The following remarks on level of analysis draw heavily on Adam Przeworski and Henry Teune, *The Logic of Comparative Social Inquiry* (New York: John Wiley, 1970), and Ashford.

most frequently, therefore, to political institutions as the easiest and most visible means for introducing a modernizing ideology.[19]

In Uganda, the evidence suggests that Obote's concern for ideology was directed at the level of institutional norms; accordingly, this will be the level of analysis here. For reasons that will be explored in detail, the options at the levels of individual beliefs and cultural values were largely closed to Obote. Lacking personal appeal and facing resilient cultures in which the traditional authorities resisted influence from the center, Obote directed his efforts at the only level readily available, though at this level he did not choose the most effective means.

As elsewhere in Africa, traditional cultures in Uganda are based on divisions and aggregations of tribes. Since in recent years the term tribalism has come into disfavor, my use of it should be clarified. For the analyst, tribalism is a social category with a variety of meanings. The adjective "tribal" is used variously to mean rural, traditional, conservative, or primitive. The assumption is that being modern precludes being tribal. There are several fallacies in this argument. Particularistic impulses at the local level and the attempt to forge national solidarities are not necessarily contradictory. They may be mutually exclusive; but they may be complementary. As African peasants migrate from rural areas to the towns, for example, tribal associations perform vital social services, offering food and housing, providing funerals, and financing marriages—services that frequently are not performed (or are performed inadequately) by governments in societies in which the extended family bears the burden of social responsibility. In cases where the government does provide for its destitute and homeless, the care is largely material (housing, allowances, and so on). Spiritual care—that is, offering a means of identification and generating a feeling of solidarity— is a more difficult commodity to supply. In this psychosociological sense, tribal associations may be assisting in some of the most arduous tasks of modern nation-building.

"Tribalism" is not necessarily equivalent to subnationalism. The validity or invalidity of that equation turns on the definition of a

19. See Ashford. Also Lloyd Fallers, "Equality, Modernity, and Democracy in the New States," in Clifford Geertz, ed., *Old Societies and New States: The Quest for Modernity in Asia and Africa* (New York: The Free Press, 1963), p. 194.

nation. If a nation is defined simply as a group of people with a common history, language, and culture, then it is correct to speak of Ibo or Ganda nationalism. In these terms, the Ibo and Ganda nations had long histories and vigorous languages and cultures, before the European balkanization of Africa. Apparently only after Ibo and Ganda nationalism was superseded by the Nigerian and Ugandan nations did the former become stigmatized as tribalism.

With the advent of colonial rule, the European administrators faced a knotty problem in attempting to extend control over numerous indigenous forms of government. In some parts of Uganda, tribal identity was virtually unknown before the European intrusion. The Bakiga of southwestern Uganda, for example, valued individualism and did not identify themselves as a common group in the precolonial period. Nor were the Basoga a single political unit. And many chieftancies that exist today, for example, amongst the Lugbara, were the products of European administration. The British found it convenient to divide colonial peoples into administrative units, and social services, rewards, and benefits were provided through these units. In this respect, colonial rule provided the incentive for tribal identity; thus, in part, tribal identity is a colonially induced phenomenon.

Concentration on tribalism as the explanation for contemporary Africa's societal problems all too often dulls observers' awareness of other, more deeply rooted sources of conflict. Cleavages along class, economic, linguistic, or religious lines may create more severe divisions within a society than tribalism does. Most typically, cleavages align in such a way that they fuse and even become reinforcing. To identify the causes of social strife is difficult, and at times the analyst sidesteps by speaking of manifestations of tribal behavior. The point to be emphasized, however, is that tribalism may be the veneer covering more deeply rooted problems.

Finally, the question must be asked, to what degree is tribalism African? Why do many commentators, and particularly the Western press, refer to Basque, Quebec, or Welsh nationalism but Ashanti, Ganda, or Ibo tribalism? The usage is widespread and clearly constitutes a double standard. Despite the differences between the politics of an industrial system, say the United States, and those of the preindustrial or industralizing societies of Africa, it would surely not be unfair to suggest that an understanding of the politics of the former turns in good part on the tribal factor. Anyone familiar with American elections is accustomed to hearing such questions as: Can candidate X carry the Irish vote? The Jewish vote? The black vote? And the political systems of Canada, Britain, and Belgium, to mention only a few, are similarly replete with tribal problems. It is in this sense that I employ the term tribalism, that is, to refer to (*1*) mythical or semimythical beliefs in common ancestry and (*2*) pandemic parochial loyalties.

In the text that follows, Chapter 2 investigates the concept of ideology. Chapters 3 and 4 review the period from independence to the initiation of the Move to the Left, and Chapters 5 and 6 analyze the documentary innovations that were intended to effect a socialist transformation. Chapter 7 explores military intervention in domestic politics, Chapter 8 the international and transnational dimensions of the coup d'état. Chapter 9 deals with the consequences of military rule, in particular the shifting emphasis to black nationalism under General Amin. In the concluding chapter, an explanation for the failure of ideology in Uganda and an assessment of the data with regard to theory-building are advanced.

CHAPTER 2

Ideology and Politics

This book seeks to assess the failure of ideology in a deeply divided country, to explain why the ruling elite was unable to turn ideas into action and mobilize the masses. The importance of ideology can be exaggerated, but the concept is of interest and deserves study.

Ideology is a major variable for analysis because it deals with the "why" question in politics. Social scientists are interested in ideology because if a community is to be cohesive its members' values must be compatible. Perhaps the best-known argument concerning the vital role of values in social change is Max Weber's contention that the explanations for economic facts are to be found in societal value systems, particularly in their religious aspects. The Weberian thesis is that Protestant values were the primary cause of industrialization.[1]

Insofar as he can distinguish between ideologically inspired and nonideologically inspired behavior, the analyst gains critical insight into social and political change. Ideological and nonideological political behavior may have the same, or at least similar, expression. An individual can act politically for ideological or nonideological reasons. Voter A may go to the polls and be influenced in casting his ballot by ideological conviction, voting, for example, for candidate X because X has promised to implement socialism. Voter B may also cast his ballot for candidate X, but because of parochial sentiment based on ethnic solidarity. Although the formal act is the same, there is an important latent distinction in behavior.

1. Max Weber, *The Protestant Ethic and the Spirit of Capitalism* (London: Allen and Unwin, 1948), pp. 181–82, also points out that values do not have the same enduring significance in industrial societies. Economic rationality itself also sustains economic and social change. Cf. R. H. Tawney, *Religion and the Rise of Capitalism* (New York: New American Library, 1958).

Ideologically inspired behavior is coherent. The political actor whose behavior is based on ideological conviction can explain his actions in terms of a cognitive scheme that makes his world intelligible. The political actor whose behavior is nonideologically inspired lacks this understanding. His behavior is liable to be based on provincialism and particularisms that may be intermittent or nondirected at the national level.

The degree to which political behavior is ideologically or nonideologically inspired has major implications for the viability of a political system. When political behavior is intermittent and nondirected, there tends to be little or no sustained commitment to the system. When the political authorities are unsuccessful, or achieve only localized success, in establishing an exchange process whereby they distribute rewards and derive commitment and support, their ability to induce the behavior required for the realization of national development goals is seriously impaired. Furthermore, there is little predictability in the course of a political system characterized by intermittent participation, low commitment, and shallow support.

The discussion thus far has considered ideology as a major variable of analysis applicable to all political systems. I contend that it offers particular advantages for the study of low income countries undergoing rapid, even drastic change. To substantiate this contention requires a brief examination of the literature on development and modernization and then a more focused discussion of the rationale for using the concept of ideology to study African political systems.

Ideology and Development

Leaving problems of definition aside,[2] at least three major criticisms of models of political development can be advanced.

2. In the "mainstream" literature, development tends to be equated with the maximization of a set of characteristics that are supposed to aid the realization of societal goals. For example, Lucian W. Pye, "The Concept of Political Development," *Annals of the American Academy of Political and Social Science*, CCCLVIII (March 1965), 5–11, presents ten elements in the "political development syndrome." Similarly, Samuel P. Huntington, "Political Development and Political Decay," *World Politics*, XXVII, No. 3 (April 1965), 387–88, itemizes four criteria of development, and Leonard Binder, "National Integration and Political Development," *American Political Science Review*, LVIII, No. 3 (September 1964), 622, lists seven "features."

First, the prescriptive and teleological biases of the analyst can be a pitfall. Many of the models reflect the ethnocentric notions of academicians, in that they assume modernity to be a singular set of conditions corresponding to those of Western societies. But development and modernization are not fixed stages. Rather, they should be viewed as fluid processes whereby societies attempt to set goals and control and adjust to severe or abrupt transitions. The problem of the analyst's biases is further complicated by shortcomings in methodologies. It is difficult to study development and modernization since many of the constructs have little utility. How, for example, are "structural specificity" or "functional differentiation" to be measured? Such constructs may be helpful as part of the theoretician's conceptual apparatus or as a pedagogical device, but they do not contribute significantly to understanding concrete situations.

Second, within the discipline of political science, study of development is placed under the rubric of comparative politics, and external determinants of domestic change are often neglected. Highly susceptible to imposed power relationships, low income countries frequently find that external factors determine internal changes. The links between internal and external affairs must be grasped if development and modernization are to be understood. Insofar as national development occurs within a world system, the political scientist's distinction between comparative politics and international relations is misleading. The conventional compartmentalization of political phenomena into subdisciplines is, as Western scholars are only beginning to realize, an anachronism.

Third, partly as a result of this compartmentalization, many theoreticians implicitly assume that the less developed countries are autonomous and really can determine their own fates. Social scientists, at least in the dominant Western tradition, have been remiss in not exploring more fully the constraints imposed by world market forces and transnational entities. Within the changing world political economy, concentrations of power and wealth often defy the juridical state. The strong and the rich are not necessarily inhibited by state sanctions. The state, especially in low income areas, is highly permeable, and social structures transcend national frontiers. Class and racial coalitions do not limit themselves to legally defined borders but operate transnationally.

In view of the limitations of development theory, the political
scientist can only advance analysis with agnostic humility. Political
scientists know very little about political development and have
made only minor contributions to understanding the larger process
of social modernization. In the present state of the discipline, to
take an entire political system as the unit of analysis is indeed
difficult. Rather than doing so, political scientists should, at this
stage, work with smaller, more manageable portions of the multi-
dimensional phenomena of modernization. Ideology is one such
portion, and to use it as a major variable for analysis offers certain
advantages. Most important, in highly fragmented societies with
severe structural inflexibilities, the introduction of an ideology of
modernization is frequently regarded as an efficient means of
motivating the masses to achieve developmental goals. As one
scholar expresses this point: "Inasmuch as ideology conceptualizes
the historical process and orients human beings for shaping it,
ideology is itself an active agent for social change."[3] To the extent
that this concept has explanatory power, however, one must avoid
reification. To mistake ideological pronouncements for values in
action is to confuse appearance with reality. Further, to attribute
undue influence or power to ideology is an error. The analyst
must select the most appropriate variable in the light of the sociopolitical conditions to be investigated and the questions to be
answered. Accordingly, the capabilities and limitations of analysis
of ideology must be evaluated in terms of the circumstances to
be studied.

In Africa, leaders strive to forge unity and to promote development as well as to pursue their own interests. As societies grow
increasingly complex, specialized institutions emerge that allow for
greater diversity in the way values relate to society. At lower levels
of development, when traditional values prevent or at least inhibit
rapid institutional change, contradictions and inconsistencies among
norms are unlikely. In societies where leaders are committed to
achieving developmental goals as quickly as possible, however,
various individuals and groups find the institutional norms inadequate. Then, if leadership is to be effective, ideological clarity must

3. Williard A. Mullins, "On the Concept of Ideology in Political Science,"
American Political Science Review, LXVI, No. 2 (June 1972), 504.

be a high priority.[4] If not, social change may be unintelligible to the common man, developmental goals lack sufficient definition, and political drift result.

A variety of social and political problems, as well as the natural impediments to nation-building in Africa,[5] make it likely that African politics will long be characterized by ideological activity representing, in good part, a response to pressing problems that defy quick solutions. Ideological innovation and diffusion is likely to assume increasing importance in the future for two reasons. Because of pervasive poverty, underdevelopment, colonialism, and white exploitation, leaders are unable to provide for the fundamental needs of their people at the pace demanded. At the same time, African elites all too frequently regard the people's needs as secondary to the achievement of personal power or the accumulation of wealth.[6]

The time is appropriate for an analysis of ideology in Africa. As state formations begin to crystallize and political consciousness is forged, an opportunity exists to gain insight into the fundamental questions that have perplexed students of ideology: Where does ideology originate? How is it formulated? How is it diffused? How does it function in a political system? There is, too, a pressing need for systematic analysis of the neglected lacuna of African ideology.[7] Few works deal with the subject in a rigorous manner, most tending to be descriptive and historical. Little empirical research has

4. Ashford, pp. 125–27, 176, 208–209.
5. Including dependency relations, agrarian backwardness that inhibits economic progress, inadequate markets and buying power, the tsetse fly, large expanses of desert, drought areas, low rainfall in some regions and excessive amounts in others. Many of these factors are discussed by René Dumont, *False Start in Africa*, trans. Phyllis Nauts Ott (Worchester: Ebenezer Bayles, 1966), pp. 29–32.
6. See *ibid.*, pp. 78, 80–85, 241, 252, 285. The principal "industry" in some West African states is administration. Personnel expenses of the leaders of Dahomey absorb 60 percent of the country's internal income. In relation to national income, the Gabonese government costs more to run than the court of Louis XVI did. In French West Africa a deputy can earn as much in one and a half months as the average peasant can in a lifetime (36 years).
7. Ali A. Mazrui, *On Heroes and Uhuru-Worship: Essays on Independent Africa* (London: Longmans, Green, 1967), p. 3, contends that to study comparative ideology makes as much sense as to study comparative government; the former is a much neglected field of inquiry.

been done on ideology in Africa, and the lack of ordering concepts is a pervasive problem.[8] Some earlier studies of Africa suggest the dangers and "blindfold effects" of ideology;[9] others suggest that there is no ideology.[10] But none specify their criteria of ideology. Is the standard a highly systematized ideology with neatly integrated assumptions and premises? Must the level of diffusion be such that the masses embrace the ideology before the ideology can be said to exist? Or is the assumption that a gelling process has yet to occur in which ideological themes congeal? Social scientists have made a valuable contribution toward understanding the substance of political beliefs, but the concept of ideology needs further refinement to be useful as an analytical tool for the study of African political systems.

What Is Ideology?

The concept of ideology is elusive, ambiguous, even chameleonic. Political scientists use and misuse the concept in a variety of ways; it is difficult to deal with in social analysis because it has been assigned so many different meanings. At least five types of definition have been advanced, which can be designated all-inclusive, configurative, functional and compositional, distortive and pejorative, and transformative. While no attempt will be made here to trace the intellectual history of the concept, an examination of the range of definitions will give some sense of the divergent theories of ideology.

The all-inclusive type of definition tends to shelter almost everything conceptual under the umbrella of ideology. Quincy Wright,

8. See the review article by Kenneth W. Grundy, "Recent Contributions to the Study of African Political Thought," *World Politics*, XVIII, No. 4 (July 1966), 674–89.

9. For example, Elliott J. Berg, "Socialism and Economic Development in Tropical Africa," *Quarterly Journal of Economics*, LXXVIII, No. 4 (November 1964), 549–73.

10. For example, David E. Apter, *The Political Kingdom in Uganda: A Study in Bureaucratic Nationalism* (Princeton: Princeton University Press, 1961), p. 6, argues: "There has been no time to develop an ideology much less a religion, since so far both have been unnecessary." With regard to political parties, Apter suggests (p. 307) that "they need both a cause and an ideology. Both are singularly lacking in Uganda." Discussing Pan-Africanism in 1966, Immanuel Wallerstein, "African Unity Reassessed," *Africa Report*, XI, No. 4 (April 1966), 44, states that Africa is characterized by the absence of a coherent ideology.

for example, uses ideology "in a very broad sense to cover all systems of ideas extending, on the one hand, to Euclid's geometry and Newton's Principia, on the other, to such complex patterns as 'nationalities' and 'culture.' "[11] Employed in this manner, ideology is too comprehensive and has little utility for distinguishing among aspects of political behavior. Since it fails to further empirical investigation, this broad type of definition has little analytic value.

In the second type, ideology is defined purely in terms of ideational configuration. Samuel Barnes uses "ideology" interchangeably with "belief system"—as "an open term referring to the set of political attitudes held by an individual, whether they exhibit strength or not."[12] According to Barnes' definition of ideology, political attitudes must be internally consistent and consciously articulated. Pierre Bonnafé and Michel Carty also employ an ideational-configurative definition: "A political ideology is a cluster of ideas, representations, and beliefs common to a specific social group but relative to the present and future structure and organization of the global society to which the group belongs."[13] The main problem with this type of definition is that, in order to assume analytic value and empirical relevance, ideology must be distinguished from such related concepts as belief system, idea, attitude, value, and theory. Furthermore, the premises of an ideology need not be consistent with one another. Ideology may come far closer to approaching reality if it is internally inconsistent, for ambivalence and discord are characteristic of humanity; men make assumptions, some of which are bound to be contradictory. Neat agreement of premises may be desired by the scholar, but such consistency is not necessarily characteristic of ideology as embraced by the masses or even by politicians.

In the third type of definition, ideology is seen in terms of function and functional components. According to David Easton, ideology consists of ethical interpretations and principles that set forth the purposes, organization, and boundaries of political life:

11. Quoted by Karl Lowenstein, "The Role of Ideologies in Political Change," *International Social Science Bulletin*, V, No. 1 (1953), 52.
12. Barnes, p. 2.
13. Pierre Bonnafé and Michel Carty, "Les idéologies politiques des pays en voie de développement," *Revue française de science politique*, XII, No. 2 (June 1962), 417.

"We may . . . interpret them [ideologies] as variable responses through which efforts are made to bring the members of a system to the point of subscribing to the legitimacy of authorities and regime or sustaining that belief once it does exist."[14]

Easton posits a general, or omnibus political ideology comprising three interwoven but analytically separable functional strands— communal ideology, partisan ideology, and legitimating ideology. The first promotes "political" identification among the general citizenry and generates "diffuse support"; the second organizes opinion for political authorities and mobilizes support in the competition for political leadership; and the third validates (or invalidates) a structure, its norms, and occupants and thus is vital to the existence and perpetuation of a regime.[15] This definition is helpful insofar as it represents an attempt to describe and explain political behavior. The problem with all functional definitions, however, is that they imply that ideology is accepted or rejected more consciously than is actually the case. Embracing an ideology does not necessarily involve a rational act of calculation but is often the result of socialization, culture, habits, and prejudice. Moreover, if ideology is defined in terms of its functions, to distinguish whether ideology is functional, dysfunctional, or neutral in the political system becomes impossible. A judgment can be made only by studying empirically the relations among variables, not on the basis of a definition that posits functional consequences.[16]

The fourth definitional category, the deprecatory view of ideology, requires greater elaboration than the first three. Those who offer definitions that fall into this category can be identified as proponents of diverse interpretations of the sociology of knowledge. The various approaches to this branch of scholarship begin with a common concern for the existential base of knowledge. Ideology is regarded as the by-product of such extracognitive factors as class, occupation, relation to means of production, and interests. There are two major, and independently developed, interpretations of the way knowledge, and hence ideology, is rooted in the strata of society.

14. David Easton, *A Systems Analysis of Political Life* (New York: John Wiley, 1965), pp. 290, 294.
15. *Ibid.,* pp. 291, 333–36.
16. Mullins, p. 502.

The French *sociologie du savoir,* as presented by Emile Durkheim, identifies the social origin of thought as group structure. In Durkheim's analysis, the origin of fundamental categories of thought is linked to the periodic recurrence of social activities, clan structure, and partial configurations of group meetings.[17] Georges Sorel, also of the French school, suggests that the role of ideology lies in the building of solidarity that constitutes the moral basis of society. Solidarity is based on myths, which in turn are based on class.[18]

The German tradition, particularly as set forth by Marx, Weber, and Mannheim, posits a more direct link between ideology and the existential base of knowledge. The Marxist position is that ideology originates in the material conditions of life, as determined by the division of labor and man's relations to the means of production. Being part of the superstructure, ideology is a "sham" and a "screen for reality." "The mode of production in material life determines the general character of the social, political, and intellectual processes of life. It is not consciousness of men that determines their existence, but on the contrary, their social existence determines consciousness."[19] Marx also attacks the concept of natural rights, as expressed in the French Declaration of the Rights of Man and some of the American state constitutions. The authors of these documents assume that natural rights are absolute or transcendent, while for Marx they establish only "bourgeois rights" with false claims to universal validity. Marx realizes, however, that influences beyond class interests are at work. So far as the petty bourgeoisie is concerned, Marx argues that it is wrong to assume that the ideology of this class is based purely on egoistic material interests. Members of a class do not pursue narrow self-interest but rather perceive the special conditions of their own existence as the general conditions for the salvation of society.[20]

17. Emile Durkheim, *Les formes élémentaires de la vie religieuse* (Paris: Aclan, 1912).
18. Georges Sorel, *Reflections on Violence* (New York: P. Smith, 1941).
19. Karl Marx, *A Contribution to the Critique of Political Economy* (Chicago: C. H. Kerr, 1904), pp. 11, 12.
20. Karl Marx, "The Eighteenth Brumaire of Louis Bonaparte," in Karl Marx, *Selected Works,* II (New York: International Publishers, 1936), 344, 347; *idem* and Friedrich Engels, *The German Ideology* (New York: International Publishers, 1947), pp. 39–43.

Max Weber, in whose analysis the correspondence between idea and interest is less direct than in the Marxist schema, suggests an "elective affinity" between ideas and interest. As patterns of authority become increasingly legal and rational, ideas are "selected out" by social groups that find them useful.[21] According to Weber, social groups in Western Europe selected religious ideas. Although Calvinist thought was based on a notion of the other world, religious doctrine was necessary to the formation of capitalism and to economic development in the West; for the ethic of Protestantism attracted and motivated certain types of personality.

Karl Mannheim's account of the social genesis of ideas, illuminating the unobserved and frequently unnoticed relationships between groups and the ideas they advocate, focuses on the historical-social situation out of which individual thought emerges. Mannheim uses the concept of ideology to bypass the collective unconscious of society in order to reveal that ruling groups can become so interest-bound that they cannot discern the factors on which their domination is based. This perspective provides the vantage point for political and social analysis. Ideologies can be exposed as illusory, and utopias are to be found in the realization of some of them. Ideas that are only distorted symbols of the past can be viewed as ideologies, while those that change the social order are utopias. Utopia represents premature truth: "Les utopies ne sont souvent que des verités prématurées."[22]

There are several problems with the fourth type of definition of ideology and some of the propositions advanced in relation to it. Marx is correct in drawing our attention to the intimate relationship between ideology and class interest, but the task for analysis is to specify how they relate to each other. Moreover, the analyst must specify and delineate a variety of such interests, some of which are not strictly economic. Political systems, particularly in low income areas, are influenced, for example, by such factors as family and kinship structure, and economic systems themselves reflect a variety of influences. The social genesis of ideas is an im-

21. Max Weber, *The Theory of Social and Economic Organization,* trans. and ed. A. M. Henderson and Talcott Parsons (New York: The Free Press, 1966).
22. Karl Mannheim, *Ideology and Utopia: An Introduction to the Sociology of Knowledge* (London: Routledge and Kegan Paul, 1954), p. 183.

portant point of departure for the study of political and economic change. The problem, however, is that those who emphasize the social determinants of knowledge advance few specific propositions about the type of relationships between social structure and ideas to be found under given conditions in particular societies. One is left with the vague impression that social structure somehow affects, orients, or makes an impact upon ideology. Clearly, if propositions and theories in social science are to be empirically relevant, greater accuracy is required.

The difficulty with the categorical view that ideologies are doctrines of power and authority facilitating the subjugation of man and perpetuating class domination is that the positive role ideologies can and do perform is ignored. Many would agree, for example, that pan-Africanism has the potential to be a positive force and play a vital role in the attempt to stem neocolonial penetration and balkanization. While nationalism in the Third World is often a guise for maintaining dependence and localizing exploitation, in some cases it has made an important contribution toward freeing colonial peoples from oppression. The major limitation to the view of ideology as distortion is that it only fits certain cases, namely, those in which social structures are inflexible and unable to adapt. In many parts of the Third World, social and economic distinctions among workers, peasants, and bourgeoisie are more pronounced than the socioeconomic distinctions of Western societies. Yet the ideological positions of these classes do not necessarily correspond to patterns of socioeconomic differentiation.[23] An ideology is frequently shared by classes whose interests conflict.

It could be objected that false consciousness explains the lack of ideological correlates, that as awareness of socioeconomic distinctions grows ideology will become more manifest. To this objection, which cannot be proven or disproven, there is no adequate reply. One can only assert that social analysis may provide a better sense of true interests than the awareness of those who are directly involved.

While socioeconomic interests may help to explain political

23. Conversely there are cases, for example, in Scandinavia, where class conflict is not severe but ideological differences are keenly felt. See Ashford, pp. 58–61.

values and beliefs, more specific questions must be posed about the role of ideology in political life. The sociology of knowledge rectifies the earlier notion that ideas need only be viewed in terms of their logic and intellectual content. Weber is essentially right in his view that interests are the tracks and switches on which the ideas must move. If they get off the track, nothing can move them.[24]

The type of definition that corrects many of these deficiencies is the fifth mentioned above, the transformative. In this definition, ideology is seen as a syndrome of functionally interrelated beliefs and values that encourages particular behavior. Beliefs, as cognitive propositions and perceptions relating the individual to the universe, produce answers to what Weber terms "problems of meaning." Values can be defined as the norms that influence human behavior. Operating in tandem with interests, ideology transforms beliefs and values into action. The elements of ideology are critique, activism, and prescription. In other words, ideology includes a theory of history, a program of action, and a conception of a desired state of affairs.

For the purposes of analysis, can ideology be regarded as an independent variable? Or is it a dependent variable? Debate on this question gives rise to two extreme views: (1) ideologies are generated by specific interests and, hence, represent intellectual dishonesty; and (2) ideologies do not camouflage interests but determine them. Put in these terms, the debate is too polarized. It would be an error to endorse the pejorative view that ideologies are merely a form of distortion. Clearly there is no constancy in the priority of existential, socially determined factors. On the other hand, the proposition that ideology is the primary cause of political behavior is facile. Only a few heirs to the Hegelian tradition would argue for the primacy of ideas. Ideology serves as a guide to behavior when it is consistent with self-interest. If predominant interests change, ideology is adjusted accordingly.

24. H. H. Gerth and C. Wright Mills, *From Max Weber: Essays in Sociology* (New York: Oxford University Press, 1946), pp. 63, 64. For a critique of the sociology of knowledge, see Merton, pp. 510–62; and Stanislav Andrezejewski, "Are Ideas Social Forces?" *American Sociological Review*, XIV, No. 6 (December 1949), 758–64. Cf. the debate that developed during the 1950s over the view that the future would be characterized by a decline of ideology. The most helpful single source is Chaim A. Waxman, ed., *The End of Ideology Debate* (New York: Simon and Shuster, 1969).

The interaction of ideology and interests is complex. Attempts to label variables generally as independent and dependent can be misleading, overlooking subtleties, nuances, and deviant cases. But to compromise by regarding ideology as an intermediate variable begs the question. Between what is it intermediate? To assert simply that both ideology and interests play a role is similarly unhelpful; the role must be specified empirically. If one acknowledges that it frequently reinforces and advances interests, then ideology can be viewed as an active agent and not merely a dependent variable reflecting economic interests. In modernizing societies, ideology may provide a vehicle for mobilization, a tool to inspire the masses, and one of the chief means of eliciting commitment. Handled adroitly, ideology represents a potentially valuable resource. Ideological modernization—the use of new norms to bring about social change—is a dynamic process.

The analysis of ideological modernization begins with the attempt to establish broad guidelines for evaluating change. What functions are performed by ideologies? How do we judge whether an ideology is operative? To answer these questions, related issues must be explored. Where does ideology originate? And how does it spread?

Guidelines for Evaluating Ideology

The six principal functions of ideology are legitimation, rationalization, interpretation, solidification, communication, and mobilization.[25] Not all ideologies perform each of these six functions in the same fashion. A variety of structures is used. Political style differs. Moreover, even if a leader intends to employ ideology for these functions, translating intentions into reality is difficult. Clearly there is neither a hard-and-fast threshold nor a clear-cut formula for evaluating the success or failure of ideology. I contend, however, that ideologies take operational form as these functions are fulfilled. An ideology is operative insofar as behavior is structured, manipulated, and justified in terms of its beliefs and values. Although ideology cannot be defined solely in terms of its functions, an operative ideology can be said to fulfill these functions, as discussed below.

25. It is not claimed that these six functions constitute a classificatory scheme. The discussion provides only a descriptive list.

Legitimation provides support for political authorities and validates action. Members of the political community appraise action in the light of shared values. Legitimation provides a link between values as internalized by the individual and the institutionalized patterns defining the structure of social relations.[26] Rationalization offers acceptable explanations for individual or group behavior. According to Freudian psychologists, ideology is uniquely personal; to understand ideology, the depths of personality must be probed. Thus, Erich Fromm advances the existential view: "Ideas can become powerful forces, but only to the extent to which they are answers to specific human needs in a given social character."[27]

Ideology adds meaning to history and makes individual participation in the historical process intelligible. It explains the events of history and the fundamental "why" of life. Conservatives, liberals, and socialists all view political activity as stemming from historical change, though conservatives see development as intuitive and social, liberals as national and progressively unilinear, and socialists as rational and dialectical. Moreover, ideology provides societal binding—solidarity. Society is possible because its members have similar ideas and expectations. As Erik Erikson suggests, an identity crisis is characteristic of the process of maturation. By providing a world image, ideology helps to resolve the search for identity, particularly as experienced by youth.[28] Conversely, when the solidification function remains unfulfilled, societal disintegration may reach the point of what Durkheim terms "anomie," a social emptiness and lack of personal meaning that is characterized by increasing suicide, crime, and general disorder. Ideology plays a central role in upward and downward communication—both within elites and between elites and masses—providing the symbols, condensations, and common understanding by which diverse groups can communicate with one another.

Marx, Mannheim, Mosca, and Pareto, among others, regard ideology as an instrument for manipulation. They argue (insofar

26. See the analysis of values by Talcott Parsons, *Structure and Process in Modern Societies* (Glencoe: The Free Press, 1960), pp. 175–77.
27. Erich Fromm, *Escape From Freedom* (New York: Holt, Rinehart, and Winston, 1961), p. 413.
28. Erik H. Erikson, *Young Man Luther: A Study in Psychoanalysis and History* (New York: Norton, 1962), pp. 20, 30, 39.

as their views can be taken together) that the political leader recognizes all political and historical ideas to be myths and values them as "derivations" (Pareto) that are used to stimulate men to action. The elites manipulate symbols to create, expand, or consolidate power and authority. As Hobbes says, "Even the tyrant must sleep." Power must be made to seem legitimate and just; it must be justified on some basis other than its mere possession by those who exercise its prerogatives.[29] In low income countries during the second half of the twentieth century, justification has typically been expressed in ideologies exhorting the masses to strive for the realization of developmental goals. Insofar as the leaders of developing countries are sincere about these goals, they attempt to manipulate political ideology for the purpose of mobilization. "The significance of ideology in mobilization is not that it 'causes one to do' but that it 'gives one cause for doing.' It provides grounds or warrants for the political activity engaged in."[30]

These functions of ideology have an international dimension as well, helping to explain the behavior of states, to justify failures and make them more bearable, to present to the public the alternative courses of action open to statesmen, to unite peoples in time of need, to provide feedback on the actions others demand and respect, and to rally people behind a cause. Of course, statesmen do not base their decisions just on ideological considerations. Nor, however, do they act purely on grounds of national interests to the total disregard of ideology. As a basis for foreign policy decision-making, ideology and national interests can be at polar extremes: "Ideology is idealistic, activist, combative, revisionist, visionary, maladaptive, and deductive; national interest is realistic, modest, constructive, conservative, emulative, compromising, adaptive, and deductive."[31] When a course of action is consistent with leaders' ideological persuasions, they opt for the ideological course of action; when it is consistent with their interpretation of national interests, they opt for action based on national interest criteria.

29. Harold Lasswell and Abraham Kaplan, *Power and Society: A Framework for Political Inquiry* (London: Routledge and Kegan Paul, 1952), p. 127.
30. Mullins, p. 509.
31. I. William Zartman, "National Interest and Ideology," in Vernon McKay, ed., *African Diplomacy: Studies in the Determinants of Foreign Policy* (New York: Praeger, 1966), p. 47.

When ideology and national interests collide, decision-makers normally opt for national interests. But it is incorrect to view ideology and national interests as dichotomous. Policies are almost always influenced by both considerations.

Related Propositions

In studying ideological innovation and diffusion one must consider not only different groups' socioeconomic interests but also elements of political culture, political socialization, and the viability of political institutions. No extended discussion of these considerations will be attempted here, but a few general remarks are offered as points of departure for subsequent chapters.

Students of political development know that problems of national integration in Western industrial societies are different from those experienced in most areas of the Third World. The citizens of Western countries generally share a common history and a common tradition, and usually a national language. Western societies have had generations, indeed centuries, to deal with the forces of modernization. In the free market economies of the West, the major problems today involve the distribution of national income and the correction of policies that discriminate against minorities. Despite the gravity of these problems, political meaning is not attached to much social conflict. In the West, widespread consensus and established national ethos allow for processes of political socialization that are implicit and require little deliberate direction from the center. Since the primary agents of socialization (especially the family) perform the major role in inculcating norms of political behavior, such secondary agents as political parties, interest groups, and government agencies bear relatively little responsibility for socialization. The primary agents are the stronger, and there tends to be congruence among agents in the sense that they are mutually reinforcing.

In comparison with the West, social change in Africa is highly politicized. The quest to realize development goals is telescoped into short time spans. Political cultures are fragmented. The overwhelming majority of the population is illiterate. At the national level, politics tends to be regarded as a zero-sum game. Give-and-take is largely absent. Associational sentiment is lacking. Consequently, political socialization is explicit, and the secondary agents of socialization—for example, the party, youth movements, and women's organizations—are assigned the major role in propagating a national ethos. Residues of colonial rule and the resilience of primary agents of socialization explain the inherently conservative bias in African politics—one of the most problematical constraints with which leaders attempting to modernize must cope. Because of the discontinuities in the process of socialization, secondary agents must be coordinated and directed. Indeed, the directed role of secondary agents might be labeled "ideological socialization" or "resocialization."

The roots of the stimulus for ideological socialization or resocialization in contemporary Africa lie in the deprivation experienced under colonialism. In the colonial context, deprivation means domination by a foreign minority, economic exploitation, de facto segregation, paternalism, and racism. As African elites reacted to the colonial intrusion, concerted efforts were made to reorient political beliefs. Hence social change, in the form of the response to colonial penetration, provided the impetus and in some instances the infrastructure for subsequent ideological innovation and diffusion.

In their attempts to win independence, politicians and intellectuals paved the way for the militant man of words. New configurations were constructed from old values and beliefs and new norms.[32] But the attainment of independence gave the new regimes little control over the agents of socialization; educational structures remained imbued with colonial values.

In Africa, as elsewhere, the primary agents of socialization are resilient, and the bias is toward traditional values. Early childhood training stresses the importance of obedience to authority and respect for traditionally rooted sources of legitimacy. The secondary agents of socialization, by contrast, attempt to induce a feeling of

32. For a discussion of opinion leaders and elements of change and an excellent inquiry into the diffusion of ideas in the disciplines of rural sociology and agriculture, see Everett M. Rogers, *Diffusion of Innovations* (New York: The Free Press, 1962). Outside the field of political science, interesting points are also made by Homer G. Barnett, *Innovation: The Basis of Cultural Change* (New York: McGraw Hill, 1953), and Eric Hoffer, *The True Believer: Thoughts on the Nature of Mass Movements* (New York: The New American Library, 1951).

political efficacy and encourage mass participation in politics. In order to propagandize effectively, postcolonial leaders try to utilize and upgrade existing means of communication. Political organizations and institutions are the fundamental mechanisms for channeling political behavior toward national development.

As the attempt is made to resocialize the masses for the tasks of development, existing norms must be aligned with a new complex of beliefs and values. As an agent of mobilization, ideology is seen as being a potentially fast and efficient (that is, capable of achieving a rapid adjustment of means to ends among the vast majority of the population) method of promoting desired forms of political behavior. For a number of Third World leaders, the role played by ideology in the People's Republic of China is exemplary; it has not passed unnoticed that Maoist ideology provides a major driving force in China's quest for modernization.

Beyond questions of speed and efficiency, however, a third aspect of ideological modernization must be considered—its absorption or penetration. The process of modernization was slower and less efficient in the West than it has been in contemporary China, for example; however, early modernizers generally enjoy the advantages (or, one might argue, the disadvantages) of a deep-rooted ideology with a long historical tradition. When a society can afford the luxury of a slow-moving, subtle means of achieving modernization, ideology is normally a mass-elite phenomenon whereas, when the means used must be quick and efficient (in the sense defined above), ideology is frequently an elite or forensic phenomenon. When ideological modernization is slow, subtle, and lasting, stability and a status quo orientation tend to characterize the political system. When this type of ideology penetrates the masses and is absorbed deeply, the process is not easily reversed.

If, on the other hand, ideological reversibility becomes characteristic of a political system, support and commitment are much more difficult to elicit. The result is a self-perpetuating mechanism that harbors instability and political decay. As pendulumlike ideological swings to left and right increase in frequency, a climate of cynicism develops. In this atmosphere attitudes that are dysfunctional for national development tend to multiply rapidly. Thus, an inverse correlation exists between frequency of ideological reverses and ability to attain national development goals. Frequent ideological reverses are associated with reduced likelihood of attaining these goals; conversely, as advances are made toward achieving these goals, sudden ideological reverses become less likely. A positive correlation can be posited between ideological credibility and the likelihood of realizing societal goals. Just as frequent ideological swings produce a climate of cynicism and skepticism, so do similar attitudes develop and become aggravated when ideological rhetoric lacks supporting political behavior. As a would-be modernizing ideology's credibility decreases, the odds on societal goals being realized are reduced significantly.

These propositions are relevant to the contrasts to be perceived in the role of ideology in Western industrial societies and the non-Western context. Table 1 summarizes the relative differences in emphasis between ideology in the West and in the Third World.

Table 1. Ideology in contemporary Western and non-Western political systems

Western, industrial	Non-Western, nonindustrial
Assumed	Created
Nondirected	Directed
Implicit	Explicit
Passive	Active
Status quo	Transformation
High penetration,	Low penetration,
high absorption,	low absorption,
modifiable but	easily reversible
relatively irreversible	

Many of these propositions can be sharpened if they are applied to African political systems. First, however, a number of fundamental questions have to be investigated. If, as Western theorists argue, ideology originates in particular groups, on which groups should we focus to identify the sources of ideological innovation in Africa? Although the terms "innovation" and "diffusion" are normally used in conjunction, it may be profitable to divide the process into two parts when analyzing ideology in highly fragmented societies with severe structural discontinuities; in parts of the Third World, innovation and diffusion should perhaps be viewed separately in terms of their relationships to such variables as ethnicity and social privilege. Furthermore, if the role of the masses is to accept or reject elite belief systems, what strategies and tactics are conducive to acceptance? What structures are utilized? What dislocations are introduced? What can one learn from unsuccessful efforts to introduce new norms? Consideration of these questions leads to a further one: Does ideological innovation and diffusion place stress on political systems in the Third World and contribute to political violence?

Understanding the links between ideology and political violence requires a stress model of social change. The model must take account of the dysfunctions as well as the functions of ideological innovation and diffusion. Little theoretical work has been done to date on the transition to socialism in Africa.[33] Clearly the transition from one social system to another involves grave problems.

Ideology that culminates in unsuccessful social transformation encourages political violence. The frequency of coups d'état has led scholars to inquire into military intervention in politics, but once again the scholarly literature displays various weaknesses. These are illustrated in Chapters 7 and 8 in conjunction with an analysis of the Ugandan coup of January 25, 1971.

33. Following the 1966 ouster of Kwame Nkrumah, some helpful works appeared on the failure of socialism in Ghana, for example, Bob Fitch and Mary Oppenheimer, *Ghana: End of an Illusion* (New York: Monthly Review Press, 1966). Valuable contributions are being made by scholars at the University of Dar es Salaam; see especially Lionel Cliffe and John S. Saul, eds., *Socialism in Tanzania: An Inter-disciplinary Reader*, 2 vols. (Dar es Salaam: East African Publishing House, 1972), and *The Silent Class Struggle: Tanzanian Studies No. 2* (Dar es Salaam: Tanzanian Publishing House, 1973). Fewer studies are available on the French-speaking countries of Africa. Samir Amin's major theoretical book, *Accumulation on a World Scale: A Critique of the Theory of Underdevelopment* (New York: Monthly Review Press, 1974), includes examples from his earlier studies of Francophone Africa.

CHAPTER 3

Sociohistorical Context

Social cleavages develop as constitutional power is transferred from the imperial authority to an indigenous elite. In most cases the structure of social cleavage is readily apparent before the formal transfer of power. In all the commissions, conferences, and hearings that mark the bargaining process between the metropole and nationlist elites, the balance of social forces tends to be the most contentious issue. With independence,[1] a new regime must deal with a variety of pressing problems. Primordial lines of social cleavage are usually the first to crystallize. They tend to be ethnic, although linguistic and religious divisions can lead to an equally volatile situation. In some instances, ethnic cleavages and class interests fuse; in others, ethnic conflict is merely a manifestation of more deeply rooted economic strife.

Following independence, the articulation of an ideology of modernization is regarded as an important task, but not necessarily the first priority. Even when a regime or an individual leader enjoys widespread support at the time of independence, the first phase of ideological modernization is usually one of apprehension. Leaders test their options. The most urgent task is to consolidate power. Insofar as the regime attempts to institutionalize new norms, the approach tends to be gradual. Subsequently, as an attempt is made to alter the lines of social cleavage, attention normally turns to the increasingly apparent imbalance between normative values and the sociopolitical environment. Regime-induced efforts to stimulate social change are disruptive for those whose values are rooted in

---

1. The term "independence," adopted here for economy of expression and clarity of style, always means "constitutional independence." The point is that formal achievement of independence does not necessarily mean effective control of affairs; more typically, in the case of the Third World, power continues to rest with the imperial authority, which forges alliances with indigenous groups.

tradition. As the previous chapter has indicated, the resilience of primary agents of socialization tends to give politics a conservative bias. The tenacity of primary socialization may breed resistance to change. Furthermore, as the regime tries to induce modernization, political authority comes to represent a threat to strongly held norms. In the absence of a sense of community at the national level, many sectors of the populace require an alternate set of beliefs and values.

There are three possible patterns to the role of ideology in the politics of low income countries. In some cases, an alternative paradigm can be introduced as an ideology of modernization without much social or any political disruption resulting. If the regime is insensitive, however, and neglects institutional change at the normative level, anomic social violence is likely to ensue. Or, if an ill-conceived attempt to articulate an ideology of modernization politicizes discontent, political violence may be directed at the regime, which is perceived as the source of grievance.

If modernization is to be successfully pursued, beliefs and values must be coordinated with changes in the political system. A rapidly changing social environment causes loss of ideological coherence. The initial stimulus for ideological modernization is exogenous to the value structure, being created by a variety of other factors. Hence discussion begins with the social and historical context of ideological modernization.

Social Structure

Uganda, a picturesque country of ten million people situated to the north and west of Lake Victoria, is often referred to, in Winston Churchill's words, as "the pearl of Africa" and "the cradle of the Nile." For a small country—only 500 miles across at its widest point—Uganda is remarkably diverse. The topography varies from the semidesert areas of Karamoja in the northeast to the rolling hills and lush savannah of Kigezi in the southwest, from the towering mountains of the Ruwenzoris (the legendary Mountains of the Moon) in the west and Mt. Elgon in the east to the scenic lakes in which the Nile finds its source.

The largest concentration of people is to be found in the area immediately north of the capital, Kampala. Most of the population are peasant farmers. Average per capita income is less than $100 per year, and population is increasing at the alarming rate of 3.3 percent annually. There are marked disparities in the development pattern of rural and urban areas and between one district and another. As a result of internal migration, the rate of growth of population in the urban areas is double that of the country as a whole. According to 1969 figures, only 7 percent of Ugandans live in towns with a population of more than 2,000; yet over 50 percent of recorded employment is in the towns.

Differences in opportunities for wage employment account for the marked variations in income levels. Among graduated taxpayers in rural areas, almost 90 percent earn less than Shs. 1,500 a year. The corresponding figure for urban areas is 20 percent. Only about one percent earn more than Shs. 6,000 per annum in rural areas, compared to 20 percent in urban centers.[2] Income- and employment-generating activities are concentrated in a belt stretching from Masaka on the western shores of Lake Victoria, through Buganda, Busoga, and Bukedi, to Bugisu. In this area climate and soil favor agricultural development; elsewhere conditions are much less favorable.

The main exports (see Table 2) are primary products: coffee, cotton, copper, and tea. The trade figures indicate an increase in the export of tea, hides and skins, animal feeding stuffs, and groundnuts, reflecting Uganda's attempt to diversify its exports. Most industrial facilities are located in the regions where agricultural activities have flourished. Uganda's light and heavy industry is found in the urban centers of Kampala, Jinja, Tororo, and Mbale—all close to Owen Falls, which provides hydroelectric power from the source of the Nile. The fact that most export earning products come from Buganda and the east is one of the major reasons for the country's regional imbalance.

Because Uganda lies on one of Africa's major historical migratory crossroads, ethnographic and demographic patterns are complex. The early precolonial period was marked by a series of invasions by nomadic tribes from the north and northeast; in many areas of what is today called Uganda, pastoralists from the north came into contact with indigenous agriculturalists. In the central

2. *Uganda's Third Five Year Development Plan 1971/2–1975/6* (Entebbe: Government Printer, 1972), pp. 93, 94. Seven Ugandan shillings are roughly equivalent to one American dollar.

Table 2. Principal domestic exports, 1965–1966 (to countries other than Kenya and Tanzania)

	1965		1966	
	Value in pounds	Percentage of total	Value in pounds	Percentage of total
COMMODITY:				
Coffee	30,421,334	24.1	34,783,274	52.6
Cotton	16,761,627	26.7	15,344,586	23.2
Copper	7,993,895	12.8	5,753,182	8.8
Tea	2,388,418	3.8	3,151,215	4.8
Hides and skins	1,258,140	2.0	1,780,249	2.6
Animal feeding				
stuffs	1,943,689	3.1	2,258,214	3.5
Groundnuts	24,595	0.04	474,553	0.8
Fish	12,562	0.02	84,978	0.1
Vegetable oils	120,123	0.20	13,485	0.02
Oil seeds	132,772	0.21	161,489	0.2
Others	1,656,666	2.6	2,130,560	3.3
TOTAL	62,713,851	—	65,935,785	—

SOURCE: *Facts about Uganda* (Entebbe: Government Printer, 1968), p. 83.

and southern regions, where climate and soil are favorable to agriculture, warfare characterized the history of the interlacustrine kingdoms.[3]

The distinction between the northern peoples and those of the south is often referred to as "the Bantu-Nilotic cleavage." The accompanying map and Tables 3 and 4 indicate the location of the different groups within Uganda, their numbers, and the percentage they constitute of the total population. The terms Bantu and Nilotic are classifications based on language, physical appearance, and forms of political organization. The Bantu peoples inhabit the area south of Lakes Kyoga and Albert (the latter renamed Lake Mobutu Sese Seko in 1973) and the connecting Nile River; the Nilotic peoples, along with the Sudanic and eastern Nilotes, occupy the area to the north. The main distinction between the two groups is that the Bantu-speaking peoples tend toward chiefly hierarchies and are more developed economically than the northerners, who are less centralized politically and have smaller, less differentiated economies. All four of Uganda's traditional kingdoms—Buganda,

3. There are exceptions to these generalizations. The early Luos were not nomads. The Bahima and the Bachwezi appear to have come from the south.

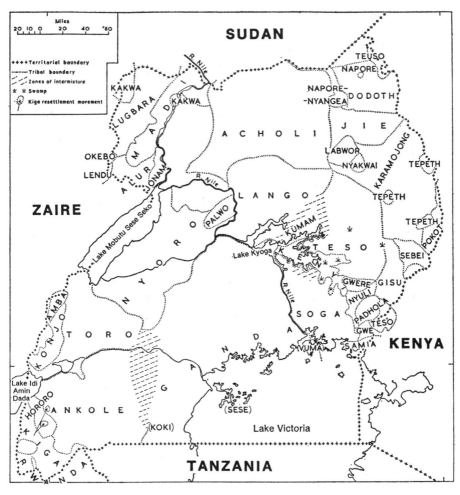

Map 2. Uganda's ethnic groups

Table 3.   Uganda population census, 1959, main tribes

Tribe	Male	Female	Total	Percentage of Grand Total
Acholi	141,643	143,286	284,929	4.4
Alur	62,274	61,104	123,378	1.9
Badama	50,721	50,730	101,451	1.6
Baganda	508,735	536,143	1,044,878	16.2
Bagisu	163,923	165,334	329,257	5.1
Bagwere	55,065	56,616	111,681	1.7
Bakiga	220,936	238,683	459,619	7.1
Bakonjo	52,073	54,817	106,890	1.7
Banyankole	253,993	265,290	519,283	8.1
Banyaruanda	212,434	166,222	378,656	5.9
Banyole	46,212	46,430	92,642	1.4
Banyoro	93,907	94,467	188,374	2.9
Basoga	246,182	255,739	501,921	7.8
Batoro	103,436	104,864	208,300	3.2
Iteso	257,134	267,582	524,716	8.1
Karamojong	63,747	67,966	131,713	2.0
Kumam	29,344	32,115	61,459	1.0
Lango	180,694	183,113	363,807	5.6
Lugbara	116,114	120,156	236,270	3.7
Madi	39,546	40,809	80,355	1.2
Rundi	87,599	51,150	138,749	2.2
Other Tribes	251,190	210,040	461,230	7.2
TOTAL	3,236,902	3,212,656	6,449,558	100.0

SOURCE: *1970 Statistical Abstract* (Entebbe: Government Printer, 1970), p. 10.

Bunyoro-Kitara, Toro, and Nkore (Ankole)—are in the Bantu areas. Although there are chieftancies in some parts of the north (for example, Acholi), the prevalent form of political organization there is segmentary lineage. Broadly speaking, the tribes in the north do not have clear-cut hierarchical political structures, and authority is vested in the clans. The poverty of north and west— reflected both in income and in the distribution of social services— has been a continual source of political grievance. Even before the colonial penetration, the centralized kingdoms had more developed economies than the segmentary societies. As subsequent discussion will show, the British policy of indirect rule affected Uganda's ethnic groups very differently. Existing patterns of uneven development were exacerbated, and the northern, segmentary societies came to resent the imposition by the British of the hierarchical structure of the interlacustrine Bantu. Contrasts in forms of political organization and differences in relative economic position certainly exist, but the problem with the concept of a Bantu-Nilotic cleavage is that Africans are unaccustomed to this distinction. The term is a social categorization that probably originated either with the colonial administration or

Table 4. Uganda population census, 1969 (provisional results)

Region and District	Population
BUGANDA:	
West Mengo	515,243
Kampala	331,889
East Mengo	844,098
Masaka	641,403
Mubende	335,599
TOTAL	2,668,232
EASTERN:	
Teso	568,327
Bugisu	398,121
Bukedi	518,922
Busoga	897,644
Jinja	47,298
Sebei	64,290
Karamoja	283,356
Mbale	23,539
TOTAL	2,801,497
WESTERN:	
Kigezi	642,300
Ankole	855,155
Toro	571,006
Bunyoro	348,031
TOTAL	2,416,492
NORTHERN:	
West Nile	579,383
Madi	89,998
Acholi	465,417
Lango	505,218
TOTAL	1,640,016
TOTAL FOR UGANDA	9,526,237

SOURCE: *1970 Statistical Abstract* (Entebbe: Government Printer, 1970), p. 14.

in early scholarly research and has been reified. More important than the origin of the notion, however, is the question of whether the cleavage has political reality. Implicit in allusions to a division between Bantu and Nilotic peoples is the idea that there is some coherence or solidarity within each group. Uganda's history reveals that these groups have experienced more recurrent strife than internal solidarity. The history of the Bantu-speaking areas (Buganda, Bugisu, parts of Bukedi, Busoga, Ankole, Toro, Bunyoro, and Kigezi) is one of intermittent struggle for supremacy. Just as conflict has marked relations among these regions, so have severe intraregional divisions existed between such Bantu peoples as the Bahima and the Bairu in Ankole and between the Baamba/Bakonjo and the Batoro in Toro. Periodic discord, at times violent, has been a feature of multitribal districts in Bantu-speaking areas, for example, among the Banyaruanda and the Bahororo in Kigezi. Similarly, strife has characterized both inter- and intraethnic relations within the Nilotic Luo diaspora as well as in other, non-Luo northern areas. Deeply rooted traditional rivalries exist among the Alur and the Lugbara, Acholi, and Langi as well as between east and west Acholi. In fact, only on one occasion in Ugandan history did conflict along a clear-cut Bantu-Nilotic axis appear to be manifesting itself in political terms. Beginning in 1964, a struggle in the cabinet seemed to be polarizing around a more radical Nilotic faction and a moderate Bantu group. The prime minister moved precipitously, however, to have five Bantu ministers arrested and detained, in effect preventing divisions from crystallizing around Bantu and Nilotic polarities.

The key to understanding ethnic cleavages in Uganda lies in grasping the significance of the historically pre-eminent position of the Baganda, Uganda's largest, wealthiest, and best-educated group. Before the colonial interlude, the Baganda had a distinct sense of national consciousness. Although the historical evidence is unclear, the various clans of present-day Buganda probably migrated into that area in about the thirteenth century. Largely as the result of a series of wars with Bunyoro-Kitara, the Baganda developed strong feelings of political solidarity and emerged as the most powerful nation in the interlacustrine region.

Traditionally, the government of Buganda consisted of a monarchy and a hierarchical system of authority. At the center of Uganda's most powerful tribe sat the kabaka, or king, the main source of legitmacy in Buganda. The locus of Ganda government was at Mengo, where the Lukiiko (parliament) met. Ganda norms have traditionally emphasized individual achievement and merit. Internalization of norms of modernity cannot, therefore, be regarded as a departure from traditional Ganda values.[4] Rather, modern norms represent a continuation and logical extension of processes of social change—for example, increasing occupational specialization—that were underway before the establishment of imperial control. In fact colonialism can be seen as having accelerated many of the changes that were already taking place.

The first Europeans came to Buganda in 1862, the year Speke "discovered" the Nile. Mutesa I was induced to request missionaries. When the kabaka's invitation was acccptcd, the Anglican Church Mission Society (CMS), the Catholic White Fathers (RCM), and the Moslems engaged in a bitter struggle for influence, which culminated in the religious wars of the 1880's and 1890's.[5]

The colonial presence may be formally dated from the Battle of Mengo (1892), when, with the British capitalizing on the existence of warring factions in Buganda, Lord Lugard and the Protestants defeated Kabaka Mwanga and the Catholics. The Imperial British East Africa Company (IBEA), a group of traders and philanthropists granted a royal charter by Lord Salisbury's government in

4. Apter, *The Political Kingdom*, p. 21, terms the Ganda polity a "modernizing autocracy," a system remarkable for its capacity to absorb change. He argues that the modernizing autocracy in Buganda could adopt instrumental values without difficulty to the point where the traditional system of authority itself was threatened. For further analysis, see Lloyd A. Fallers, ed., *The King's Men: Leadership and Status in Buganda on the Eve of Independence* (London: Oxford University Press, 1964); Semakula Kiwanuka, *A History of Buganda: From the Foundation of the Kingdom to 1900* (New York: Africana Publishing Company, 1972); and Donald A. Low, *Buganda in Modern History* (Berkeley: University of California Press, 1971).
5. A Jewish community was also established in Uganda. Founded by a Ugandan, Semei Kakungulu, at the beginning of the twentieth century, the Bayudaya initially left the Christian Church because of differences with the British and because they adhered to a more literal interpretation of the Old Testament than other Afro-Christian groups. They are a small community, numbering about 800 in 1971, and reside near Mbale. Arieh Obed, *The Bayudaya: A Community of African Jews in Uganda,* Occasional Paper, The Shiloah Center for Middle Eastern and African Studies, Tel Aviv University (Tel Aviv, 1973).

1888, withdrew from Buganda in 1893 as a result of the religious wars and disruptions in commerce. Financial interests in London argued for formal colonial acquisition, and the British protectorate was established in 1894. Following a period when Baganda Christians and the British collaborated against Bunyoro-Kitara, the imperial power gave its support to the bakungu (senior chiefs) in Buganda. In 1897 Kabaka Mwanga joined forces with Kabalega, the omukama (king) of Bunyoro-Kitara, his traditional enemy. But their combined resistance to imperial expansion could not equal the might of the British, with their Indian and Nubian troops, and the majority of the Christian and Moslem chiefs. The revolutionary decade of the 1890's culminated with the deportation of Mwanga and Kabalega to the Seychelle Islands.

The British and their collaborators placed Daudi Chwa, the infant son of Mwanga, on the throne of Buganda. The British then signed a series of agreements, with Buganda and Toro in 1900, with Ankole in 1901, and with Bunyoro in 1933. By the agreement of 1900, the Baganda accepted British sovereignty over the protectorate of Uganda; in return they retained de facto control over their internal affairs, and their status as first among equals in the protectorate was formally recognized. In order to impose their control on the segmentary societies, which lacked administrative hierarchies, the British dispatched Baganda as the agents of imperial authority. Their task was to establish Gandalike structures in the other regions of Uganda.

The 1900 agreement with Buganda also provided for grants of large landed estates to senior chiefs. The introduction of the freehold land system (mailo tenure) and the development of coffee and cotton as cash crops created a wealthy group of holders of land titles within Ganda society. The buying and selling of land titles led to a flurry of commercial activity and even capital investment in Buganda, a phenomenon not paralleled anywhere else in the protectorate.

As the agents of indirect rule and the group with the greatest exposure to Europeans, the Baganda had greater opportunities for formal education than the other peoples of Uganda. Between 1922 and 1953 over 50 percent of the students entering Makerere College, Uganda's most advanced educational institution, were Baganda; and the Baganda held three-fourths of the top civil service service jobs.[6] Thus the proclivity of the Baganda for modernizing norms, the emergence of commercial activity in Buganda, the fact that Buganda is the heartland area and had most contact with Europeans, the preferential treatment accorded the Baganda within the colonial educational system, and the disproportionate access to government jobs that followed, all contributed to a structural imbalance that manifested itself politically as Buganda versus the others. Just as the Baganda developed a sense of being apart from the rest, so did Uganda's other peoples come to resent Ganda-centric politics.

Within Buganda, despite increasing social complexity, differences were not perceived in terms of class antagonisms. Social strata never assumed corporate identities. For the majority, the most important distinction continued to be between royal and common clans. A powerful indigenous middle class did not emerge. In terms of perceptions, the main differentiation, other than tribe, was between emerging elites and the mass of peasants.

These social distinctions must be seen in the context of racial stratification. In Uganda, unlike Kenya, the European community remained small, never numbering more than 11,000. There was no white settler community and little land alienation. As in other parts of Africa, however, the Europeans constituted the top tier of the racial hierarchy. The Asians, that is, people of Indian and Pakistani origin, were in an intermediate position between the Europeans and the Africans. Asian traders first appeared on the coast of East Africa well before the British arrived there. The Asian presence was not felt in the interior until the British began recruiting indentured laborers to construct the railway between Mombasa and Kampala, a project that was completed in 1901. When the British realized that the African population could not supply enough skilled artisans, the colonial administration began importing Asian masons, carpenters, clerks, and mechanics. Some Asians were also brought to Uganda as soldiers to help subdue resistance to colonial rule. Since Uganda was a protectorate and not a colony, the British had no statutory right to sell land to

6. M. Crawford Young, "The Obote Revolution," *Africa Report,* XI, No. 6 (June 1966), 13.

Asians. Not being able to acquire land to farm, Asians went to the towns and became traders; thus Uganda developed a nonindigenous middle class. Below the Asians, composing the bottom tier of the racial hierarchy, came the African majority, although members of African elites often interacted, both socially and economically, with the Europeans.

This pattern of racial stratification was the product of British paternalism. Wittingly or unwittingly, the British, a people accustomed to rigid social distinctions themselves, established racial ordering in the colonies. Asian and African children attended their own schools, and the school systems were separate but not equal. The 1959 figures, for example, indicate that expenditure in the schools was at the rates of £186 per European, £38 per Asian, and £11 per African in aided schools.[7]

Under the British, Asians and Africans doing identical jobs were paid at different rates. The correspondence between race and income carried over well into the postcolonial period. In 1969, cash wages for non-Africans employed in private industry totaled Shs. 75,679,000 for 2,154 Europeans and Shs. 148,515,000 for 9,448 Asians.[8] An aggregate figure for Africans' earnings is not provided in the *Statistical Abstract;* however, a computation by wage groups shows that just over 90 percent of Africans employed by private industry earned less than Shs. 400 per month. The mean income for Africans in private industry was about Shs. 150 per month. In the public services 90 percent of the Africans employed received less than Shs. 500 per month; the mean was about Shs. 175. In other words, the average wage of Europeans working in private industry was 19.5 times the mean for Africans in private industry and 16.7 times the mean for Africans working in the public services. Asians earned more than Africans by multiples of 8.7 in private industry and 7.5 in the public services. It must be remembered, too, that vast numbers of Africans had not entered the cash economy (and many still have not).

That racial conflict should eventually have surfaced in Uganda

7. Sheldon Weeks, *Divergence in Educational Development: The Case of Kenya and Uganda* (New York: Teachers College Press, 1967), p. 5. The figure per Muganda would be higher than the average expenditure per African; however, these data are not available.
8. Figures computed from the *1970 Statistical Abstract,* pp. 106–108.

is, therefore, hardly surprising. The ill feeling became apparent in the boycott of Asian shops during the 1940's and 1950's and culminated in General Amin's order of August 1972 expelling non-citizen Asians.

As regards linguistic patterns, Uganda has no lingua franca.[9] Luganda is the most widely spoken indigenous language, but only 16 percent of the population learn Luganda as their first language (see Table 5). No other African language (save Swahili) is spoken by half that many, and only 7 other languages are spoken by more than 5 percent. One-third of the population speak Eastern Bantu languages; almost as many Western Bantu languages; 15 percent Western Nilotic; 11 percent Eastern Nilotic; and 5 percent Central Sudanic.[10]

With the extension of British rule by Baganda agents, Luganda became the language of administration. The use of Luganda outside Buganda provoked considerable resentment. In parts of the north, Luganda was later replaced by local languages in education and administration, but in some of the eastern areas Luganda has remained the official language of government and in the schools. Discontent has arisen not only from the use of Luganda but also from the selection of Acholi in Lango schools and Lutoro in parts of Toro.

Largely because use of any one African language causes resentment among peoples who speak other vernaculars—though also because English would be more useful than a local language in facilitating extranational communication, work, and travel—English was adopted at independence as the national language. The vast majority of Uganda's population, however, has never had a command of English, and there has been psychological and cultural dissatisfaction about using the language imposed by colonial rule rather than an African tongue.

The pros and cons of employing Swahili as Uganda's national language have been much debated. Swahili is widely spoken in

9. In 1973 General Amin's government adopted Swahili as a national language; discussion of usage of Swahili follows.

10. Clive Criper and Peter Ladefoged, "Linguistic Complexity in Uganda," in W. H. Whiteley, ed., *Language Use and Social Change: Multilingualism with Special Reference to Eastern Africa* (London: Oxford University Press, 1971), p. 149; and Peter Ladefoged *et al., Language in Uganda* (London: Oxford University Press, 1972).

Table 5. Official status of the major languages spoken in Uganda

Language	% population native speakers	Hours/week radio	% non-English radio time	Literacy campaign	Newspapers: % of total circulation	Officially used in primary schools	Agriculture information services	Law courts
WESTERN NILOTIC								
Lango	5.60	12.75	11.00	X	2.10	X	X	
Acholi	4.40	3.25	3.00	X	0.20			
Alur	1.90	0.50	0.50	X				
Dhopadhola	1.60	0.50	0.50	X				
Kumam	1.00			X				
GROUP TOTALS	14.50	17.00	15.00	5	2.30	1	1	
EASTERN NILOTIC								
Ateso	8.10	12.75	11.00	X	0.90	X	X	
Akaramojong	2.00	3.25	3.00	X				
Kakwa	0.60	0.75	0.50	X				
Sebei	0.60	3.00	3.00	X				
GROUP TOTALS	11.30	19.75	17.50	4	0.90	1	1	
CENTRAL SUDANIC								
Lugbara	3.70	5.25	4.00	X	0.20	X		
Madi	1.20	3.50	3.00	X	0.10			
GROUP TOTALS	4.90	8.75	7.00	2	0.30	1	0	
BANTU (E)								
Luganda	16.30	34.00	29.00	X	40.00	X	X	

Lusoga	7.80	6.25	5.00	X			X
Lumasaba (Lugisu)	5.10	4.50	4.00	X			
Lugwere	1.70	—	0				
Lunyole	1.40	—	0	X			
Lusamia/Lugwe	1.30	3.50	3.00	X		X	
GROUP TOTALS	33.60	48.25	40.00	4	40.00	1	1
(W)							
Runyankole	8.10	9.75 }	8.00 }	X		X	
Rukiga	7.10			X	0.80		
Runyaruanda	5.90	—	0				
Rutoro	3.30	9.25 }	8.00 }	X			
Runyoro	2.90				0.80	X	X
Rurundi	2.00		0				
Rukonji	1.70	—	0	X			
Rwamba	0.50	—	0	X			
GROUP TOTALS	30.50*	19.00	16.00	5	1.60	2	1
NON-UGANDAN							
Swahili	—	—	0		2.40	(X)†	
English	0.20	50.75	—		50.50	X	X
Gujerati	1.00	—	0		2.00	X	
Hindustani (Hindi/Urdu)	0.10	5.00	4.00				

SOURCE: Clive Criper and Peter Ladefoged, "Linguistic Complexity in Uganda," in W. H. Whiteley, ed., *Language Use and Social Change: Multilingualism with Special Reference to Eastern Africa* (London: Oxford University Press, 1971), p. 148.

* The figure presumably intended here is 31.5.

† Vigorous opposition to the use of Swahili in the schools caused it to be dropped from the curriculum first in Buganda and later in the north.

Tanzania and Kenya, and to a lesser degree in Zaire, Rwanda, Burundi, Mozambique, and Somalia. Within Uganda, Swahili has long been the working language for the army, police, and prison service. It is as widely spoken as Luganda among the male population, but fewer women speak it. For cultural and religious reasons, many Ugandan Christians opposed Swahili as a national language, Swahili being viewed as the language of the coast and, hence, as an agent of Islam. The Baganda have regarded the move to introduce Swahili as designed to diminish the influence of Luganda. Among the Baganda the issue also became linked with the controversy over the East African Federation (EAF); the Baganda feared that federation would dilute Buganda's privileged position in Uganda and grant Kenya's white settler community an entree into Uganda. Many Ugandans would prefer a vernacular as the national language, but no local language is acceptable to the majority.

The final source of cleavage in Uganda is religion. The intimate relationship between religion and politics has produced an enduring pattern of denominational politics. When Arab traders and European explorers first came to Uganda, traditional religion was in flux. Of the two world religions to gain large numbers of converts, Islam was the first to arrive. Sheikh Ahmed bin Ibrahim met Kabaka Suna and introduced Islam in 1844. The influence of Christianity dates from 1877 and 1879, when the CMS and the RCM accepted the kabaka's "invitation" to Buganda. The three faiths battled for adherents through two decades of intense rivalry and managed to survive the religious persecution of Kabaka Mwanga. The Catholics gained most converts, but at the governmental-administrative level the British created a Protestant establishment, allocating civil service positions on a denominational basis in order to extend Protestant control; Protestants were also granted a majority of posts in the hierarchy of appointed chiefs. As Uganda approached independence, religious groupings—of the total population 34.5 percent were Catholic, 28.2 percent Protestant, 5.6 percent Moslem, and the balance observers of traditional religions[11]—

11. *Uganda Census 1959: African Population* (Entebbe: Government Printer, 1963), p. 31. The corresponding percentages for Buganda are 49, 27.5, and 7.3. The 1959 census may have underestimated the number of Moslems.
Religious groupings in Uganda must be regarded as overlapping cate-

were one of the most important factors in the formation and subsequent behavior of political parties. The salience of religious distinctions is illustrated by Uganda's 1961 elections. Commenting on these elections, and the close correlation their data indicate between religion and voting behavior, Donald Rothchild and Michael Rogin say: "The greater the percentage of Protestants in a district, the higher the vote for the UPC [Uganda Peoples Congress]. The greater the percentage of Catholics, the higher the vote for the DP [Democratic Party]."[12] In the elections of a year later, religion again was a major factor. In his study of the importance of religious distinctions for politics in Uganda, F. B. Wellbourn notes: "Although it may to some extent have misrepresented the facts, it was no accident that during the election campaign of 1962, the Democratic Party was known popularly as *Dini ya Papa* (Religion of the Pope), and the Uganda Peoples Congress as 'United Protestants of Canterbury.' "[13]

At various times in Uganda's history, religious divisions have been extensions of other cleavages. At other times, religious distinctions have cut across or even redirected lines of social strain. Since independence, one problem for Uganda's leaders has been to manage these distinctions so that their impact would be integrative rather than disintegrative. Scholarly analysis, accordingly, must address the issue of cleavage alignments. Given the pluralism of Uganda's social structure—in terms of ethnic, regional, economic, linguistic, and religious distinctions—the question is, how do the lines of cleavage relate to one another? Are they reinforcing? Do they crosscut? Or are they merely social distinctions that are not translated into sources of political conflict?

The question that is of fundamental importance for this inquiry can be stated as follows: In what way, if at all, does an attempt to introduce an ideology of modernization affect patterns of cleavage? In order to assess the reciprocal impact of social cleavage and attempts at ideological modernization, Uganda's history will be briefly

gories. As elsewhere in Africa, many individuals who profess to be Christians or Moslems also adhere to traditional religions.

12. Donald Rothchild and Michael Rogin, "Uganda," in Gwendolen M. Carter, ed., *National Unity and Regionalism in Eight African States* (Ithaca: Cornell University Press, 1966), p. 380.

13. F. B. Wellbourn, *Religion and Politics in Uganda, 1952–1962* (Nairobi: East African Publishing House, 1965), p. 1.

reviewed. Since the late colonial period and throughout the twentieth century, one ineluctable theme has dominated developments: the heartland tribe's fear of eclipse of its privileged position, and the concomitant problems of power generation and management at the center.

Historical Background

Although after signing agreements with the kingdoms Britain sought to extend indirect rule throughout the protectorate, direct rule was practiced for the most part in the nonkingdom states. In the heartland area, the imperial power faced a resurgence of local nationalism. Throughout the late colonial period, Britain's attempt to impose the centralist Westminister model met resistance from the Baganda. The imperial authority and the government at Mengo adhered to different interpretations of the 1900 agreement, each stressing its own prerogatives and rights. Antagonism mounted in the 1920's over the controversy concerning the power of the katikkiro (prime minister within Buganda) vis-à-vis the protectorate government and increased still further during the riots of 1945 and 1949 in Buganda directed at chiefs who were regarded as following British dictates. The Baganda consistently refused to yield to what they regarded as interference with their right of internal autonomy and in 1944 won further concessions by which the role of the European provincial administration was reduced to an advisory one.

Then, in the early 1950's, when the British made new overtures toward establishing unitary government in Uganda, the full vigor of Ganda separatism was provoked. With the advent of a liberal governor, Sir Andrew Cohen, in 1952, grievance in Buganda became more politicized than ever before. Convinced that Uganda had to begin to prepare for self-government, Sir Andrew introduced a series of progressive but unpopular reforms. Determined that indigenous government should be democratized and granted greater scope, the new governor attempted to turn the protectorate into a unitary state with a popularly elected legislature. His objective was to relieve the traditional leaders, particularly the kabaka, of a major portion of their administrative and political responsibility. As one scholar notes, Sir Andrew was attempting to pave the way for nationalist politicians in Uganda: "If, as Cohen foresaw,

Uganda was likely to advance to self-government far faster than had been imagined, then it seemed essential to concentrate on developing institutions that could hold the country together. After decades of a government policy which had a directly opposite bias, he was attempting to win the nationalists' struggle for them."[14]

Early in 1953, using a comment by the secretary for the colonies about an eventual East African federation as a pretext, the kabaka notified the British of his intention to block popular elections in Buganda to the Legislative Council. The governor responded by declaring a state of emergency in Buganda, removing the kabaka, Sir Edward Mutesa, from his position as native ruler of Buganda, and deporting him to the United Kingdom. When the British allowed him to return, eighteen months later, Sir Edward enjoyed greater popularity than ever before, and the kabaka became the symbol of opposition to imperial authority. A new agreement in 1955 assured Mengo of control of its own affairs and recognized the kabaka as constitutional monarch.

To defend the kabaka's cause, Ignatius Musazi, a Muganda, formed Uganda's first national party, the Uganda National Congress (UNC). After the UNC was founded as a neotraditional party (in March 1952 in Buganda) a number of other political parties emerged. Tending to represent the interests of specific geographical areas, these were parties of local notables, rather than mass parties, and were incapable of attracting large followings.

In 1958 seven members of the Legislative Council joined forces to form the Uganda Peoples Union (UPU), an anti-Ganda party. One year later, the first group to have a large membership, the Uganda National Movement (UNM), organized a boycott of Asian shops, declared its opposition to the Legislative Council, and argued for government by traditional rulers. Initially refusing to join the UNM-organized boycott, Apolo Milton Obote (a member of the Legislative Council from the north) and Abu Mayanja (a Muganda Moslem) opposed Joseph Kiwanuka's group of Baganda within the UNC. The Obote group emerged victorious in two intraparty leadership crises in 1959. Following the expulsion of Musazi, president general and original founder of the UNC,

14. R. C. Pratt, "Nationalism in Uganda," *Political Studies*, IX, No. 2 (June 1961), 161.

Obote's supporters succeeded in suspending both the party's chairman, Joseph Kiwanuka—who was criticized for having backed the colonial government against the UNM and for failing to mobilize large numbers of Baganda—and the secretary-general, B. N. Kununka. Then the Obote faction sought new allies, joining in 1960 with a number of Catholic leaders from within the UNC and the UPU, which had substantial backing in the West, to form the Uganda Peoples Congress (UPC). Despite its lack of strength in Buganda, the UPC claimed to be interdenomininational and to be the successor to the original UNC.

As the 1961 elections approached, two other parties assumed increasing importance. Benedicto Kiwanuka's Democratic Party (DP), established in 1954 as an antineotraditional party, tended to attract Catholic members, in contrast to the UPC, which, despite the Catholics among its leaders, derived its backing largely from the Protestant community. Kabaka Yekka (KY, Kabaka Only) was a neotraditional movement rather than a political party (because politicians in Buganda realized that defense of their interests required organization but feared that political parties would have a divisive impact on the kingdom). Formed primarily through the efforts of Masembe-Kabali, it stood for unity in Buganda, supported the kabaka as the embodiment of Ganda tradition, and included members of all religious denominations.

A year after threatening secession and demanding independence for Buganda, the kabaka's government refused to cooperate in elections for an interim government during the period immediately before independence. Less than 2 percent of eligible Baganda turned out for the March 1961 elections, and the DP won a majority of seats in the Council on the eve of independence. For a brief moment in Uganda's history it seemed possible that local Ganda nationalism could be reconciled with modern Ugandan nationalism. Yet the fissiparous tendencies of Ugandan politics were not so easily cured.

Uganda's first prime minister, Benedicto Kiwanuka, was a Muganda in a country whose peoples harbored strong grievances against this historically predominant tribe; he was also a Catholic in a country whose elite was recruited from the Protestant establishment. While these factors were important, they did not present insurmountable problems. The main difficulty was that issues within Buganda became polarized in terms of Kiwanuka versus the kabaka, and for the average Muganda it was heresy to conceive of a peasant holding a position above the traditional leader. This inherent difficulty within Buganda was aggravated by Kiwanuka's abrasive personality and his penchant for employing inflammatory tactics. Increasingly the DP was marked by serious divisions within its ranks, and these divisions came to a head in 1962 when Benedicto Kiwanuka's support within Buganda dwindled to the extent that his constituency elected another M.P. to the National Assembly. Basil Bataringaya assumed the mantle of leadership within the parliamentary party and proceeded, unsuccessfully, to challenge Kiwanuka for the party presidency.

As Ugandans attempted to arrive at a mutually acceptable balance of forces at home, deliberations with the metropole continued. The Munster Commission (1961) endorsed Buganda's demands for a federal position in the central state and the right to hold indirect elections to the National Assembly through the Lukiiko. The Commission recommended "semifederal" status for the kingdoms of Bunyoro, Ankole, and Toro and suggested that the remaining districts be under a unitary government. When the constitutional conference opened in London in December 1961, the battle lines were drawn. Fearing that indirect elections would give all of Buganda's votes to the KY, Benedicto Kiwanuka and the DP argued for direct elections. But the UPC supported Buganda's demands, Obote agreeing that indirect elections through the Lukiiko should determine Buganda's twenty-one members of parliament.

Responding to the DP's show of strength in the elections of March 1961, Obote startled the country in September by allying his populist, predominantly northern-based UPC with the royalist, Ganda KY. For the sake of electoral convenience, an antineotraditional party and a neotraditional movement joined forces. The quid pro quo included the kabaka's agreement to support Obote as prime minister in exchange for the UPC's endorsement of federal status for Buganda and the Lukiiko's right to elect members to the National Assembly. In *Desecration of My Kingdom,* Sir Edward Mutesa gives his reasons for concluding the alliance and his impressions of Obote:

An alliance between Buganda and U.P.C. was suggested, with innumerable promises of respect for our position after independence. He [Obote] would step down, and I should choose whoever I wished to be Prime Minister. Though I did not particularly like him, for he is not a particularly likeable man, I agreed to the alliance without misgivings. He understood our fears for the position of Buganda; we shared his hopes for a united, prosperous and free Uganda. Kintu was alone in opposing this new friendship. Obote had said that he meant to crush the Baganda, and Kintu would not forgive or trust him. We waved it aside as an impetuous remark made to please crowds. Now we thought him reformed, the obvious and best ally against Kiwanuka and the hated D.P. . . .

. . . Obote assured us that all the details would be ironed out later in discusions between the relevant Minister of the Lukiiko and of the National Assembly. We could count on him. "Trust me," he said and smiled reassuringly. With only faint misgivings, we did.[15]

The UPC and the KY found common ground in the Protestant ascendancy and opposition to the DP. The UPC's main aim was to prevent the KY from upsetting or delaying independence, and Obote was willing to make substantial concessions in order to persuade Buganda to enter a new state of Uganda; the objective of the Protestant establishment in Buganda was to keep the Catholics— in the guise of "the hated D.P."—out of power. Alliance achieved both ends and also served as a device for two suspicious partners to check on one another—the UPC had to contain Buganda, and Buganda was concerned about the UPC's antimonarchical tendencies.[16]

One provision of the UPC-KY agreement stipulated that Obote's men would not contest constituencies in Buganda. The result was that in direct elections for the Lukiiko in February 1962—elections that were marked by intimidation and violence directed against DP members and supporters—the KY won sixty-five of sixty-eight seats. Subsequently, in April 1962, Ugandans went to the polls to determine the composition of their first postcolonial government. The results gave the UPC thirty-seven seats, KY twenty-one, and the DP twenty-four. (In accordance with the 1962 constitution, which provided that elected members would choose

15. Sir Edward Mutesa, The Kabaka of Buganda, *Desecration of My Kingdom* (London: Constable, 1967), pp. 160 and 166.
16. Wellbourn, p. 35.

specially elected members, the UPC total in the first session of the National Assembly reached forty-three, the KY twenty-four.) The new prime minister, Milton Obote, proposed that Uganda's president and vice-president be selected from among the hereditary rulers and constitutional heads of state. Initially, the heads of state were opposed to an arrangement whereby a Bantu king would become president. The smaller kingdoms also had reservations about the kabaka assuming the presidency. However, when deliberations were concluded, the nonexecutive positions of president and vice-president were filled by Sir Edward Mutesa, kabaka of Buganda, and Sir Wilberforce Nadiope, kyabazinga (traditional ruler) of Busoga.

The neofederal arrangements of the 1962 constitution and the UPC-KY alliance proved incapable of withstanding the centrifugal forces of Ugandan politics. When Uganda became independent, in October 1962, the constitution provided for four kingdoms (Buganda, Bunyoro, Toro, and Ankole), one territory (Busoga), and ten districts (West Nile, Madi, Acholi, Lango, Karamoja, Bugisu, Bukedi, Kigezi, Sebei, and Teso). The difficulty of the task facing Obote cannot be overestimated. The prime minister's objective was to convert a minority into a majority by playing two opposed groups off against one another. This course had to be pursued without alienating the radical and anti-Ganda wings of his own party (which overlapped but were not identical). Furthermore, given the intrigue of Ugandan politics, a KY-DP alliance could not be ruled out. With these considerations in mind, Obote formulated his strategy, which was to wear down DP support outside Buganda, maintain the alliance with the KY, and work to strengthen the UPC in parliament to the point where it could achieve a majority without KY support.[17]

As Obote attempted to build a majority in parliament, a more urgent problem was the need to generate and manage power at the center. In formulating his policies, Obote was necessarily constrained by the fact that the UPC-KY coalition gave the kabaka de facto veto power. Tension between the UPC and the KY would increase the likelihood of a KY-DP partnership. The alliance was

17. Colin Leys, "Present Relations between the States of East Africa," *International Journal*, XX, No. 4 (Autumn 1965), 515, 516.

indeed tenuous. In addition, fissiparous tendencies threatened not only interparty relations but intraparty unity as well. With independence, the UPC, like other ruling parties in Africa, faced the problem of scarce trained and qualified personnel. In such a situation, a party competes with the government and the bureaucracy for human resources; as a ruling party attempts to Africanize government, parastatal bodies, and civil service posts, its own ranks are depleted of the most highly qualified. The Ugandan experience followed the pattern of events elsewhere in Africa: the scope and power of the government and the bureaucracy increased in relation to that of the political parties, and shortly after independence Uganda's one-party dominant system began to atrophy.

Factionalism and lack of discipline, both in relations between local branches and national headquarters and within the central organization, were problems the UPC experienced from its inception. Even before independence, a series of expulsions and reinstatements indicated disorganization and lack of control. The party's relations with the trade unions and with its own youth wing were particularly difficult. Strikes and labor unrest became an issue between the top echelon of the UPC and the unions. The UPC's labor policies were aimed primarily at maintaining stability and unity. In the spring of 1963, Obote joined ministers Felix Onama and Adoko Nekyon in attacking the unions for their failure to abide by UPC policies. The prime minister contended that "foreign hands" were controlling the Trade Union Congress (TUC) and announced that appropriate action would be forthcoming.[18]

The youth wing of the UPC, too, was displaying increasing militance and deviating from official party policies. The election of the UPC secretary-general in 1964 provoked a bitter struggle for power in the party, with leaders of the Youth League throwing their support to John Kakonge, the incumbent candidate. Kakonge leaned toward the East in foreign affairs and derived his support from the trade unions as well as youth. The challenger and other major contestant, Grace Ibingira, a young cabinet member from Ankole, received the endorsement of most of the party bosses in the cabinet and parliament. As far as Obote was concerned, the issue in the election was the need for the party to pursue an inde-

18. Rothchild and Rogin, pp. 388, 389.

pendent course of action; accordingly, he supported the more moderate Ibingira. When Ibingira triumphed, the Obote strategy seemed to have succeeded, at least insofar as intraparty factionalism abated temporarily.

Fragility was characteristic of other political institutions in Uganda as well as parties. Preserving the inviolability of civil-military relations was a constant source of concern, but an elusive goal. Throughout East Africa, in the early years after independence, the military was staffed largely by expatriates. Localization of the officer corps was slow, and enlisted men were not well paid. In Uganda, military affairs were highly politicized; the ethnic basis of recruitment, in particular, has long been a source of concern. The kabaka placed his trust in the Etesot and other Bantu elements in the army; Obote solicited support from high-ranking northerners. Politicization was aggravated by rapid expansion of the size of the army and by frequent reshuffling and dismissal of officers. And, in addition to ethnic divisions and personal rivalries, tensions between direct-entry, educated officers and experienced NCO's increased.

The army mutiny of January 1964 was precipitated by grievances over wages and the rate of Africanization of the officer corps. While definite links between the events are difficult to establish, the Zanzibar revolution of January 12, 1964, appears to have triggered crises in civil-military relations throughout East Africa. Beginning nine days after the revolution, military unrest spread through the area. In Uganda, the battalion stationed in Jinja mutinied on January 23, holding the minister of defense, Felix Onama, prisoner. The mutinous soldiers pressed for redress of specified grievances; the officers neither planned a coup d'état nor intended to march on the capital. The government dealt with the mutiny essentially by meeting the army's demands. It agreed to accelerate localization of the officer corps and to increase wages; at the same time, however, it dismissed a number of officers involved in the mutiny.

By mid-1964, Obote appeared to have succeeded beyond all expectations. In his handling of two major crises—the struggle for power within the UPC and the army mutiny—he had amply demonstrated his political sagacity. By the end of 1964, seven KY and fourteen DP M.P.'s had joined the UPC, giving that party a two-thirds majority in the National Assembly; in August 1964

Obote was able to bring the precarious UPC-KY alliance to an end. The demise of the alliance that had ushered in Ugandan independence was precipitated by the prime minister's decision to hold a referendum to determine the fate of the "lost counties" of Buyaga and Bugangazi. These counties had been transferred from Bunyoro to Buganda early in the colonial period in gratitude for services provided to the metropole. The issue was an emotional one in Bunyoro, for the traditional kingdom, including the tombs of former kings and national shrines, was located in Buyaga and Bugangazi. When Obote presented a bill providing for a referendum in the lost counties, the kabaka, as president of Uganda, would not sign it, and subsequently he contested its legality in the Uganda High Court and Privy Council. The government at Mengo refused to sanction the referendum and alleged that the provisions concerning voting qualifications were invalid. When the referendum was held, on November 4, 1964, after seventy years of separation, an overwhelming majority voted for reunion with Bunyoro.

Having built an electoral majority, ended the UPC-KY coalition, and returned the lost counties to Bunyoro, Obote faced a crisis more serious than any with which he had been presented before. The secretary-general of the UPC, Grace Ibingira, was expanding his power base and increasingly divorcing himself from the policies of the prime minister. Members of the UPC who were critical of Obote began to gravitate toward Ibingira, adopting a strategy of opposing the prime minister not from without but from within the party. A significant group of KY, who in effect controlled the Buganda UPC, threw their lot in with the secretary-general, whose faction attempted to mobilize further support by capturing power in the party's district organizations. Rumors circulated that Ibingira cohorts, in collusion with the KY, were contemplating a coup d'état.

Obote's strategy of centralizing power was increasingly challenged by centrifugal tendencies within his own party. In 1966, several no-confidence motions were introduced in UPC-controlled district councils. Factionalism was rife both in the central party organization and in the parliamentary party. Links between UPC central headquarters and the party's district branches were at best intermittent and in some cases nonexistent. Against this background of institutional weakness and personal insecurity, Obote faced a major challenge from Buganda. The crisis that ensued is normally seen as representing a collision between two irreconcilable aims—the heartland tribe's attempt to redress its grievances, and the central government's effort to forge unity. More probably, however, Obote's response to Ganda provocation reflected his belief that the only way to repair the divisions in his party and compensate for a general lack of support was to strike against the Baganda.

The events leading up to the crisis began with a parliamentary motion on February 4, 1966, moved by Daudi Ocheng—an Acholi and secretary-general of the KY—that a commission of inquiry be established to investigate charges that Colonel Idi Amin, the second highest ranking officer in the army, was smuggling gold and ivory from the Congo. Producing a document that he described as a photograph of Amin's bank account, Ocheng maintained that Amin was being paid for his efforts as well as converting gold and ivory into money for his own use. Ocheng further alleged that Amin was instructing a group of youths, based near Mbale, who were planning to overthrow the constitution. According to Ocheng, although Amin's activities were well known, he had not been brought to justice because others would be implicated. On October 7, 1965, Ocheng claimed, he had informed the prime minister that new information was available concerning Amin's affairs but Obote had dismissed the matter, saying that politics were divorced from security matters. Ocheng's final charge was that Amin was acting in collusion with high-ranking politicians, including the prime minister, Obote's cousin, Adoko Nekyon (minister of planning and community development), and Felix Onama (minister of state for defense).

A vigorous debate followed in the National Assembly. It quickly became apparent that the UPC was not supporting the prime minister. C. J. Magara (UPC member for Bunyoro) claimed to have evidence confirming certain aspects of Ocheng's allegations; on a recent visit to London he had been surprised to learn the rate at which Uganda was exporting gold. A. K. Mayanja (UPC, Kyagwe Northeast) was disappointed that action had not been taken earlier; he affirmed that grounds had certainly existed for moving the motion before Ocheng's proposal in the National Assembly was actually made. J. W. Kiwanuka (UPC, Mubende

North) and F. C. Sembeguya (UPC, a specially elected member[19])
called for the immediate suspension of Colonel Amin. On the other
side of the floor, A. A. Latim (DP, Acholi Northwest, leader of
the opposition) submitted evidence that Amin had threatened his
and Ocheng's lives. Ocheng demanded Obote's resignation and
called on the UPC to appoint another prime minister. When the
issue was put to a vote, the National Assembly approved the
motion to create a commission of inquiry with only one dissenting
vote—that of John Kakonge. In accordance with a parliamentary
directive, Abu Mayanja announced that a letter had been delivered
to Colonel Amin giving him two weeks' holiday.

The prime minister appeared to be further isolated by the
election of February 13, 1966, for the position of UPC branch
chairman in Buganda, in which E. Lumu, a Muganda identified
with the Ibingira faction, defeated Godfrey Binaisa, also a Muganda
but a staunch Obote supporter. Only then did Obote respond
publicly to the allegations made in parliament. At a press conference in Entebbe on February 13, more than a week after
Ocheng's initial accusations were presented to the National Assembly, Obote insisted, "This is a frameup to present me as the most
dirty man in Uganda. . . . I have led the country with clean
hands and with a clean heart."[20] Shortly thereafter he arrested five
ministers, suspended the constitution, assumed all powers of government, and appointed himself president. In April he called the
National Assembly into session, presenting the members with an
interim constitution without any chance for discussion or debate.
After the opposition and four government members had walked
out, the 1966 constitution was adopted by a vote of fifty-five to four.
The purpose of the new constitutional provisions was to move
Uganda away from the pluralism embodied in the neofederal
arrangements of the 1962 constitution. Obote sought to use the
constitution to achieve political change, and the 1966 version

19. According to the 1962 constitution, the party having the greatest
numerical strength in the National Assembly would choose as many specially
elected members as required to give that party a majority of not more
than ten.
20. "Dr. Obote Denies Allegations," *Uganda Argus* (Kampala), February
14, 1966.

augmented the power of the center at the expense of the kingdoms, the territory, and the districts. Among the most important provisions, Buganda's right to hold indirect elections for the National Assembly was ended, the four kings were reduced to ceremonial positions, and the offices of president and prime minister were combined.

Mengo was not prepared to accept these measures. As far as the kabaka's government was concerned, Obote's action was a violation of Buganda's social contract with the state of Uganda. On May 20, 1966, the Lukiiko passed a resolution calling for the government of Uganda to remove itself from Buganda soil. Rioting and battles with the police ensued. Four days after the Lukiiko resolution, Deputy Commander Amin led the national army in an assault on the kabaka's palace. The kabaka escaped and lived as an exile in London until his death in November 1969. (Alcoholic poisoning was the official cause of death, but many suspected foul play.)

Reminiscing about the events of 1966, the kabaka admitted that he had held talks with Brigadier General Shaban Opolot, the Iteso commander of the Ugandan army, and with the British high commissioner. He denied, however, that extralegal plans to replace the prime minister had been formulated.

But, though I would have liked to see him destroyed, I took no part in moves against him; perhaps I was foolish not to do so.

Assuming that he had something to hide from the investigation, Obote was now in a desperate position. The country was against him; his party was against him; he retained the control of only the Army. . . .

I remained in Kampala very much aware that it was my turn next. My curious position as President of a country without a Government or Constitution would not last. I did not know whether I would be arrested or accused first, but I could do little but wait.[21]

Obote has argued, however, that the kabaka, acting in collusion with Opolot, tried "to jump the gun by once more attempting to effect a change of Government by using the Army. I had, therefore, to take drastic action."[22]

21. Mutesa, pp. 188–89.
22. A. Milton Obote, *Myths and Realities: A Letter to a London Friend* (Kampala: African Publishers, November 16, 1968), p. 27.

Obote attempted to consolidate his maneuvers in the 1966 crisis with the adoption of a new constitution a year later. Unlike the interim constitution of 1966, the document of September 1967 was carefully scrutinized and debated by a constituent assembly. The republican constitution, as it came to be called, was designed to remove the vestiges of regional autonomy and centralize the powers of government in a unitary state. Its most notable feature was the abolition of monarchies. Executive power was vested in the president, who, subject to the provisions of the constitution, was to serve as head of state, head of government, and commander in chief of the armed forces and to enjoy general exemption from judicial proceedings.

From the adoption of the republican constitution in September 1967 to the launching of the Move to the Left in October 1969, political activity in Uganda was subdued and lacked the intensity that the events of the preceding years had generated. By 1967 the Youth League had, in effect, been disbanded. After the adoption of the republican constitution, the UPC annual delegates conference was not held until June 1968. A new UPC constitution was proposed and adopted by which the structure of the party was brought into line with the government through greater centralization. Obote was elected president of the UPC for seven years, and Felix Onama was named secretary-general. In short, little activity could be observed within the UPC. Meanwhile, members of the DP continued to cross over to the major party. Emergency regulations covering Buganda were renewed every six months. In Uganda generally, the power of preventive detention was used to stifle opposition, and no elections were held.

The major incident during the 1967–1969 period was the *Transition* affair. On July 5, 1968, *Transition,* a Kampala-based magazine with international circulation, published an article by Picho Ali stressing the need for the judiciary in Uganda to toe the party line. "The argument for ideological parity is based upon the necessity to re-examine the judicial set-up in the country so as to make the judiciary an organ of the people for administering justice in conformity with the aims and objectives of the State of Uganda."[23]

23. Picho Ali, "Ideological Commitment and the Judiciary," *Transition,* VII (v), No. 36 (1968), 47.

In the following issue of *Transition,* Abu Mayanja attacked Ali's argument and reported a rumor that tribal considerations were responsible for the failure to Ugandanize the judiciary—the implication being that Obote did not want Baganda (as the majority of trained lawyers have been) in the courts.[24] Subsequently, Mayanja and Rajat Neogy, editor of *Transition,* were charged with sedition; although acquitted of that offense, they were then rearrested and detained under the emergency regulations.

Throughout the 1962–1969 period, Obote's policies and style of power management were directed above all at increasing central power. Whenever independent sources of power developed, they were regarded not as complementary or contributory to power at the center but as jeopardizing national interests. Obote's tactics can be faulted on grounds of poor execution, and many of his individual decisions can be criticized in terms of measures employed. Given the traditional rivalries, the fragmentation, and the structural inflexibilities of politics in Uganda, however, it is problematical whether a national leader could have pursued any other strategy. Even if this issue remains open to debate, it is certain that, following independence, Uganda, like other countries in Africa, suffered from a lack of power, in both relative and absolute terms. If Uganda was to embark on a viable program of national development, establishing control at the center had to be the first task. Only then could decisions be made about development strategies and an ideology of modernization be introduced. In such a process, timing is clearly of fundamental importance: if the attempt to articulate an ideology of modernization is premature or ill conceived, ideology can activate or exacerbate economic cleavages and primordial loyalties.

Obote's first concern, therefore, was power management. From 1967 to 1969, he showed himself to be a clever and astute politician, not only surviving designs intended to remove him from leadership of the body politic but even augmenting his power at the expense of the ambitions of critics, challengers, and sycophants. By 1968–1969, Obote felt more secure than at any time since independence. Writing in 1968, he went so far as to boast about the state of national unity in Uganda: "We have had two years without a Kabaka at Mengo and we have not had a 'Biafran'

24. Letter to the editor, *Transition,* VII (vi), No. 37 (1968), 15.

situation."[25] The same year saw him displaying greater abandon and daring to use terms that had generally been avoided previously: "The Uganda revolution of 1966 was a revolution of the masses against the forces of feudalism and tribalism whose design was to divide Uganda into personal domains with the aid of imperialist forces outside Uganda."[26] The unlikely partnership with a royalist party was buried in a problem-ridden past. The power of Buganda had been crushed. The monarchies were abolished. Factionalism in the governing party seemed to have abated, and opposition parties were no longer of concern. Major dissidents were in exile, detention, or held within the confines of the governing party. Feeling increasing certainty about his own position and Uganda's future, displaying renewed self-confidence, and enjoying far greater constitutional power than ever before, Milton Obote was about to engage Uganda in an attempt to mold a medley of traditionally oriented peoples into a modern socialist state. And ideology was selected as a principal agent for social transformation.

25. Obote, *Myths and Realities,* p. 7.
26. *Idem,* "The Footsteps of Uganda's Revolution," *East Africa Journal,* V, No. 10 (October 1968), 13.

CHAPTER 4

Toward an Ideology
of Modernization

There are two distinct phases to ideological modernization in Uganda. The first, covering the period from independence (October 1962) to the launching of the Move to the Left (October 1969), was a time of ideological quiet, particularly in comparison with the ideological activity of some of the other African states in these years. Although particular ideas and policies of African leaders who win acclaim as ideologues may be faulted, most observers agree that such statesmen as Nkrumah and Nyerere, to name but two, enhanced their prestige by establishing reputations as prominent spokesmen for the African revolution. Obote, by contrast, was reluctant in the 1960's to advance Uganda's version of the African revolution, preferring to be circumspect in exercising his ideological options. Prudence and restraint were the watchwords. "Uganda seemed to be, in relative terms, ideologically dormant. . . . In the visionary centralizing sense, the country's ethos was almost anti-ideological."[1]

In the first phase, the Obote government possessed neither the legitimacy nor the coercive capacity to establish an operative ideology of modernization. From a normative perspective, modernization refers to choice. If government decisions on development strategies are to be implemented, either a sense of political community must supply binding force, or the government must be able to compel the necessary behavior, or there must be an adequate combination of the two conditions. Neither condition obtained in Uganda in 1962–1969; accordingly, this phase represented a prelude to themes that were to emerge in the 1969–1971 period. Ideological innovation was muted during the first phase because

1. Engholm and Mazrui, p. 593.

structural constraints limited the options open to leaders. Given the extent of social fragmentation and the hostility among groups, the channels normally employed for ideological diffusion—for example, the party system, the bureaucracy, women's leagues, youth groups, the trade union movement—were regarded as unreliable if not hostile. In some cases, these potential mechanisms for ideological diffusion atrophied during the 1960's; in others institutionalization never advanced to the point where atrophy could occur.

This period of ideological quiet was also a time when Ugandans were attempting to establish their identity and, above all, a preparatory period of pragmatism and consolidation. Consolidation of power is indispensable for the introduction of an ideology of modernization, for ideological innovation and diffusion unleash disruptive forces as well as offering new avenues of success. Conversely, a modernizing ideology can help in generating and managing power. The first phase was, therefore, critically important in terms of the later ideological sequel. What some observers came to regard as the radical departures of an individual political leader proved to be, at least in part, the crystallization of values and beliefs adumbrated in the earlier years. Certainly in the period after independence Obote had to feel his way, both in determining his own patterns of thought and in dealing with the volatile political situation in Uganda. In the absence of an appropriate mythology, there was no Ugandan identity when constitutional power was transferred to an indigenous elite. Some of the reasons for this lack of a distinctive Ugandan mythology—economic divisions, interethnic rivalries, the paramount position of the Baganda, religious and linguistic cleavages—have already been discussed; but there are others.

Comparison of Uganda with some of the other states of Africa reveals a number of differences that indicate the constraints on ideological innovation and diffusion in this small East African country. Unlike parts of West Africa, Uganda has few large towns, and not many Africans live in these urban areas. It is difficult, therefore, to produce large crowds for political gatherings. Furthermore, without a large urban population, mass media cannot be effective in spreading ideology. The problem is compounded by the absence of a lingua franca. No one language in Uganda is functionally equivalent to Hausa in parts of West Africa or Swahili in

Tanzania. Moreover, literacy in English is limited, and little literature exists in the vernacular languages.

Unlike Kenya, Northern Rhodesia, Southern Rhodesia, Nyasaland, and South Africa, Uganda had no non-African political movements or trade unions to serve as a threat—or perhaps a model—and thereby stimulate organization of Africans. The number of expatriate Europeans resident in Uganda remained small. In contrast to the African territories that were victimized by entrenched white power, the absence of a white settler community in Uganda was a mitigating factor in the relationship between Ugandans and colonialists. Grievances against the imperial authority never resembled the highly politicized discontent of neighboring Kenya, and this relative lack of widespread, deeply rooted outrage weakened the force of potentially unifying issues. Nor was there, under colonial rule in Uganda, much feeling of economic affliction or dissatisfaction; the educated African elite was small, and its members had little difficulty in gaining access to avenues of upward mobility in traditional political structures, the church, and the school system.[2]

The lack of an appropriate mythology and the structural factors inhibiting ideological innovation and diffusion in Uganda made the context for ideological modernization largely transnational, continental rather than Ugandan. If during the period 1962–1969 (and particularly in the years before 1966) the ruling elite had taken bold steps to resurrect and reconstruct specifically Ugandan traditions as the basis for a national mythology, their efforts would probably have been abortive; for Uganda's history is marked more by internal heterogeneity and conflict than by shared tradition or cooperation. Instead the ruling elite, steering away from the divisive course, turned toward what it regarded as a safer option. In the first phase of ideological modernization Uganda's leaders tended to derive their ideas from the greater African context, in which they sought to discover and legitimize a new identity.[3]

For the sake of coherence in analysis, the substance of ideological

2. Donald Anthony Low, *Political Parties in Uganda, 1949–1962* (London: University of London, 1962), pp. 13–17; J. E. Goldthorpe, *An African Elite: Makerere Students 1922–1960* (London: Oxford University Press, 1965).

3. Also see Wellbourn, p. 62.

modernization is best approached by examining six ideological themes that are significant in the broader African context: nationalism, pan-Africanism, antineocolonialism, neutralism and nonalignment, African socialism, and négritude and the African personality. Insofar as one can legitimately speak about a specifically African paradigm of political values and beliefs (for statesmen subscribe to significantly different interpretations), these six themes represent the major motifs of African political ideology. In different parts of Africa, particular themes are more or less salient or intensive; nevertheless, the substantive intent of individual pronouncements (for example, the call for racial equality), is often one of mutual reinforcement, despite differences in semantics, the nature of the colonial experience, and cultural patterns.[4]

Nationalism

Nationalism in Uganda has been colored by two factors. First, Ugandan nationalists did not have to wage a pitched battle for independence. Britain was not recalcitrant in acceding to demands for a constitutional transfer of power to local elites. Granting indigenous elites the right to occupy positions of nominal authority was consistent with the interests of the metropole, and there was no white settler community with which to contend. Hence, neither the kind of violent struggle experienced in Algeria nor the political agitation waged in Ghana or Nigeria was necessary in Uganda. Second, in the heartland area before and during the transition to self-government, anticolonialism and traditionalism were regarded as complementary; in other parts of Africa nationalists generally viewed anticolonialism and traditionalism as opposed.

On the eve of independence, Ugandan nationalists gained inspiration from the fervor of anticolonialism elsewhere on the continent and throughout the Third World. The increasing strength of anticolonial sentiment in the United Nations, the growing demand of blacks in the United States for racial equality, the realization of self-government in parts of Asia and North and West Africa, the campaign launched by Mau Mau in Kenya, and the accession

4. The rationale for using this paradigm is abbreviated in the text; for a more complete explanation see my "Ideological Modernization: An Approach to the Study of African Political Systems" (unpublished Ph.D. dissertation: Cornell University, 1971).

to independence of Uganda's other neighbors (Sudan, Congo, Tanganyika, and Rwanda) all fired the enthusiasm of Ugandan nationalists. In many of the African states that attained independence before Uganda, nationalist movements had attempted to mobilize mass support. In Uganda, however, the imminence of independence obviated any sense of urgency. Rothchild and Rogin argue that, so far from nationalism producing independence in Uganda, the relationship was reversed: the imminence of independence was responsible for the emergence of nationalistic parties.[5] This view is largely correct, but two qualifications can be added. First, Rothchild and Rogin do not make explicit allowance for a Fanonist devolution of power. Independence may be more apparent than real. Reference has already been made to constitutional independence, or false decolonization, in which a national bourgeoisie joins in an alliance with external capitalist forces. Local elites replace expatriates in exploiting the masses, perpetrate internal colonialism, and contribute to the maldistribution of wealth, both internationally and domestically. No allegation that these were Uganda's circumstances can, of course, be leveled a priori, but the issue will be raised again in the chapters that follow. Second, Uganda had a long-standing tradition of local nationalism before independence. Rothchild and Rogin's argument is valid insofar as it refers to modern nationalism, but it must also be remembered that local nationalism engendered fierce resistance to the imposition of colonial rule. When Colonel Colville defeated Kabalega in western Uganda in 1893, the omukama of Bunyoro-Kitara was forced to retreat to the north, from where he conducted five years of guerrilla warfare against imperial supremacy. In 1894 and 1895 Captain Thurston and Major Cunningham continued the British offensive, but Kabalega stubbornly held on to the area north of the Nile. He was not captured until 1899, when British agents found him still fighting despite a bullet wound that required amputation of the arm. When seized, the omukama was with the kabaka of Buganda, who by 1897 had also rejected alien rule. These two kings—Chwa II Kabalega of Bunyoro-Kitara and Mwanga II of Buganda—were nationalists who preferred the honor of battle to acquiescence in the indignities of imperial control. The imposition of colonial rule was fiercely resisted in other parts of

5. Rothchild and Rogin, p. 351.

Uganda as well. In Ankole, the king of Igara decided on suicide. His neighbor, the king of Kajara, withdrew to Tanganyika. In Busoga cooperation was won only by threatening the ruler with deposition and deportation. In Teso, Lango, and Acholi, resistance to imperial authority culminated in the Lamogi rebellion of 1912.[6] Even the oligarchy in Buganda, propped up only with external support, became increasingly independent and steadfastly protected the kingdom from further inroads. The Lukiiko demanded an end to practices that allowed European and Indian cotton-buying monopolies to exploit African farmers. In the 1940's a series of riots expressed further protest against economic exploitation as well as opposition to the older, more obsequious chiefs; and the boycott of non-African shops organized in Buganda and the Eastern Province at the end of the 1950's had as its target the expatriate middle class—primarily Asian traders and a few European merchants.[7]

For both the Ugandans and the Colonial Office, as early as the mid-1950's, the real issue was not winning independence but devising an acceptable formula for the period after the transfer of authority. In 1953, Lord Chandos, British colonial secretary, stated that at some (unspecified) time in the future Uganda would be self-governing as a "primarily African state." When the kabaka returned from exile in 1955 there was little doubt that Uganda would attain independence without pitched battle. And after Ghana obtained its independence in 1957 the speculation was that Uganda would be next, many thought before the end of the decade.[8]

6. M. S. M. Kiwanuka, "Uganda under the British," in B. A. Ogot and J. A. Kieran, eds., Zamani: A Survey of East African History (Nairobi: East African Publishing House, 1968), p. 314. On nationalist resistance, see John Beattie, The Nyoro State (Oxford: Clarendon Press, 1971); Low, Buganda in Modern History; Nykatura; and Godfrey N. Uzoigwe, "Kabalega and the Making of a New Kitara," Tarikh, III, No. 2 (1970), 5–22, and Revolution and Revolt in Bunyoro-Kitara: Two Studies, Part 2 (London: Longmans, 1970).
    7. M. S. M. Kiwanuka, "Nationality and Nationalism in Africa: The Uganda Case," Canadian Journal of African Studies, IV, No. 2 (Spring 1970), 236; Dharam P. Ghai, "The Buganda Trade Boycott: A Study in Tribal, Political, and Economic Nationalism," in Robert I. Rotberg and Ali A. Mazrui, eds., Protest and Power in Black Africa (New York: Oxford University Press, 1970), pp. 755–90.
    8. Low, Political Parties, p. 41; Kiwanuka, "Nationality and Nationalism," p. 238.

As a result of the inability of political parties to resolve their differences, the lack of a sense of urgency amongst the elites, and Britain's increased appreciation of the benefits to be gained by transferring authority, nationalism in Uganda during the late 1950's and early 1960's was marked by fluidity, shifting alignments, and unprincipled maneuvering. There was considerable dissension among aspiring politicians. Values that were widely accepted and could be used to mobilize the masses and forge unity were absent. In searching for issues, "politicians migrate[d] from party to party and from principle to principle in a depressing search for political status."[9] Unlike countries (for example, Kenya) where the heartland tribe (in Kenya's case, the Kikuyu) spearheaded the drive for independence, Uganda became self-governing without the support of the dominant tribe. For the vast majority of Baganda, the success in 1955 of the campaign to have the kabaka returned was sufficient proof that tribal institutions were the most viable form of political organization. The restoration of the kabaka was regarded as symbolic: the Baganda could be both anticolonial nationalists and loyal to their own traditional institutions.

Most Uganda nationalists reasoned that the first task was to win independence; the issue of Buganda could be faced after that. For the Baganda, however, the primary question was their own future position; the independence of Uganda was secondary. Speaking to this point, the kabaka is unequivocal:

The wind of change had started to blow in West Africa and there was no doubt now that Uganda would become independent. For most Africans in such a position the question is "When?" For us it was "Whither?" We had struggled long and hard to retain our integrity during the life of the Protectorate Government. Now the situation was to be different and we looked ahead to see if there were different dangers. Where would we stand in an independent Uganda? . . .

At first we thought we would be held back by our more backward neighbours; later we feared that a combination of the rest of the country might from motives of self-interest and jealousy seek to destroy us. Both fears proved well-founded. Of course, we desired to be independent as soon as possible, but it was essential to settle our relationship with the central government in advance, not simply to allow it to emerge haphazard. This necessity became the theme of our demands from my return until independence.[10]

9. Pratt, p. 173.
10. Mutesa, pp. 148–49.

Reference was made earlier to the neofederal arrangements of the 1962 constitution. During the early and mid-1960's, the Obote government attempted gradually to align values and beliefs with newly created national institutions. In the first phase of ideological modernization, the issue of institutionalizing national norms was widely debated in press and parliament. Two controversies in 1964—concerning the West Nile district administration, and members of the KY who crossed the floor—indicate the flavor of the discussion. In July, G. O. B. Oda (DP M.P. for West Nile and Madi West) moved a motion asking the government to appoint a commission to inquire into the "unsatisfactory state of affairs in the West Nile District Administration." S. W. Uringi (UPC, West Nile and Madi South) countered with statistics on religious representation in government indicating that the recruitment policies of the district council of the Appointments Board were nondiscriminatory. He accused the DP of urging people not to carry out the government's policies, advising chiefs not to collect taxes, and arranging a strike by Catholics that would paralyze the machinery of government. Noting the gravity of the allegations of religious discrimination, George Magezi, minister of state, argued that the strike was engineered as a political maneuver by the DP; according to him, the underlying causes were "a complete absence of nationalism in Ugandan people."[11] Similarly, when Eriabu Lwebuga, the former KY organizing secretary, and Peter Kasujja (KY M.P. for Mubende South and Gomba) announced their intention of joining the UPC, the debate that ensued centered on the nature of national unity in Uganda. Their statement emphasized that a Muganda must realize that Buganda is an integral part of Uganda. "KY is not a national party but a tribal party with no manifestation and as such it would be useless to any farsighted person willing to serve independent Uganda remaining in an opportunistic party." They further questioned the logic of a party that supported the kabaka—Uganda's head of state—sitting on the opposition side. They urged other KY members to join a national party and build a strong Ugandan nation.[12]

The government's strategy of gradualism included emphasis on

11. "So Tribe and Religion Are Used to Achieve Political Objectives," *Uganda Argus,* July 15, 1964.
12. "Mubende MP Crosses," *Uganda Argus,* December 23, 1964.

the importance of inducing national norms in socialization and forging national unity through Africanization. Obote realized that if Ugandans were to share a common mythology the agents of political socialization would have to assume some of the responsibility, or even carry the whole burden. Addressing a group of primary school teachers in 1963, the prime minister spoke of the need to redirect the agents of socialization to aid in creating a sense of national unity: "Our reconstruction of national education must . . . aim at creating a unity of purpose among all our nationals, and developing in them a common outlook which will transcend and harmonize in an attractive pattern the differences in history, background, language and culture, that exist among various sections of the people."[13] National loyalties could not be left to chance, and teachers were made aware of their special responsibilities.

In Uganda, as elsewhere in Africa, independence produced demands that high-level posts in the civil service, military, and schools be localized. There was little disagreement among Ugandans about the need to replace European personnel with Africans; but the rate at which localization should proceed proved to be more contentious. Some argued that the turnover should be slow, in order to ensure that competence was maintained, while others regarded national pride and dignity as the higher priorities. Obviously a balance had to be struck, and there were bound to be individuals who were discontented with their share of the national pie. Replying to charges of nepotism leveled against the government in 1964, Felix Onama, then minister of internal affairs, quoted facts and figures to show that preference was not given to members of the UPC or northerners. The government had to make the best of what staff it had, said Onama; in May of 1962, only 12 Ugandans were in the "superscale," while by late 1964 151 had been advanced to that rating.[14]

Pan-Africanism

If the government's attempt to synchronize normative values with national institutions was gradual, policies on pan-Africanism

13. Speech at the Annual Conference of the Uganda Education Association, Jinja, August 14, 1963.
14. "Mr. Onama Denies 'Baganda Favoured by Imperalists,' " *Uganda Argus,* December 4, 1964.

in the first phase were even more guarded. A distinction can be made between the government's policies regarding continental pan-Africanism and regional pan-Africanism. In the former, the government was less restrained. Since realization of continental unity would necessarily be more arduous, less likely, and certainly less imminent than the establishment of a federation among the three East African states, the Obote government could afford to issue rhetorical, if at times vacuous, statements on the need for pan-Africanism at the continental level. For continental unity was regarded in Uganda as less threatening than regional integration, and therefore the government was less constrained by domestic political considerations. On the issue of regional pan-Africanism, however, Ganda fears had to be placated. From the outset the major obstacle preventing Obote from pressing for federation was the objections of the kingdoms—especially Buganda, whose people feared that their historically paramount position in Uganda would be diminished in a greater East Africa. The Baganda were also dismayed at the possibility of being in a federation dominated by Kenya's white settlers, arguing that regional unity would provide a mode of surreptitious entree for the settler community. Uganda's disadvantaged position vis-à-vis its East African neighbors also raised apprehensions. The forces championing the minimalist pan-African position prevailed; the Obote government, responding to the heartland tribe's fear of cultural submergence and judging national unity to be of greater importance than regional integration, reluctantly consented to proceed with measured steps.

The history of regional planning in East Africa dates back to the early 1900's. As long ago as 1899, Sir Harry Johnston recommended the amalgamation of Kenya and Uganda. Although federation never took place, functional cooperation did, in the form of combined postal services (1900), the King's African Rifles (1902), the Uganda and Kenya customs union (1917), extension of the customs union to Tanganyika (1927), the East African Common Market (1927), an interterritorial high commission (1948), and the East African Common Services Organization (EACSO, 1961). As the research of other scholars indicates, the prelude to independence in East Africa produced sufficient social integration to form the bare outlines of a transnational process.[15]

15. See Donald Rothchild, "A Hope Deferred: East African Federation,

Buganda's formal opposition to federation dates from 1931, when a delegation went to London to argue against it before the Joint Select Committee on Closer Union in East Africa. In 1953 a UNC resolution claimed that Uganda must develop in its own way and called for the country's withdrawal from the high commission. When Nyerere appealed for East African union immediately on independence, the response in Uganda was negative; not only the kabaka but also Obote (who was not going to jeopardize the UPC-KY coalition, at least until the UPC had forged a parliamentary majority of its own) and the DP argued that Uganda was not yet ready for federation.

With the Emergency in Kenya still in force and desires for independence becoming stronger, Nyerere's warnings went unheeded and the East African countries became self-governing separately— Tanganyika in December 1961, Uganda in October 1962, and Kenya and Zanzibar in December 1963. Following the Addis Ababa conference of May 1963, which established the Organization of African Unity (OAU) and generated euphoric pan-African feelings, Nyerere, Kenyatta, and Obote pledged themselves to pan-Africanism in the Nairobi Declaration of June 5, 1963. This declaration announced the three countries' intention of federating by the end of the year and of discussing a constitution. At the first summit conference of African heads of state, Obote, as well as offering Uganda as an anticolonial training ground for African liberation forces, called upon his fellow heads of state to surrender some of their countries' sovereignty in favor of an African central legislature. Discussing East African federation in late June 1963, Obote said: "Unless we are prepared to venture into the unknown world, we shall never progress. . . . To remain small and independent countries we become weak, but when we come together we are fairly strong and can face the world with our heads held high."[16]

Less than a month after the Nairobi Declaration, however, Buganda began to bring pressure to bear on Uganda to change its position. In an open letter to the president of Tanganyika and the prime ministers of Uganda and Kenya, Abu Mayanja stressed that Buganda, while anxious to go forward to freedom and reconstruc-

---

1963–1964," in Gwendolen Carter, ed., *Politics in Africa: Seven Cases* (New York: Harcourt, Brace and World, 1966), pp. 219–23.
    16. "Big '3' Meet," *Uganda Argus,* July 1, 1963.

96 IDEOLOGY AND POLITICS IN UGANDA

tion, preferred to build a new edifice on an "old and tried foundation." According to Mayanja, Obote had agreed to allow Buganda to preserve its traditional identity and institutions while playing a "full part in the wider set-up." He concluded: "Buganda's tribalism is positive and looks outwards to wider horizons and greater roles."[17]

Negotiations among the three East African states had begun to break down by October 1963. Following the election of the kabaka as president, the Ugandan government moved toward accepting the kingdom's objections to federation. Obote decided not to attend a meeting in September with Nyerere and Kenyatta in Nairobi that had been called to salvage the attempt at federation. On October 24, Joseph Murumbi, minister of state in the Kenya prime minister's office, told members of the Nairobi Rotary Club: "I don't know whether we will succeed in bringing about an East African Federation, but I think we will at least bring about a Federation of Tanganyika and Kenya, and Uganda might come in at a later stage."[18] The *Uganda Argus'* report of the speech went on to say that "he [Murumbi] did not agree with the theory that Pan-Africanism had been the driving force behind the independence movement in African countries. Each nation had a national desire to be free, while Pan-Africanism was an ideological belief that tried to bring people together." Speaking eight months later on behalf of Tanzania, Oscar Kambona, external affairs minister, said: "We would prefer to federate with both our East African neighbours, but we are prepared to federate with one or the other."[19] Meanwhile Obote's ministers were warning that the interests of smaller units had to be protected. Replying bluntly to Kambona's remarks, Uganda's minister of internal affairs, Felix Onama finally closed the door: "Political federation is not feasible. If an East African Federation were established hurriedly there would be bloodshed within two years."[20]

17. "We Must Retain Our Identity—Buganda," *Uganda Argus,* July 4, 1963.
18. "Federation Forecast," *Uganda Argus,* October 25, 1963.
19. "Tanzan Would Link up with Both or Just One Neighbour," *Uganda Argus,* June 24, 1964.
20. "First Step Must Be to Strengthen E.A.C.S.O.," *Uganda Argus,* June 25, 1964; "Big Trouble If Federation Is Hurried," *Uganda Argus,* June 27, 1964.

In order to legitimize and rationalize their position, Ugandan leaders turned to another interpretation of pan-Africanism. Adopting the Nkrumahist position that regional integration would be dysfunctional for continental unity, Obote allegedly told a diplomat that the problem of reconciling East African federation with the Addis Ababa resolutions was an "embarrassment."[21] By November 1963 Obote was saying that the government had reservations about establishing an East African federation without taking into consideration the views of other members of the Pan-African Freedom Movement of East and Central Africa (PAFMECA).[22] And by mid-1964 the trend in government pronouncements was toward aspirations to unity at the continental level. The distinguishing characteristic of these statements was their lack of concrete proposals. Speaking on African Unity Day 1964, Obote commented on the signing of the Addis Ababa Charter: "We were convinced that the signing of the Charter would give us the way to translate our determination into a dynamic force in the cause of human progress. This determination we agreed was to be safeguarding and a consolidation of our hard-won independence as well as the sovereignty and territorial integrity of Africa."[23] Similarly, George Magezi, minister of state, expressed general admiration for Kwame Nkrumah's ideas. He told an audience in Accra that Uganda was prepared to do anything possible to support the OAU, "because we are convinced that it is only when we have a Central Government of Africa that we can ward off neo-colonialist exploiters."[24]

Uganda's sudden shift in position after June 1963 reflected the extent to which Obote's freedom of action was circumscribed by the fragility of his position. As a practical politician, Obote was concerned with maintaining the precarious balance of forces at home and holding his country together. The September meeting in Nairobi was scheduled at a time when constitutional revisions were being made in Uganda, which necessitated Obote's maneuvering his

21. Joseph Nye, *Pan-Africanism and East African Integration* (Cambridge: Harvard University Press, 1965), p. 197.
22. A. Milton Obote, "His Excellency the President's Speech from the Chair to the National Assembly on the 4th November, 1963."
23. "Freedom Day Struggle Is Not Yet Over, Premier Tells Unity Day Crowds," *Uganda Argus*, May 26, 1964.
24. "We Are Proud of Nkrumah—Magezi," *Uganda Argus*, August 15, 1964.

party into continuing its support of the kabaka.[25] Quite apart from Baganda opposition, the UPC was divided over the issue of federation. Some members were reluctant to sacrifice Uganda's national interests, which they regarded as threatened because of its smaller population and weaker party organization, Kenya's strength in terms of civil service personnel, and the logic of locating the federal capital (which in turn would attract industry) in Nairobi or Arusha.[26] Bowing to these pressures, the Uganda government insisted not only that the right of secession be included in any constitution but also that agriculture, higher education, and trade union affairs be reserved as concerns of the individual states.

After the failure of negotiations in 1964, the issue of federation played less part in events. In 1965 the government of Kenya seized a shipment of arms in transit from Dar es Salaam. The two governments exchanged harsh words, and the EACSO Central Legislative Assembly was suspended indefinitely. One month later, in June 1965, Tanzania withdrew from the currency union.

In 1967, East African leaders moved to counter fissiparous tendencies when the three heads of state signed the East African Treaty for Cooperation and subsequently launched the East African Community. The treaty of 1967 is generally regarded as a landmark in the forging of East African unity. A more realistic assessment is that the establishment of the Community in 1967 marked the point at which East African leaders said, in effect, that divisive tendencies had gone far enough. It is beyond the purposes of this discussion to review the exact provisions of the treaty, but broad concessions were made to national interests, a decentralized structure was provided for, functional cooperation among member states was emphasized, and political unity was embraced as an ultimate goal. At Independence Day ceremonies in 1968, when not only had the Community been established but also Uganda's new republican constitution was in effect, Obote hailed the recent moves toward East African unity. He acknowledged that in the past internal

25. Leys, p. 520.
26. Nye, pp. 189–92. Another interpretation is presented by J. H. Proctor, Jr., "The Effort to Federate East Africa: A Post-Mortem," *Political Quarterly*, XXXVII, No. 1 (January–March 1966), 46–69, who suggests that the Nairobi Declaration may have been a ruse to facilitate Kenyan independence and save face for the British.

federation had limited Uganda's options regarding any East African federation; now that the internal federation had been abolished, however, "we are in position to give East Africa the maximum we can offer. If this is the view of Dar es Salaam and Nairobi, Uganda is ready."[27] When Obote made this statement, he understood that recent events in East Africa had made federation unlikely; indeed, since 1964 the trend had been away from federation. Obote had just successfully disposed of one federal structure; it is doubtful that his government was seriously prepared to join another one in 1968.

Antineocolonialism

While pan-Africanism was emotionally evocative and, too, a theme that many Ugandans understood to be proximate to their interests, other foreign policy issues were seen as more remote. Although Obote had to move slowly on East African federation, he could afford to be more forceful on antineocolonialism and neutralism and nonalignment. Throughout the first phase of ideological modernization in Uganda, the trade union movement and the youth were consistently the groups that pressed most strongly for firm policies against neocolonialist intrigue. Despite other differences between the UPC, the unions, and the youth, Obote, spoke for all of them when, at Addis Ababa in 1963, he inveighed against neocolonialist influence: "The principal driving force that motivated our ex-colonisers in their colonial adventure was economic and political power. . . . The predominant consideration in their present attempt to maintain their influence in Africa is still the same."[28]

On the policy level, the issue of antineocolonialism was raised even before Uganda became independent. At the Commonwealth summit talks in September 1962 the central points of discussion were Britain's entry into the European Economic Community (EEC) and, closely related, the possibility of associate membership for African countries. English-speaking Africans debated the pros and cons of association. Would an economic relationship with the

27. *Africa Research Bulletin* (Political, Social and Cultural Series), V, No. 10 (November 15, 1968), 1203A.

28. A. Milton Obote, "Address to African Summit Conference," Addis Ababa, May 1963.

EEC involve political strings? Would associate status be an obstacle to African unity? Should association be regarded as a transcolonial subterfuge whereby the Europeans would insure that African economies remained dependent upon primary products and ill-suited for industrial development? Or, on the other hand, would nonassociation disadvantage the exports of Anglophone states relative to those of the Francophone states? When Obote returned from London his position was unequivocal; he opposed the idea of institutionalizing a relationship between Africa and Europe, especially with the latter moving toward unity. Speaking at a time when East Africa was clamoring for independence, the Ugandan prime minister asserted, "Africa is not going to be an appendage of any other part of the world."[29]

Despite strong words against formal association with the EEC, the government's policy during the first phase was to reassure sources of private and public foreign investment that their interests were safe and would be protected in Uganda. When measures were taken to insure that foreign investment would be used on projects that would benefit Uganda, the government's statements were apologetic in tone. There was no mention of any leftward move; rumors of nationalization were denied; and when militant elements in Uganda called for a vigilant policy on foreign investment, ministers were quick to call such sentiments out of place.

At the 1963 annual meeting of the Uganda Chamber of Commerce, Malik Kassim Lakha, the organization's retiring president, asked the prime minister for a clear statement of government policy on private investment. Obote replied: "I would reiterate that the Government does not seek to place any restriction on the repatriation of profits earned on foreign investment in Uganda, nor the repatriation of foreign capital invested in Uganda."[30] On the occasion of a visit by six American businessmen soon after, J. S. Mayanja-Nkangi, the minister of commerce, announced that the government would offer five incentives to outside investors: tariff

29. "London Trip Was 'Successful,'" *Uganda Argus,* September 26, 1963. Subsequently, in September 1969, Uganda, Kenya, and Tanzania all concluded trade agreements with the EEC. The Europeans agreed to suspend customs duties on most East African products; in return, Uganda granted tariff preferences on about fifty European products.
30. "Reassurance for Private Investors," *Uganda Argus,* April 5, 1963.

protection, duty-free capital equipment and raw materials, readily available foreign exchange and credit facilities, generous tax inducements, and a government policy that did not stipulate that a given percentage of profits must remain in the country. The minister assured the American ambassador that the government would seriously consider drawing up an investment guarantee agreement between Uganda and the United States.

Once again, the trade unions and the youth called for the government to be on guard against neocolonialist intrigue. Typical of union sentiments were the remarks of Frederick Kasumba, general secretary of the Uganda Textile Worker's Union, who, reacting to a dispute between the union and Nyanza Textiles, criticized expatriate employers "who have no regard for African achievements" and the Uganda Development Corporation (UDC) for its "backward approach" to industrial and human relations. Kasumba was also reported to have said that his union deplored the "colonial and anti-African attitude" of both the textile firm and the UDC.[31] The UPC's national youth organizer, Raiti Omongin, called for the nationalization of all major industries, companies, banks, and firms as the first step toward economic independence. In words that came to typify the Obote government's style of power management, Grace Ibingira, minister of state and UPC secretary-general, retorted that the Youth League had no right to pursue a policy independent of the party:

> I wish to make it abundantly clear that the UPC Youth Wing is part and parcel of the UPC proper. It has no right to pursue an independent policy because then it would become a distinct party such the KY or DP. It is therefore imperative that the parent party, and in particular the headquarters of the UPC, will in the future be more directly responsible for the issue of statements concerning policy matters of the party, and the statement such as that made by Mr. Omongin is no more than an expression of opinion of an individual.[32]

Certainly Omongin's statement diverged from the party's official position. Whatever the merits and demerits of its policy, the UPC maintained a consistent posture on foreign investment during the

31. "Union Man Lashes Out at the U.D.C.," *Uganda Argus,* January 3, 1963.
32. "Mr. Ibingira Slaps Down Youth," *Uganda Argus,* September 5, 1964.

period of the first phase. Its position was set forth as early as spring 1962: "The Party shall . . . ensure that if the foreign investor is more efficient and cheaper than his domestic competitor, neither he nor his customer will be artificially prevented from reaping the reward of his superior ability."[33] While it may well be imperative that a central party organization and its youth wing act in tandem, whether such a highhanded approach to youth's dissent from party policy is either necessary or advisable is another matter. The imperious stance adopted by the central organization of the UPC undoubtedly did little to endear it to the youth and probably served to broaden the chasm.

The government's definitive statement on foreign investment during the first phase was advanced in the Industrial Charter of 1964. The general tone was one of restraint, the content largely repeating assurances to foreign investors. Paragraphs 6 and 7, dealing with security of investments, remittance of profits, and repatriation of capital, contained lengthy quotations from Section 22 of the 1962 constitution, which guaranteed adequate compensation for nationalized property; and the appendix to the Charter—"The Foreign Investments (Protection) Act"—provided that no approved enterprise should be acquired compulsorily except in accordance with the constitution.

Regarding taxation, approved enterprises were entitled to an initial "investment deduction" allowance of 20 percent and "annual deductions," which together permitted deductions totaling 120 percent of investment expenditure. They were liable for local rates and graduated tax or other personal taxes levied by local government authorities; however, the Charter indicated that the government of Uganda would "use its good offices on behalf of an Approved Enterprise if it appears that a local government authority is discriminatory against the Enterprise in respect of the tax levied."[34]

Provision was made for increasing the number of shareholdings or partnerships available for Ugandans to purchase, the expectation being that at least 25 percent of shareholdings attributable to capital invested in Uganda should be locally owned within five

33. Uganda Peoples Congress, *Policy Statement* (Kampala, 1962), p. 7.
34. *Industrial Charter: Sessional Paper No. 1 of 1964* (Entebbe: Government Printer, 1964), p. 3.

years. Although the Charter called for the training and employment of as many Ugandans as was "reasonably possible," the
government promised to be "generous" in issuing employment permits to non-Ugandans. As for industrial facilities, not only was
tariff protection offered but in addition consideration was to be
given to permitting duty-free import of necessary machinery, equipment, materials, and components. The Charter pledged that if
difficulty arose in securing land title the government would, under
certain conditions, help approved enterprises; should an enterprise
be required to relocate, the government would make appropriate
concessions to offset the extra expenses. The concluding paragraphs reiterated the theme that overseas-owned, approved enterprises were to receive the same treatment, facilities, and assistance
as wholly Ugandan-owned enterprises.

Insofar as foreign enterprises had any intimation during the first
phase that Uganda's policy might change, it came as a result of
the activities of foreign investors, not in Uganda, but in a neighboring country. When copper-rich Katanga Province attempted to
secede from the Congo, considerable apprehension was expressed
in Uganda about the implications for would-be secessionist movements there. And it was generally recognized that Tshombe's
activities in Katanga were dependent upon, if not directed by, a
foreign business enterprise—the Union Minière du Haut-Katanga.[35]
With these considerations in mind, Obote announced that: "Uganda
has agreed to take steps, if necessary, against business concerns in
the country who have had head offices of their origins in Britain,
Belgium, France or Portugal to enforce Katanga's reunification
with the Congo." The Ugandan prime minister claimed that "the
Katanga situation had been caused by commercial interests rather
than M. Tshombe's great belief in tribalism."[36] The situation became more worrying, both for Uganda and for other African
countries, when Tshombe came to power in Leopoldville in July
1964 and anticentral government forces captured Stanleyville in
August. For Uganda, these events were particularly ominous be-

35. Cf. the view that white settlers, a constant irritant to Brussels, pushed
Tshombe to secede even though this was against the interests of the metropole; Arghiri Emmanuel, "White Settler Colonialism and the Myth of Investment Imperialism," *New Left Review*, No. 73 (May–June 1972), p. 38.
36. "Companies Warned," *Uganda Argus,* January 24, 1963.

cause European military forces had reappeared in East Africa earlier in the year; when the Tanganyikan, Kenyan, and Ugandan armies mutinied in January, Nyerere had requested the British to send troops, and cold war politics cast a shadow across East Africa.

From Uganda's perspective, the Congolese situation took a marked turn for the worse in November with the American-Belgian Stanleyville paratroop drop. In reaction to the Stanleyville operation, the UPC Youth League drafted a memorandum to be cabled to the U.S. president. Members of the Youth League accused the U.S. of installing Tshombe as a puppet, killing innocent civilians, and violating the sovereignty of the Democratic Peoples Republic of Congo. Charging that America was interested in the Congo because of its uranium deposits, the prime minister alleged that the American government had been responsible for putting Tshombe in power. In February 1965, military action was extended to Ugandan soil with the bombing of two villages, Goli and Paidha, by Tshombe forces. Although the American State Department denied involvement in the matter, a series of debates followed in the Ugandan press and parliament on neocolonialism. J. O. Anyoti (UPC M.P. for West Teso), for example, suggested that the government should reconsider the pros and cons of American aid. He said that the schools were "flooded with American teachers and I think some of them are spies and they should leave the country." Concluding that the United States wanted to neocolonize Africa, he warned that Uganda must not allow itself to become a second Vietnam.[37] The bombing of the two villages in West Nile was also the cause of a demonstration at the American Embassy in Kampala. A crowd of thousands, which included ministers and members of parliament, was dispersed only when Uganda's Special Forces fired tear gas. Three ministers presented a 600-word protest to Embassy officials asserting that Uganda would not become a battlefield for U.S. ideology.

The Americans wanted to start where the British, French, and Belgians had left off, and turn Africa into another South America where, for the last fifty years, the U.S. had supported reactionary and fascist regimes.

37. "Bomber May Have Been Shot Down Parliament Told," *Uganda Argus,* February 16, 1965.

Their desire is to exploit Africa's wealth for the financial adventurers and speculators of Wall Street who thrive on war, murder, and human suffering as long as these do not occur on the sacred soil of the United States.[38]

It was revealed later, in Obote's testimony before the commission of inquiry investigating the Ocheng allegations in 1966, that the Uganda government had provided assistance to anti-Tshombe forces in the Congo, the Ugandan army training Congolese personnel and providing supplies.

In the case of the conflict in the Sudan, Uganda's northern neighbor, the Uganda government did attempt to maintain a policy of impartiality; but its Congolese policy was decidedly partisan. In both cases the Uganda government sought to use its good offices to effect a political settlement; and in both instances, as well as in the case of the Rwandese conflict, Uganda's policy of granting asylum to political refugees was generous. The Sudanese imbroglio was seen as a war between two groups of nationalists—the Khartoum government and the southern Sudanese—who were struggling over their differing interpretations of self-determination. Many Ugandans sympathized with the plight of the southerners, particularly because of feelings of ethnic solidarity between northerners in Uganda and southerners in the Sudan. The dilemma for the Obote government was that to sanction a secessionist movement in the Sudan, or anywhere else in Africa, would be to open a Pandora's box in Uganda. It therefore based its policy on what it regarded as a fundamental difference between the Congolese and Sudanese situations, the distinction being that what was happening in the Congo was not a struggle between two groups of nationalists but a clear-cut attempt by imperial powers to reassert their control in Africa. The immediate danger for Uganda came from refugees, for with Tshombe supporters seeking admission to Uganda, the specter was raised of neocolonial attitudes penetrating the country.[39]

38. "U.S. Flag Is Hauled Down," *Uganda Argus,* February 17, 1965.
39. Yashpal Tandon and A. G. G. Gingyera-Pinycwa, "Uganda-Sudan Relations and Uganda-Congo Relations, 1962–1966: A Comparative Examination" (paper presented to the University of East Africa Social Science Conference, Nairobi, December 1966).

Neutralism and Nonalignment

In its relations with the great powers, Obote's government consistently enunciated a foreign policy based on neutralism and nonalignment. Even before independence, the UPC sounded the Nkrumahist theme of positive nonalignment: "The Party shall follow a policy of positive non-alignment. The Party shall not accept aid from any quarter which may be an instrument in introducing or imposing alien and undesirable political doctrines or systems, or any aid which could undermine the country's political and economic independence as well as the integrity of the country."[40] Like many other countries in the Third World, Uganda eschewed entangling alliances and military pacts with great powers. Policy-makers reserved the right to pick and choose, siding with the West on some issues and the East on others. At all times, the government insisted on avoiding foreign ideologies. In other words, at the verbal level, most of the themes of the 1960's that were embraced by developing nations claiming to be nonaligned were heard in Uganda as well. But many of the government's statements on neutralism and nonalignment were little more than verbiage, lacking substantive content. In terms of nonverbal behavior, Uganda's policies in the first phase displayed a pro-Western bias. An example is provided by the 1962 UPC policy statement, which, as well as calling for positive nonalignment, in the terms quoted above, also contained the following passage: "In addition to Makerere and other colleges of Higher Education in East Africa, the Party shall provide scholarships for higher studies tenable in universities outside East Africa. Preference shall be given to those students going to Britain and the U.S.A."[41]

That Uganda should have been more closely tied to the West than the East during the first phase is hardly surprising. During the colonial period, which lasted until October 1962, Uganda had no ties with the East whatsoever. Unless Uganda was prepared to embark upon an extreme course, similar to that followed by

40. UPC, *Policy Statement*, p. 6. In the late 1950's and early 1960's Kwame Nkrumah was Africa's most articulate advocate of "positive nonalignment." By the mid-1960's, however, Nkrumah was saying that nonalignment was obsolete and that developing countries were either revolutionary or counterrevolutionary; see Nkrumah, "African Socialism," pp. 3–9.
41. UPC, *Policy Statement*, p. 14.

Guinea in West Africa, the most rational procedure seemed to be to reduce dependence on the West by gradually diversifying Uganda's economic and diplomatic ties. In any attempt to formulate a balanced foreign policy, one precluding dependency relations, Obote was subject to constraints imposed by domestic politics as well as by external interests. Even after independence, colonial attitudes continued to be widely held. The kingdoms, in particular, were wary of the socialist orientation of Eastern countries. Despite these restrictions, however, the Obote government succeeded in dissociating itself from the position of many other former British colonies in two major policy areas: from 1962 on, Obote's government actively opposed America's attempt to isolate the People's Republic of China; and on issues of decolonization Uganda consistently refused to compromise its principles.

Ugandan diplomats have played an active role in the UN, the OAU, and the Commonwealth. The demand for more effective African representation on the principal organs of the UN has been a recurrent theme in Uganda's foreign policy. At the second conference of heads of state and government of nonaligned countries, which convened in Cairo in 1964, Uganda took a strong stand on implementation of the Declaration on the Granting of Independence to Colonial Countries and Peoples, adopted by the UN General Assembly in 1960. Uganda also served on the Provisional Secretariat of the OAU and as a member of the Liberation Committee from its inception.

Uganda's major trading partners have been Western states. Table 6 indicates the countries of origin of Uganda's imports, and Table 7 the direction of exports, for 1965 and 1966, the middle of the first phase. Commonwealth countries supplied one-third of Uganda's net imports, and Britain alone provided 75 percent of Commonwealth commodities. After Britain, West Germany and Japan competed for second place. Italy, India, France, and the People's Republic of China were also important sources of imports. On the export side, the U.S. bought the most. But as a grouping, the Commonwealth topped the list once again. Commonwealth countries purchased a quarter of Uganda's exports, half of that total going to Britain. In 1966 Canada replaced India as the second largest Commonwealth buyer. American imports from Uganda

Table 6. Origin of net imports, 1965–1966 (unit, £'000)

	1965	1966
COMMONWEALTH COUNTRIES:		
United Kingdom	15,679	15,488
India	1,946	1,963
Hong Kong	807	1,305
Pakistan	797	732
Australia	407	246
Rest of Commonwealth Countries	839	1,011
TOTAL FOR COMMONWEALTH COUNTRIES	20,475	20,745
NON-COMMONWEALTH COUNTRIES:		
West Germany	3,812	4,803
France	1,575	1,900
Netherlands	993	985
Belgium	648	664
Italy	1,636	2,194
Luxembourg	22	42
U.S.A.	1,937	1,650
Japan	4,157	2,314
China	974	1,707
U.S.S.R.	34	176
Iran	108	193
Sweden	550	492
Switzerland	327	482
Austria	182	169
Denmark	305	379
Norway	166	124
Others not mentioned above	1,487	2,504
TOTAL OF ALL COUNTRIES	40,870	42,947

SOURCE: *Facts about Uganda* (Entebbe: Government Printer, 1968), p. 82.

amounted to £17,000,000 in 1966, or about a quarter of Uganda's exports to non-Commonwealth countries.

Comparable country-by-country data on foreign aid is not available.[42] However, in the 1960's the government's official policy was to diversify in both trade and aid. Among the Western powers, Israel played a major role in training the Ugandan military, constructing roads, and bringing students to its kibbutzim for applied studies. On the other side, from 1962, when diplomatic relations were established, Uganda consistently supported recognition of the

42. Foreign assistance is also discussed in Chapter 7, pp. 180–81, where figures on economic aid from U.S. and Eastern bloc countries are cited.

Table 7. Direction of trade exports, 1965-1966, outside Kenya and Tanzania (unit, £'000)

	1965	1966
COMMONWEALTH COUNTRIES:		
United Kingdom	10,694	12,271
India	3,477	1,817
Canada	2,165	2,972
Hong Kong	1,372	1,674
Australia	1,185	1,778
Rest of the Commonwealth	1,126	1,105
TOTAL COMMONWEALTH COUNTRIES	20,022	21,617
NON-COMMONWEALTH COUNTRIES:		
West Germany	1,902	2,542
France	779	533
Netherlands	1,076	1,817
Italy	951	1,974
Belgium	7,017	1,321
U.S.A.	14,092	17,039
Japan	1,635	3,265
China	6,237	1,209
U.S.S.R.	—	69
Jordan	1,148	666
Israel	1,118	1,145
Others	26,759	34,356
TOTAL	62,714	65,936

SOURCE: *Facts about Uganda* (Entebbe: Government Printer, 1968), p. 84.

People's Republic of China and voted for that country's legitimate right to a seat in the UN. Obote visited Peking in 1965 and was given a particularly warm reception by Chou En-lai. The following year Uganda and China concluded a trade agreement worth about £250,000.

On issues relating to decolonization, Uganda has always taken a strong stand. The Obote government supported liberation movements, refused diplomatic relations with Portugal, Rhodesia, and South Africa, and was outspoken in its opposition to Pretoria's presence in Namibia. It backed sanctions against South Africa and demanded an effective boycott against all South African goods. Responding to the unilateral declaration of independence by the minority white regime in Rhodesia (November 1965), Uganda strongly condemned Britain's failure to act in accordance with the principle of independence on the basis of majority rule but did not follow Tanzania in severing diplomatic relations with Britain.[43]

African Socialism

In Africa there is generally a correlation between a state's foreign policies and its domestic development strategies. The countries most committed to socialism—Tanzania, Guinea, Congo-Brazzaville, Somalia, Ghana under Nkrumah, and Mali under Keita—have forged ties to the East. Conversely, countries with the least commitment to socialism internally—Ivory Coast, Gabon, and Malawi— are usually the most pro-Western externally. In Uganda during the 1962–1969 phase, aspirations toward socialism were articulated but limited to the rhetorical level. Greater militance was shown in foreign than in domestic affairs; and there were many occasions when Obote deemed it tactful to assuage fears of socialist construction in Uganda. Just as with antineocolonialism and neutralism and nonalignment, the theme of African socialism was heard during the first phase but meant little to the average Ugandan; for, in contrast to ideas of nationalism, which are concrete and fairly easy to grasp, the universal principles of socialist thought can appear abstract and generalized during the early period of ideological innovation and diffusion.

In the early 1960's a few guarded hints were given of socialist inclinations in Uganda. However, the rhetoric remained vague; the more explicit pronouncements of Nyerere in Tanzania were lacking. The realities of this period included traditional monarchies, which were still very much alive until 1966, a free enterprise economy, private ownership of land and major industries, overseas exploitation of resources, and non-Ugandan control of the means of production, distribution, and exchange. Yet in mid-1963 Obote's speeches began to have a prosocialist flavor. In his May Day speech that year, he extended fraternal greetings to the "labouring masses of Uganda" and to "the workers' movement the world over" and expressed solidarity "with all the progressive forces struggling against exploitation and human indignity."[44] Exactly when Obote

43. Only nine African countries—Tanzania, Mali, the United Arab Republic, Algeria, Mauritius, Guinea, Sudan, Ghana, and Congo-Brazzaville— respected the OAU's directive that member states break diplomatic ties with the United Kingdom.
44. "Premier's May Day Plea," *Uganda Argus,* May 2, 1963.

first mentioned the need for socialist construction in Uganda is unclear, but he made an explicit statement on the issue during the
1964 debates on one-partyism. While assuring businessmen that
nationalization was not in the offing, Obote spoke of his socialist
proclivities and the implications for Uganda's party system:

> We have decided to follow a Socialist line of development. Conse-
> quently Socialist principles must inform, guide and govern the basis,
> form and content of all the institutions of our society. Our lives,
> thoughts and actions must reflect the same trend.
>
> Discipline, order, control and planning are elements of the Socialist
> code of action, behaviour and approach. Organised opposition against
> the Government is a typical capitalist notion and concept and under
> capitalism the laws are those of the jungle, namely free for all, laissez
> faire, and the survival of the fittest. We have rejected capitalism once
> and for all.[45]

By the time of the party conference in Gulu, in late April 1964, a
determined group within the UPC was making its intention to
move toward socialism known. But the nature of Ugandan socialism
remained undefined, its advocates embracing diverse interpretations.
For some, to endorse socialism meant little more than to support
a minimalist policy of increased government prerogative. For
others, building socialism in Uganda meant completely transforming society, and even deriving inspiration from the Chinese
experience in doing so.

In the debates of 1964, the youth and the trade unions were
staunch advocates of socialist construction. The major contestants
in the polemics that ensued were the Youth League and Grace
Ibingira. When Ibingira replaced the more radically minded John
Kakonge as secretary-general of the UPC in 1964, he became an
object of the youth's discontent. Not only did he succeed in gaining
the prime minister's support for expelling a section of militant
youth from the party, but in addition he was regarded as being pro-
American in foreign relations and too conservative in domestic
affairs. Beyond their general opposition to Ibingira, the youth were
inclined toward radical politics because of a variety of social
grievances—in particular, the burgeoning problem of school drop-
outs, lack of employment opportunities, and the rapidly increasing

45. "Capitalism Rejected 'Once and for All,'" *Uganda Argus,* January 8,
1964.

flight from rural areas to urban centers. Those in control of the party attempted to check the militance of the Youth League by breaking its organization. Their strategy was to create another group, the National Union of Youth Organizations, which was placed under the strict direction of the Ministry of Culture and Community Development.[46] The dissolution of the Youth League demonstrated the ineffectiveness of those few individuals who supported socialism in Uganda as well as the opposition by top government leaders.

The trade unionists, who also called for the introduction of socialist measures, were even less effective than the youth. The unions in Uganda suffered from internal rivalries and differences over external alignments. In the early 1960's, union-government relations were marked by a series of acrimonious exchanges. From the government's point of view, the trade unions were conducting their own foreign policies in their relations with the international labor movement and thereby jeopardizing Ugandan nonalignment. Labor leaders argued that the issue of external alignments was being used by the government as a cover for its attempt to monopolize power. When Humphrey Luande (president of the TUC and a UPC M.P.) left the party in 1964, he charged that, "it has become glaringly apparent that the Government's policy is to interfere in the liberty and freedom of organized workers' movements and to turn them into Governmental tools."[47] In 1966 the government suspended trade union activities in Uganda and created the Uganda Labour Congress as a replacement for the old organizations. A government commission (the Binaisa Commission) then made a series of recommendations for increasing control of the labor movement. The government's action in crushing the Youth League and the unions signified that it would not tolerate independent initiatives toward socialism. Insofar as the government favored introducing measures for building socialism, such measures would have to derive from its own invention.

The government's tactics and rhetoric concerning socialism were not greeted with equanimity in all quarters, opposition being expressed by the KY, the DP, and even elements in the UPC. React-

46. Akiiki B. Mujaju, "The Demise of the UPCYL and the Rise of NUYO in Uganda," *African Review*, III, No. 2 (June 1973), 300–301.
47. "Luande Quits U.P.C.," *Uganda Argus*, October 9, 1964.

ing to the prime minister's January 1964 statement on socialist construction, Enoch Mulira, president of the Uganda National Union, labeled Obote's ideas "Nkrumahism," while Abu Mayanja, the kabaka's minister of education, affirmed the KY's belief in the right of private property, the need for a mixed economy, and the importance of private enterprise. Benedicto Kiwanuka, president general of the DP, warned that socialism would mean the abolition of kingship and discourage foreign investment. Within the UPC, the most important figure to resist socialism was Grace Ibingira. In the following years the dissidents were joined by A. A. Nekyon, a relative of Obote's and a onetime minister and member of the UPC, who publicly criticized the government's position on several issues, including one-partyism, the postponement of general elections after 1966, and the tactics to be used in dealing with the DP.[48] In the 1964 debate on the budget, Obote sought to allay the fears of his opponents, explaining that the terms "capital" and "capitalism" have different meanings. Citing the example of such countries as Portugal, Obote argued that freedom of speech, worship, and the press are not necessarily an integral part of capitalism, and he reminded fellow Ugandans that there were socialist countries, namely, Denmark, Sweden, and Norway, that maintained democratic institutions, enjoyed freedom of the press, and retained their kings.[49]

After hinting at socialist construction, the government began to turn its attention to the agents of political socialization. When Uganda became self-governing, the schools were controlled by private sectarian groups, and the UPC committed itself to preserving this state of affairs. "The UPC," said the 1962 policy statement, "shall maintain the existing system of education whereby the schools are mainly privately owned."[50] However, beginning with Sessional Paper No. 4 of 1963 (*Memorandum by the Government on the Report of Uganda's Education Commission, 1963*), steps

48. "And Now the Reaction," *Uganda Argus*, January 9, 1964; "D.P. Leader Hits out at Government Policies," *ibid.*, May 9, 1964; "Communism Is Condemned . . . by Mr. Nekyon," *ibid.*, April 30, 1964; and A. G. G. Gingyera-Pincywa, "Prospects for a One-Party System in Uganda," *East Africa Journal*, V, No. 10 (October 1968), 18.
49. "Outside Governments Prefer Africa to Follow Socialist Pattern," *Uganda Argus*, June 26, 1964.
50. UPC, *Policy Statement*, p. 14.

were taken to rationalize the school system. Obote's government asserted that its authority took precedence over the long-standing right of private agencies to operate schools in Uganda. Henceforth, not only would there be efforts to make the schools interdenominational, but also all teachers were to be employees of the Ministry of Education rather than agents owing loyalty to sectarian interests. Although the stated policy was laudable, de facto policy was inconsistent. While sessional papers were calling for measures to localize the school system, the government continued to extend invitations to expatriate teachers,[51] who usually enjoyed more favorable contract terms than Ugandan teachers. Despite considerable talk about Africanizing the school syllabus, few concrete measures were taken. As has frequently been observed, Ugandan students learned more about English constitutional history and Shakespearean drama than they did about their own customs and traditions; essentially, the elites continued to be European-trained and European-taught.

Négritude and the African Personality

Insofar as socialism embraces an egalitarian ethic, négritude and the African personality are intimately related to it. With the heightened anticolonialism of the 1950's and 1960's went an increase in exhortations calling for pride in things African. In Uganda, indeed throughout East Africa generally, the themes of négritude and the African personality may have been played less loudly than in West Africa. Nevertheless, even if their ideas did not achieve the notoriety of Léopold Senghor's (of Senegal) poetic notions of Africanness, there is ample evidence to suggest that Ugandans held similar values. Clearly English-speaking Africans do not dwell on the Francophone aspect of the Senghorian concept of négritude; however, many do believe in what he calls "antiracial racialism." The semantics may differ, but the sentiment is much the same.

In Uganda during the first phase of ideological modernization there emerged a subtle but nonetheless clear tendency to couch arguments in egalitarian terms based on notions of racial equality. This tendency was most evident in the realm of cultural affairs.

51. See, for example, "More Peace Corps Workers Wanted," *Uganda Argus,* January 5, 1965.

This phase was marked by countless discussions, debates, and conferences on how best to promote things African in Uganda. The issues ranged from localization of school curricula and further utilization and teaching of African languages in the schools, through schemes to maintain an African Studies Programme at the University, to support for the Uganda Museum and Nomo Art Gallery and promotion of the National Theatre and the "Heartbeat of Africa" (Uganda's internationally renowned dance troupe). Most notably, the 1963 annual delegates conference of the UPC Youth League recommended establishment of a Ministry of Cultural and Social Relations, which would be responsible for determining ways in which "the country's tribal institutions could be accommodated in the African Personality"; encouraging traditional dancing and handicrafts, "which had been crippled during the last thirty years"; revolutionizing the school curricula "to cater for the teaching of African history and cultural relations"; and nationalizing the school system and Africanizing all headmasters' posts.[52]

In Uganda, the themes of négritude and the African personality (or the sentiments these ideological motifs stand for) normally occur in relation to, or are provoked by, particular incidents, typically but not exclusively in foreign relations. Two incidents that took place in 1963 are illustrative. While on a tour of Africa, American Senator Allen Ellender of Louisiana said that Africans were unable to govern themselves without white assistance. In the uproar that followed, the senator was not permitted to enter Uganda, and leaders of the UPC called for a re-examination of the role played by such non-African groups as the Peace Corps and AID. Six months after the Ellender incident, the UPC Youth League staged a demonstration outside the American Embassy in Kampala, the purpose of which was to express solidarity with the black struggle in the U.S. Responding to the killing of black school children in southern Alabama, John Kakonge, then secretary-general of the UPC, presented a petition to the ambassador that read in part:

We on the African continent, who have been the major victims of imperialism and colonialism, have come to see nothing but sheer hy-

52. "Culture Ministry Is Sought by UPC Youth," *Uganda Argus,* April 30, 1963.

pocrisy in American declarations about democracy and the rights of men.

If there were any amount of sincerity in the American declarations, the energy, dollars, Peace Corps and Crossroaders which are lavishly being spread all over Africa, would now be diverted to the Southern States of America where millions of blacks are not only unemployed, persecuted, discriminated against, but constantly live in fear of losing their lives because they happen to be black in colour.[53]

Calls for black pride and racial equality were not sounded only in response to American prejudice and discrimination; Britain, too, provoked Ugandans' anger, most particularly in March 1968, when the Smith government of Rhodesia hung three black Africans and Britain stood passively by. Students from Makerere University College marched to the British High Commission in Kampala bearing placards (for example, "Hang Wilson and Smith and Save Africa") and demanding an audience with the deputy high commissioner. The envoy refused, and the students agreed to hand over their statement to another official. The text served notice on Mr. Wilson: "The forces of oppression will be crushed, the pretenders will be exposed and the African people will sing with joy at the arrival of real freedom."[54]

A question that provoked continuing debate about the meaning of Africanness was that of Arab domination from the North. The issue arose most poignantly over Uganda's Sudan policy. After Uganda began to accept and provide for refugees from the Sudan, relations between the Uganda government and southern Sudanese political leaders deteriorated rapidly. The southern leaders, and advocates of their cause in Uganda, argued that Obote's government should press the cause of racial solidarity harder. The dominant sentiment in the government in Kampala was that southern Sudanese leaders were taking advantage of Uganda's good will. Some M.P.'s complained that not only were military activities being planned in Uganda but also that the Anyanya (southern Sudanese soldiers) were launching their operations from the country's northern areas. The dangers for the Uganda government were two. First, Obote wanted to maintain cordial relations with Khartoum, and with the North African states in general. Second, he was concerned

53. "Riot Police Sent to Embassy," Uganda Argus, September 18, 1963.
54. "Text of Protest," Uganda Argus, March 18, 1968.

about the implications for ethnic relations in Uganda. If his government gave overt support to the southern Sudanese cause, the forces of local nationalism in Uganda would argue that they were entitled to an equal right to self-determination; and in denying their claim the government would surely lay itself open to accusations of double standards. The prime minister had had his fill of secessionist movements and wanted, above all, to avoid provoking another domestic crisis. Voicing Obote's concerns, Akena Adoko, a top aide and confidant, provides a narrative of the events of 1966. Akena's post-mortem of the 1966 crisis begins with a section on "Imperialism, Feudalism, and Nationalism" acknowledging the importance of racial pride and the value "of things purely African":

> Ugandans were demanding,
> That the table should be turned,
> That there be revolutions,
> That the old order of aping
> And imitating Europeans
> Were fit only for the slaves.
>
> . . . . .
>
> Gone were all those olden days
> When Uganda depended
> On European culture,
> European diplomacy,
> European double-crossings,
> And European expertise.
>
> Independence ushered in
> The era of expression
> Of things purely African:
> Our thoughts and our deeds,
> We had to be ourselves
> Whether for better, for worse.[55]

The argument to this point has been that the initial stimulus giving rise to an ideology of modernization is external to the value system. A lack of ideological coherence is normally the result of a rapidly changing social and political environment. If changes in the political system are to be linked to values and beliefs, an alternative paradigm must be introduced. In Uganda after indepen-

55. Akena Adoko, *Uganda Crisis* (Kampala: African Publishers, 1968), p. 19.

dence, the social and political environment was one of severe and highly politicized cleavages. The regime, like many others in the Third World, lacked power, both absolutely and relatively. Holding, and then augmenting, power at the center therefore took top priority. In 1966, Obote's strategy of increasing centralization appeared to have triumphed beyond his fondest expectations. Many observers shared the view that Uganda had surmounted some of the major challenges to national development, that this country was succeeding where others had failed.

Yet the Obote regime lacked legitimacy and support. Clearly, if a direct attempt had been made to achieve ideological modernization in the 1962–1969 phase, it would have been premature. To invoke a Ugandan national mythology engendered more hostility than unity. Many of the structural mechanisms that have facilitated ideological diffusion elsewhere—such as a relatively educated populace, an urban tradition, developed mass media, a lingua franca, and locally based non-African movements serving either as organizational models or as targets of discontent—did not exist in Uganda during this phase. Since the political climate was one of pragmatism and consolidation, it is hardly surprising that the most characteristic feature of the first phase should have been gradualism. The analysis of six major ideological themes offered above has indicated that the regime was hesitant and reluctant to advance a comprehensive ideology of modernization. Such ideological motifs as were introduced tended to be vague, abstract, ad hoc, and more often rhetorical than substantive. The regime's circumspection has two explanations: first, the leaders' need to determine their own ideological proclivities; second, the political and economic circumstances limiting alternatives. The dominant pattern of ideological innovation was, accordingly, one of government pronouncement, extreme caution or even vacillation in nonverbal behavior, and frequent apologia to cushion the impact of intended actions. A distinction must be made, however, between foreign and domestic affairs. Save on the issue of East African federation, the Obote government was more ideologically militant in the realm of foreign policy than in internal politics. The ideological themes of continental pan-Africanism, antineocolonialism, and neutralism and nonalignment were more remote, and hence generally regarded as less threatening to entrenched domestic interests, than the themes of African nationalism, socialism, and négritude and the African personality.

If one sought to define the dominant trends of the first phase, Obote's ideological initiatives, side-stepping, and withdrawals might seem to constitute a course similar to that steered by the statesman-revolutionary who first guided the Soviet Union toward modernization. Lenin's program of "two steps forward, one step back" proved a skillful strategy for utilizing ideology, in combination with pragmatic interests, as an agent to induce modernization. But Obote was not Lenin, nor the kabaka the czar. And despite the pretensions about revolutionary change, the crisis of 1966 was not Uganda's 1917.

CHAPTER 5

Documentary Innovations

The second phase of ideological modernization in Uganda began with the Move to the Left, in October 1969, and ended with the coup d'état of January 25, 1971. In this period, Obote sought to set forth an explicit ideology. The diffidence, want of confidence, and apprehension of the first phase were no longer present. Rather, the regime took concerted steps to restructure beliefs and values. A series of ideological pronouncements formalized long-term development goals and established strategies intended for their realization.

The second phase, then, was a period of ideological assertion during which Obote attempted to Ugandanize ideological themes found elsewhere in Africa. Having looked to other "progressive" African leaders for inspiration, Obote tried to make ideology more concrete and to establish "Uganda's contribution to the 'African revolution.'" Accordingly, if efforts toward rapid ideological modernization were to be made, further structural change was required. New norms had to be institutionalized. As Obote said in a memorandum to the UPC delegates conference of August 1970, "a new ideology cannot be implemented through the institutional structure of an old system."[1] The comment was made in reference to the debate about presidential elections; however, its applicability extends to the 1969–1971 period in general.

During the second phase, Obote attempted to hasten the rate of change through socialist construction. In the wake of resolutions passed by the UPC delegates conference of June 1968, he launched Uganda's Move to the Left. The proposals that followed (issued in 1969 and 1970) consisted of five ideological documents blueprint-

---

1. A. Milton Obote, "Memorandum by the President of the UPC, Dr. A. Milton Obote, to the Delegates Conference to Be Held at Mbale on 28th August, 1970" (Kampala: UPC Headquarters, August 21, 1970).

ing the "new political culture." The analysis of the second phase begins with discussion of these five documents, the measures adopted to implement them, and the regime's intentions in promoting an ideology of modernization. The government's program in the second phase produced ideological stress. Examination of the structural mechanisms for ideological innovation and diffusion indicates some general questions that Obote's proposals left unanswered and the nature of the dysfunctions that resulted.

The Documents

The first document to be made public, the "Proposals for National Service," came to be known as Document No. 2. The "Common Man's Charter," released on October 8, 1969, and entitled Document No. 1, provided the foundation for the second phase. (The complete text is provided in the Appendix to this book.) While the Charter deals with all six of the ideological themes set forth in Chapter 4, the emphasis rests with nationalism and socialism. The critique advanced identifies the malaise in Ugandan society as being caused by capitalism, the well-to-do, entrenched interests, the educated, foreign influence, feudalism, and neofeudalism. The latter element—the survival of privilege based on heredity and landed wealth, and particularly, by implication, continuing support for monarchy—is singled out as the major obstacle to the creation of a socialist revolutionary society.

Beginning with the premise that political and economic power should be vested in the majority, the Charter points toward "a new way of life" for Ugandans: "The Move to the Left is the creation of a new political culture and a new way of life, whereby the people of Uganda as a whole—their welfare and their voice in the National Government and in other local authorities—are paramount. It is, therefore, both anti-feudalism and anti-capitalism."[2] The prescription for the future is the generation of new attitudes. Just as Nyerere's earlier pronouncements stressed that socialism can be defined by the extent to which certain specified attitudes toward the sharing of property and other resources exist, rather than by objective measures of income, Obote maintained that

2. A. Milton Obote, *The Common Man's Charter with Appendices* (Entebbe: Government Printer, 1970), p. 4.

answers to the challenges posed by rapid social change begin with the generation of new attitudes to life and wealth: "Much as the laws might assist in preventing such crimes [corruption, nepotism, and abuse of authority] being committed against the nation, it is our view that the answer lies in tackling the root of the problem, namely to generate a new attitude to life and to wealth, and new attitudes in exercising responsibilities."[3]

While the Charter can be regarded as a fairly typical statement of a leader's decision to opt for socialism, the implications of the "Proposals for National Service" were more far-reaching and could have had greater consequences for political development in Uganda. Document No. 2 focuses on the twin problems of rural life and elitism. The Obote regime was attempting to make rural life more attractive and thereby stem the migration from the countryside to urban areas. The strategy was to confront these problems both in the countryside and in the towns. New values and attitudes would have to be forged, not only among the peasantry but also among a parasitic elite. Attitudes were to be changed, first by promoting "African Revolution, Culture and Aspirations," and second —and here the tone again echoes Nyerere's approach to nation-building—by encouraging "self-reliance" in problem-solving. The emphasis of the Proposals is on national integration, mobilization, and socialization. The general tenor is given by Article 9:

It is proposed that these Camps should collectively, and as far as possible individually, be a "miniature Uganda" in that all the agricultural, animal husbandry and related activities, together with cultural activities, which may be found in any part of Uganda, may also be found there. They will be centres in which basic training in increased production, national consciousness and the promotion and advancement of African culture will be undertaken. It is further proposed that those called up to do their National Service in each of these Camps, should come from all parts of Uganda, and arrangements will be made particularly for those engaged in crop production and mixed farming, to advance their knowledge in their occupations during their service in these Camps. Any person, irrespective of educational standard, may be called up to do National Service in any of these Camps.[4]

3. *Ibid.*, p. 7. Cf. Julius K. Nyerere, *Freedom and Unity: Uhuru na Umoja* (Dar es Salaam: Oxford University Press, 1967), pp. 162–71.
4. Obote, "Proposals for National Service," in *The Common Man's Charter*, p. 15.

Except during a national emergency, every able-bodied Ugandan was to be obliged to do national service. The Proposals recommend establishment of a Ministry of National Service, whose main work would be in the field rather than in the office, and provide for national training camps, constituency training centers, subcountry camps, state farms, and "other centres." The document is most explicit on the national training camps and constituency training centers. The four national training camps (one in each of the four regions of Uganda) are seen as emphasizing rural development, offering courses on national consciousness, and promoting African culture. The constituency training centers (one to each rural parliamentary constituency) would deal with primary school leavers and the fourteen to twenty-one age group generally. Youths would be called up for a period of two to four years and be subject to recall for "twelve or more continuous months." All school leavers and recent graduates, irrespective of status, would be required to do national service; thereby, individuals who were at least functionally literate would be reoriented toward the tasks of nation-building.

The next document, "His Excellency the President's Communication from the Chair of the National Assembly on 20th April, 1970," represents an attempt to sharpen and give substance to some of the more general themes expressed in the Charter. Document No. 3 is far-ranging, in that it touches on all six of the ideological themes discussed in the previous chapter, but also includes a number of specific suggestions. In order to forge a specifically "Ugandan political culture," Obote announced in this communication, there should be one public service, with a uniform salary structure, for all officers in the government, district administrations and urban authorities, the teaching service, and parastatal bodies; further consideration would be given to extending the same conditions to the cooperative unions and societies, the trade unions, and the UPC. To encourage maximum effectiveness and competence in the public service, the president proposed the establishment of "efficiency bars" that would check on employees every five years, abolition (except under special circumstances) of extra allowances for public officers, termination of car loans to persons employed in the service, the ending of overtime pay for public employees, and a change in the system whereby promotion could be achieved purely on the basis of seniority. Increasing attention should be given to the Ugandanization of the public service; efforts to this end would include the just and speedy application of the Trade Licensing Act and the Immigration Control Act, which were intended to insure that citizens managed, directed, and controlled local concerns and export-import businesses. Finally, improvements should be made in the social services, particularly the police force, markets for cash crops, health centers, social networks, the cooperative movement, and general economic planning.

Document No. 4, the president's 1970 "Labour Day Speech"—the "Nakivubo Pronouncements" or "May Day Pronouncements," as it came to be called—is the shortest of the five documents but, as a declaration of intent, the most decisive. Accordingly, it provoked most reaction, both at home and abroad. This document can be regarded as a logical sequel to Article 38 of the Charter, which establishes the guiding economic principle that the means of production and distribution should be in the hands of the people. The Pronouncements state that, effective from the day of the speech, the government is assuming 60 percent control of the 84 major industries in Uganda, including all oil companies, the Kampala and District Bus Services, Kilembe Mines, and every major manufacturing industry, plantation, bank, credit institution, and insurance company. Foreign business interests would be compensated out of repatriated profits over the following fifteen years.

The Nakivubo Pronouncements came as a surprise to many of Obote's colleagues in the cabinet. There was no public debate before the decision to nationalize, and the policy took effect from the time of the president's speech. One interpretation of the nationalization measures is that they were directed primarily against politicians and civil servants engaged in profiteering. As Obote was well aware, some of Uganda's foremost capitalists occupied high level posts in the government and the party; their ostentatious self-seeking was a blemish on the socialist image that the president was attempting to portray. Another reaction, expressed on a BBC "World Today" program entitled "Changes in Uganda," was that unless Uganda issued negotiable bills guaranteeing payment at any of the world's banks the Nakivubo Pronouncements amounted to little less than outright expropriation. Voicing their concern at a meeting with British government officials, London's financial interests encouraged Whitehall to view the measures as an "opening bid" and to strive for a better deal.[5]

The fifth document, dealing with electoral proposals, was the most specific of the five and undoubtedly the most original. Its major objectives were use of the party as an agent of mobilization and the electoral system as a device to induce national integration. Document No. 5 proposes that every candidate for parliament should stand in one basic and three national constituencies. The basic constituency would be in the candidate's home region and the three national constituencies in the three other regions of the country. The percentages won in each constituency would count as electoral votes, and the winning candidates would be those with the highest totals for their four constituencies. The proposals claim that such a scheme would avoid representation of parochial interests and encourage national unity.

Obote's ideas on election of members of parliament were widely hailed as a bold and imaginative effort to regulate conflict and build loyalty to national institutions. Some observers applauded what they regarded as an outstanding contribution to constitutional theory. Ironically, however, the debate centered, not on these novel provisions, but on the procedure for electing a president. Document No. 5's recommendations for presidential elections are for a procedure similar to that followed in some other parts of Africa. After the dissolution of parliament, either the party should summon a delegates conference to select a candidate or the party's current president should automatically become the candidate. Each voter would then cast a ballot for or against the candidate. When the votes in favor and against in each constituency had been computed, constituency percentages would count as electoral votes; if the total in favor of the candidate was greater than the number against, the candidate would be elected.

The proposals for electoral reform became the subject of vigorous debate in the party and throughout the intellectual community. Convening in August 1970, the national council of the UPC and the UPC delegates conference approved the measures

5. "Let Them Try: The Risk Is Theirs," *People* (Kampala), May 15, 1970; and "On Views on the Nakivubo Pronouncements," *People,* May 30, 1970.

providing for election of members of parliament. The national council also decided to form an electoral commission, composed of presidential appointees, whose task would be to establish constituency executives, each of which, in turn, would nominate up to three candidates for selection as prospective M.P.'s. With an arrangement that gave the commission control over who would be selected, allegations were made that it had been vested with authority to pass judgment on prospective candidates' ideological qualifications and economic activities.[6]

But the proposals concerning election of a president provoked greater opposition. Some argued that genuine competitive elections, involving two or more candidates, should be held; others that, at a delicate time in Uganda's history, maintaining the impetus for revolution was more important than democratic representation. Spokesmen for the UPC suggested that genuinely competitive elections would not only inject divisions into the party but also dilute the ideology.

Surprisingly, when the national council of the UPC met on August 12, 1970, Articles 26–34 of the proposals (those dealing with election of a president) were voted down, the top echelon of party officials counseling that acceptance would violate the decision of the 1968 UPC delegates conference to name Obote party president for a seven-year term. Ignoring the stated wishes of its president, the council passed a resolution stipulating that "the President of the Party, elected in accordance with the provisions of the Party Constitution, shall be the President of the Republic of Uganda, Head of Government and Commander in Chief of the Armed Forces."[7] Party officials were widely criticized. Okello Oculi and other members of Uganda's intellectual community warned that the president was making his political career dependent on the party rather than the masses and that this dependence could lead to his downfall. Indeed there was a distinct possibility that Obote might become the prisoner of high level officials within the UPC, many of

6. D. L. Cohen and J. Parson, "The Uganda Peoples Congress Branch and Constituency Elections of 1970," *Journal of Commonwealth Political Studies,* XI, No. 1 (March 1973), 49.
7. "Election of the President: Council Says It Cannot Tamper with Decision of Supreme Organ of the Party," *People,* August 13, 1970; and "Resolution on Head of State," *Uganda Argus,* August 14, 1970.

whom—most notably, Felix Onama, secretary-general of the party and Uganda's minister of defense—expressed little remorse about their aggrandizement of wealth and had the most to lose from a move to the left.

Responding to the challenge from within his own party, Obote made a dramatic appeal to face the electorate. In his memorandum to the delegates conference due to meet in Mbale on August 28, 1970,[8] he reminded UPC officials that the masses, not the party, were the most important entity in Uganda. Noting the party's supremacy as a political institution, he asserted that it must embody the will of the people. And the party's performance could be tested by holding direct presidential elections. Obote further argued that in the struggle to implement a socialist ideology direct presidential elections were essential if party and president were to be united with the masses against the forces of reaction.

Having made the case for direct elections, Obote then drew back. The last paragraph of his memorandum suggested that the council's decision be accepted for the next election and his recommendations adopted thereafter. At the conference in Mbale, the president did not fight for the ideas in his memorandum but gave the appearance of being passive and remote from the infighting that ensued. The fact that he chose not to engage in the intraparty dispute added to the impression that he was not intent on pursuing his recommendations. Party officials saw to it that the memorandum was not circulated to conferees, and many delegates confessed that they had not read it. Despite Obote's protestation that he wanted to face the electorate, only four delegates voted for the motion advancing his cause. On August 28, the conference endorsed the recommendations of the national council and overrode the president again.

What accounts for such an occurrence? Although the UPC had frequently suffered from factionalism, never before had it so flagrantly violated the expressed wishes of its leader. Intraparty disputes were nothing new, but the public airing of the tensions and rivalries generated in mid-1970 assumed a pitch unequaled since the crisis of 1966. Why should the issue of presidential elections have brought these schisms and such dissension to the surface?

8. See n. 1 above.

There are a number of plausible explanations. One accepts the situation as it appeared to the public: the dominant sentiment in the UPC was against open, mass elections for the presidency, and Obote gracefully bowed to the wishes of his party cohorts. This line of reasoning suggests that the UPC was a mass party open to all, that a delegates' conference represented the will of the people, and that, therefore, there was no reason why the candidate selected by such a conference should not be regarded as the popular choice. Obote accepted this decision in the interests of minimizing the visibility of his dispute with the UPC national council, healing the wounds within the party, and gaining party support; the last paragraph of his memorandum was, thus, a practical compromise by which the president offered to respect the wishes of high level UPC officials.

A second explanation focuses on the fact that even contradictory motives could unite opponents of the president's proposals. As already noted, a number of top officials had major reservations about the Move to the Left. Fear that Obote would win his election, and that a victory at the polls would spur on measures to implement socialism, led this group to adopt a strategy of trying to contain the prerogatives of leadership by insuring the president's loyalty to the party. But their efforts to prevent direct presidential elections were seconded by those who feared that Obote might lose. For, ironically, another group maneuvering against the proposals was motivated by what was regarded as the paramount need to safeguard the revolution. The members of this group reasoned that Uganda was undergoing revolutionary change, that a president provides leadership for the revolution, and that decisions to implement revolutionary measures are not always popular. There is little doubt that, from its inception, the Move to the Left generated considerable opposition. And Obote's electoral prospects were uncertain. Conceivably, he could have been defeated. Even if he were returned to office, his mandate might have been marred by either widespread abstention or a negative vote by key ethnic groups. The specter of 1961 cast its shadow over 1970; the Baganda boycott of the 1961 elections had detracted from the legitimacy of Uganda's first government, and the prospect of Buganda refusing to participate in the elections scheduled for 1971 was worrying for a government seeking a mandate. While Obote might manage to be elected to office without the support of the heartland tribe, he could scarcely, in such circumstances, claim an electoral "victory"; rather, the elections would have dramatized patterns of ethnic discord in Uganda.

A final interpretation is that Obote stage-managed the debates.[9] This view attributes Machiavellian motives to the president and also assumes that he was astute enough to make a realistic appraisal of the extent of popular opposition to his recommendations for electoral reform. According to this argument, if Obote had truly wanted the proposals accepted, the party could not have acted in such a high-handed manner; had he had strong convictions, he would not have stood by without making a vigorous defense of his proposed measures. Those who accept this interpretation suggest that Obote wanted to be known above all as a democrat and that the only way to foster this image was by making it look as if the party had vetoed competitive elections against his expressed wishes.

Amidst growing speculation, Obote reopened the presidential debates.[10] In December, to both the national council and the delegates conference (reconstituted by virtue of the branch and constituency elections in October and November), he issued a compromise proposal in the form of a new report.[11] The original yes-no arrangements, set forth in Document No. 5, were revised in this report, but the new scheme was not to affect the agreement, reached previously, that the president would not be required to stand in the forthcoming elections. After that, direct competitive elections would be called only if more than one candidate was nominated. A candidate would be able to secure nomination by establishing a majority in thirty-two of ninety-six parliamentary constituency conferences. Theoretically, therefore, there could be as many as three candidates; but if one candidate was nominated by sixty-five constituencies, he would be elected unopposed. If three candidates were to run, the candidate securing most votes

9. This argument is referred to by Selwyn D. Ryan, "Electoral Engineering in Uganda," *Mawazo,* II, No. 4 (December 1970), 11.

10. The best account of these events is provided by Akiiki B. Mujaju, "The Uganda Presidential Election Debate Re-examined" (mimeo, a revised version of a paper presented to the Universities of East Africa Social Science Conference, Dar es Salaam, December 1970).

11. A. Milton Obote, "Election of the President of the Republic: Report to the Delegates Conference" (Mbale, Uganda, December 18, 1970).

would win. In the event of either no registered candidate or a tie, the UPC delegates conference would determine who should be president.

Obote's strategy was to insure the role of the party in forthcoming elections and to provide a popular base. In other words, he sought to fuse control by the party with mass participation. At the same time, Obote clearly sensed the need to deal with a mounting challenge from within his party. He no longer stood aloof, as he did during the August deliberations, but assumed personal command of the UPC branch and constituency elections. Felix Onama was relieved of the responsibility of organizing the December delegates conference and Basil Bataringya put in charge of the arrangements. At the conference, the president succeeded in marshaling support for his new proposals.

While Obote was, therefore, ultimately successful on this issue, a larger lesson was emerging from the controversy. The opposition to the proposals contained in Document No. 5 provided ominous warning of antagonistic political forces' determination not to accept the new departures of the second phase. The increasingly vigorous maneuvering against the Move to the Left made it clear that the objectives of ideological modernization could not be realized without severe divisions in the body politic.

Related Measures

As the president and his top aides continued to draft ideological documents, other stalwarts called for implementation of the new principles. Measures were taken to achieve the goals set forth in the documents. Time and again, however, they were either insufficient or ill-conceived; or, in those cases where measures were adequately planned, officials charged with implementing them lacked commitment or were even opposed to the Move to the Left.

Attempts to give substance to the documents began with legislation to speed up the rate of Africanization. Many Ugandans resented the anomaly of being discriminated against in their own country, either by or on behalf of noncitizens. The government sought to change the situation by insuring rapid localization of both governmental and nongovernment posts. Efforts were made to provide commercial opportunities for African Ugandans by restricting the privileges of Asian traders.

As has already been noted, the economic power and social exclusiveness of Asians in East Africa has long caused resentment. Representing less than one percent of the population, the Asian community in East Africa came to control over 80 percent of regional commerce.[12] One observer has estimated that in the 1960's individuals of Indian and Pakistani descent provided 25 percent of East Africa's professional and managerial personnel and approximately 40 percent of the area's highly skilled clerical and manual workers.[13] In that decade the average earnings of Asians were eight times higher than those of Africans. Moreover, as figures compiled in 1968 for banking and industry demonstrate (see Table 8), the number of Africans holding senior executive positions was still very small.

Clearly, neither European-controlled nor Asian-controlled firms were pushing localization. The explanation for the slow progress centered on the lack of qualified personnel of local origin. With reference to the Asians, Ugandan Africans argued in return that these traders regarded their business enterprises as family firms providing sustenance for an extended family and that, since they were attempting to keep as much wealth as possible within the family, Asian businessmen did not want to take on partners of a different cultural or racial group. The African population was piqued at what it regarded as the Asians' self-serving approach to life in Uganda, their aggrandizement of wealth at the expense of the masses and refusal to throw in their lot with the nationalist cause.

The 1968 *Report of the Committee on Africanisation* is indicative of heightened feelings about the economic and cultural role of noncitizens residing in Uganda. The committee was distressed about "the non-indigenous character and appearance of our towns and trading centres which to a first visitor to the country would look like a transplanted Bombay, Calcutta or Madras except that

12. *Speech by His Excellency the President of the Republic of Uganda General Idi Amin Dada at the Commonwealth Heads of State and Government Meeting Held at Ottawa, August, 1973* (Entebbe: Government Printer, 1973), p. 4; Juliet H. Zaidi, "The Asian Community in East Africa: Its Geographical Distribution and Economic and Social Characteristics" (unpublished M.A. Thesis: University of Denver, 1967), p. 59.
13. Anirudha Gupta, "The Asians in East Africa: Problems and Prospects," *International Studies*, X, No. 3 (January 1969), 277.

Table 8. Upper level staffing of banking and industry in Uganda, 1968

Name of firm	Number of senior executives	Number of Africans	Number of non-Africans
EUROPEAN-CONTROLLED:			
Nyanza Textiles	20	3	17
Barclays Bank	38	3	35
B.A.T.	12	0	12
Uganda Company	15	1	14
Kilembe Mines	72	4	68
A.E.L.	36	11	25
Gailey & Roberts	33*	8	27
National & Grindlays Bank	13	2	11
A. Baumann & Co.	11	2	9
Standard Bank	8	0	8
Uganda Cement Industry	11	1	10
Uganda Breweries	13	4	9
Uganda Shell	11	3	8
Tororo Chemicals	8	0	8
ASIAN-CONTROLLED:			
Mulco Textiles	21	3	18
Steel Corporation of East Africa	16	2	14
Other Madhvani Group Industries	66	3	63
Mehta Group	50	1	49
Sikh Saw Mills	12	1	11
Sango Bay Estates	8	0	8
Bank of Baroda	6	0	6
Damodar Jinabhai	6	0	6
Dayalbhai Madanji	10	0	10

SOURCE: *The Report of the Committee on Africanisation of Commerce and Industry in Uganda* (Entebee: Government Printer, 1968), p. 19.
* The figure presumably intended here is 35.

they would perhaps be tidier and less populated."[14] Recommending a five-year period for foreign firms and parastatal bodies to recruit Ugandans as replacements for noncitizen employees, the committee also advised abolition of racial differentials in salary and termination of promotions and appointments disingenuously designed to make Africans visible in executive positions.

The Obote government made a concerted effort to correct the legacy of British paternalism in commerce by increasing the African share of the wholesale and retail trade. Among the most

14. *The Report of the Committee on Africanisation of Commerce and Industry in Uganda* (Entebbe: Government Printer, 1968), p. 3.

important steps taken before the Move to the Left, the establishment of African Business Promotions in 1963 and the National Trading Corporation (NTC) in 1966 were to bring about increased opportunities for Africans in commerce. The reasons behind the creation of such entities as the NTC were laudable, but the organizations themselves were singularly unsuccessful. The NTC suffered from inept leadership, rampant corruption, lack of business know-how, inadequate funding, and attempts at subterfuge by African politicians and Asian businessmen whose interests opposed those of the organization.

In March 1969 the president approved the Trade Licensing Act, which enabled the minister of commerce to insure that trade was controlled by firms in which citizens were the predominant shareholders. A number of restrictions were placed on the trading activities of noncitizens; in particular, their business concerns had to be licensed by the government. And certain business centers and trading activities were to be reserved exclusively for Ugandans.

Measures were also taken in the realm of banking. The Banking Act of 1969 required banks in Uganda to maintain a cash capital of no less than Shs. 200,000,000 and banks incorporated outside Uganda to have at least Shs. 10,000,000, with assets of at least 5 percent of total deposit liabilities in Uganda. In order to demonstrate their ability to meet their public liabilities, each bank would be further required to show evidence of a reserve fund equal to paid-up capital. An amendment to the act—approved by the National Assembly in October 1969—declared that all banks operating in Uganda must be incorporated locally and that a cash capital of Shs. 20,000,000 must be held in securities as stipulated by the government.

In December 1969, declaring that Uganda was to be a one-party state, the UPC adopted the "Common Man's Charter" as its official ideology. Opposition parties were banned, and members of the DP were detained under emergency regulations. In accordance with Document No. 2, a Ministry for National Service Camps was established. Four camps were set up, the intention being that members of the National Union of Uganda Students should be the first entrants. As specified in the Nakivubo Pronouncements, an Export-Import Corporation was created through which trade should eventually be channeled. The cooperatives were strengthened and granted a monopoly over processing coffee. A Produce Marketing Board was designed to counter exploitation and to offer farmers a higher return. Legislation passed in 1970 provided that corruption should be punishable by up to twenty years' imprisonment, a Shs. 20,000,000 fine, or both. The Companies (Government and Public Bodies Participation) Act of 1970, which was to become the first amendment to the 1967 constitution, filled out the scheme whereby nationalized enterprises were to be compensated from profits. One of the most controversial measures was the order of October 1970 repatriating unskilled laborers from neighboring countries. The largest number of these were Luos from Kenya; government spokesmen argued that, East African unity notwithstanding, they had to act against Kenyans who were absorbing jobs that should be available to Ugandans and thereby aggravating the unemployment problem. In a subsequent act that stirred considerable reaction in Kenya and Tanzania, government-imposed currency restrictions ended the Uganda shilling's convertibility in the other East African countries.

In order to carry out the recommendations set forth in Document No. 5, new constituency boundaries were drawn that would expand the National Assembly from eighty-two to ninety-six members. When the military coup took place in January 1971, the changes that were under way for elections were rendered superfluous; at that point, the government was amending the Electoral Act, making administrative arrangements for new voting procedures, ordering materials from abroad, preparing the Government Printer's office, and planning to train officials and register voters.[15]

In the realm of school reform, educational expenditure was increased to 28 percent of the 1969-1970 budget. On August 18, 1969, the president, speaking at the opening of the annual conference of the Educational Association of Uganda,[16] argued that, although education was being given top priority in Uganda's development program, little had been accomplished in reorienting the schools. Education was the most important instrument for pro-

15. Cohen and Parson, p. 54.
16. A. Milton Obote, "Policy Proposals for Uganda: Educational Needs," *Mawazo*, II, No. 2 (December 1969), 3–9.

moting national consciousness, Obote stressed; but the continuation
of a European-oriented curriculum amounted to a rejection of
African culture. Warning against formation of a parasitic class of
educated men, Obote concluded that Uganda's school system must
not make the citizen a foreigner in his own country.

The most radical proposals for changing educational practices
were advanced by the Visitation Committee to Makerere University College, whose report criticized Makerere's colonial heritage,
the College's policy of recruiting expatriate teachers to instruct
Ugandans, and its syllabus, which lacked relevance to Uganda's
needs. Echoing the president's speech to the Educational Association, the committee foresaw such factors leading to a situation that
would tend "to make the graduate an alien among his own society."[17]
The members of the committee suggested that, although the college
was founded in a colonial era, when capitalism, feudalism, and
foreign domination flourished, the new Makerere University was
a specifically Ugandan institution, born in a "revolutionary
socialist era."[18] If it could not change of its own accord, they
warned, the government would step in to change it. Emphasis was
laid on the role of the University as an agent of ideological
socialization:

Since the high-level manpower requirements of Uganda both in quality
and quantity must be defined by the State, we feel that their fulfillment
through training by the University must follow a well-defined pattern
based on the commitment and implementation of Uganda's ideology.
The definition of Academic freedom in the University of East Africa
Act is, however, diametrically opposed to this approach and is a relic
of colonialism.[19]

The Visitation Committee made specific recommendations for
syllabus revision in each department. In the case of the Department
of Political Science and Public Administration, their recommendations gave rise to considerable debate among faculty members on a
number of fundamental questions: What is the proper role of a
department of political science in a developing country? When
there is only one university, and therefore only one political science

17. *Report of the Visitation Committee to Makerere University College*
(Entebbe: Government Printer, 1970), p. 3.
18. *Ibid.*, p. 5.
19. *Ibid.*, p. 7.

department, what are the special responsibilities and potential contributions of that department to the country's development? When
a government opts for socialist construction, should political scientists at the university be charged with the task of instilling the
official ideology? Should the university resist pressures to become
an ideological institute? In the context of development, is academic
freedom a right, a privilege, or a luxury? Are other goals more
important in periods of abrupt transition?

The eight units outlined in the syllabus recommended for the
political science curriculum included some that appeared to be
based on part of one committee member's syllabus at Cambridge in
the 1930's, with a flavoring of topics from current affairs relating
to Uganda added. Some members of the Department of Political
Science were not pleased at being told what to teach, especially at
being instructed to include such "traditional" subjects as constitutional development and comparative constitutions, which "modern"
political scientists tend to omit from their syllabi. Others were perplexed by the notion of presenting an entire course (one year at
Makerere) on the eleven-page "Common Man's Charter."

With the adoption of the Makerere University, Kampala Act
(October 6, 1970), the University was placed under national control. The most portentous provision of the act may well have been
Section 12, which gave the minister of education the power to
appoint deans. The University retained the right to select professors,
but subject to ministerial veto; the minister was also granted power
to give directions to the University Council, Senate, and other
authorities.

Intended Ideological Functions

The examination of Obote's proposals and the measures adopted
to implement them provides evidence of certain implicit assumptions
about the way in which ideology was intended to function. The
attempt to advance an ideology of modernization in Uganda entailed a strategy that aimed at utilizing all six of the functions of
ideology that were discussed in Chapter 2. This is not to say that
Obote thought in the same analytical terms employed by the social
scientist; to assume an automatic correspondence with the classificatory scheme would be to err by reifying categories of analysis.
Yet these six functions can be seen to be helpful in assessing the

activities of the second phase. Intended functions, however, are not the same as the actual impact of an ideology.

In other parts of Africa, efforts to establish legitimacy included appeals based on charisma, tradition, and nationality. In Ghana, for example, Nkrumah sought legitimacy in the messianic fervor surrounding the president, in the idea of the Convention People's Party being the successor to the medieval African empire of Ghana, and in the notion that the regime was the guardian of the best features of African tribalism.[20] In Uganda, however, these potential sources of legitmacy were absent: Obote aroused no charismatic fervor; the UPC could hardly claim to be the successor to a great medieval empire; and to recall tradition was to encourage deeply rooted ethnic animosity rather than to provide the foundation for national unity. Therefore Obote sought to establish legitimacy in newly institutionalized norms. During the second phase his efforts centered on developing notions of "Uganda's contribution to the 'African revolution,' " "the new political culture," and the creation of a "socialist revolutionary society."

Ideology was frequently employed as a convenient way of rationalizing problems, some of which were the inevitable by-products of rapid social change. Failures were explained not as the result of mistaken UPC policies or the blunders of inept ministers but in terms of the mischief and cabal of reactionary forces. "The reactionary forces all over the world are on the run. In Uganda they have attempted and still attempt to frustrate the successful implementation of The Common Man's Charter in a desperate death-bed endeavour to remain economically alive. It will be recalled that the reactionaries tried to murder the Common Man's Charter on the very day it was born." When "reactionaries" disagreed with the "Party's ideology as enunciated in The Common Man's Charter," they were to be considered the enemies of the people of Uganda and Africa.[21]

The major instruments through which the general populace was to be exhorted to pursue the goals set forth in the Charter were to be the party and the electoral system. The idea that a new ideology cannot be implemented through old institutions was a recurring

20. Donald MacRae, "Nkrumahism: Past and Future of an Ideology," *Government and Opposition*, I, No. 4 (December 1966), 537.
21. "Democracy Appeal by Dr. Obote," *Uganda Argus*, August 22, 1970.

theme in Obote's speeches. According to Akena Adoko, one of
Obote's closest confidants, the revolution in Uganda required
manipulation and organization of agitation from the top: "In all
countries where socialist revolutions have taken place, the population has always been stirred up from their passive state into an
active state by government policies designed to that effect or by
groups of organized agitators and revolutionaries."[22]

To encourage use of the official ideology for purposes of social
change the regime turned to myth-making. Of course, with myth-
making, the critical factor is not whether the myth is true or false
but whether it is believed. Just as leaders in Kenya glorified the
Mau Mau experience in order to appeal to the citizenry, the Obote
regime employed a distorted, or, perhaps better, a selective, view of
history.[23] The Kenya example has an interesting sequel, which may
hold a lesson for other African states. While Mau Mau provided
the basis for nationalist appeals in the early years after independence, references to this phase of Kenyan history are less frequently
heard today; and the reason is heightened ethnic tension in Kenya.
Mau Mau was primarily a Kikuyu affair, and other ethnic groups—
most notably, the Luo—are increasingly antagonistic to resurrection
of this myth. More important, Mau Mau was also a Kikuyu civil
war, which created bitter divisions among the Kikuyu. The point is
that in a climate of generalized economic and ethnic tension, an
ideology that relies on historical myth-making may offend major
groups and thereby alienate potential sources of support.

In Uganda, the myth of the "new political culture" was designed
to capitalize on what was regarded as the logic of the independence
movement and postcolonial efforts to consolidate power. All previous attempts to generate a sense of solidarity in Uganda had
failed miserably. Christianity was incapable of providing a sense of
Ugandanness.[24] The attempt to operate a modern nation-state in
tandem with traditional kingdoms under the umbrella of a neofederal structure was never likely to succeed. Political parties had
failed to aggregate interests at the national level and served only as
reference groups. There was no one leader behind whom a large
majority of the people could unite. In the search for yet another

22. "Revolution to Bring Social Justice—Akena," *People,* March 25, 1970.
23. Mazrui, *On Heroes and Uhuru-Worship,* p. 21.
24. Wellbourn, pp. 58, 61.

road to solidarity, Obote turned to ideological modernization, and attempted to move his country to the left accordingly. In the terms of the Charter, "the meaning of the phrase 'people of Uganda' is always clear and definite. It is, One People under One Government in One Country."[25]

Ideology, then, was to become the language of political consciousness and of protest. Increasingly, it was used as a device by which leaders explained to and interpreted for the masses. At times, rhetoric became an esoteric communication code in which the leaders addressed the general citizenry:

> The African Revolution in general and the Ugandan Revolution in particular have had a very difficult birth. The newly born revolutionary and republican child requires nursing. It is the duty of the masses, under the guidance of the Party, to nurse that child. The child must not be given to the heartless exploiters of the African womb. The Party must therefore ensure that Uganda of the future is free of those exploiters by arousing the masses to support the successful implementation of the Common Man's Charter.[26]

Intending ideology to serve as an agent of change, Obote exhorted the people to meet the duties and challenges of modernization. Obote's task became, above all, manipulation, or, less pejoratively, mobilization. Genuine personal conviction, self-interest, lack of viable alternatives, and the nature of Uganda's problems led Obote to turn to ideology as a device for mobilizing the masses.

25. Obote, *The Common Man's Charter*, p. 4.
26. "Democracy Appeal by Dr. Obote," *Uganda Argus*, August 22, 1970.

CHAPTER 6

Ideological Stress

In the attempt to utilize ideology as the agent of mobilization, a massive campaign was launched to spread the message. The Charter was translated into a number of vernacular languages and distributed to shops and government buildings. Radio, television, and newspapers featured excerpts from the Charter and other ideological documents. In party meetings, the Charter became a frequent topic for discussion. The Chinese example of circulating the sayings of Chairman Mao could not have been far away from the minds of Obote's men.

Unlike China, however, Uganda lacks the infrastructure for ideological diffusion. The Chinese Communist Party (CCP) expended immense effort over decades to build political institutions, including leadership bodies and cells at the grass roots level. After expelling the foreigners and the forces of Chiang Kai-shek, the CCP had an infrastructure that could be used for ideological diffusion. Uganda, on the other hand, had never experienced the bitterness of sustained struggle against foreign domination and lacked a developed political infrastructure.

In Uganda, most of the local newspapers that grew up after World War II did not survive independence. Of those that did survive, *Munno* gradually became known for its bold editorial policy, its independent line leading it to frequent identification with the DP on matters of party politics, persistent attacks on corruption, advocacy of reform, and support for the peasants against the chiefs. The other major newspapers since 1962 have been the *Argus*[1] (1970 circulation, 27,000) and a Luganda publication, *Taifa Empya* (1970 circulation 8,000). There was no challenge to the near monopolistic position of these publications

1. Under Uganda's Second Republic, beginning December 1, 1972, the *Uganda Argus* became the *Voice of Uganda.*

until "committed" newspapers were established. The *People* was founded by the UPC in 1964 as a government daily. During the Obote years, newspaper coverage was almost entirely minister- or party-oriented. Stories about the common man were rarely featured, and newspapers therefore had little appeal to the literate or semi-literate at the local level. Although direct government censorship was not imposed, the threat of censorship served to restrict criticism. In general, the press was characterized by an elite orientation, a failure to mobilize support for the government, and a tendency to treat the words of high level officials as infallible.[2]

Radio and television came much later to Uganda than to some other African countries. Sound broadcasting began on March 1, 1954; the service, known originally as Uganda Broadcasting Service, Kampala, changed its name to Radio Uganda after independence. The main programs have been news (local and international), discussions for women and children, items for farmers, veterinary talks, listeners' favorite songs, religious services, outside broadcasts, football commentaries, and coverage of ceremonies. In 1960, 90,000 sets were in use; by mid-1964, over 145,000. In the late 1960's Radio Uganda claimed a listening audience of about three million people. From its inception in 1963, Uganda Television (UTV) has carried 50 percent of its programs live. Coverage of news, both national and international, has been featured prominently—two Luganda bulletins and two English bulletins were telecast each evening in the 1960's. As of June 1968, 9,137 television sets were in operation.

Both Radio Uganda and UTV have faced problems of language, finance, lack of skilled personnel, and scattered distribution of population. Radio and television have been government-operated and -owned, and the audience has frequently complained about the boring and frivolous nature of programs. Throughout the Move to the Left, the Ministry of Information, Broadcasting, and Tourism continued to condone the use of foreign programs. Although these broadcasts conveyed the values of Western societies, the Ugandan government made little attempt to limit their use. As one observer puts it, "the various weaknesses . . . make it rather difficult to see

2. Daniel Nelson, "Newspapers in Uganda," *Transition,* VIII (iv), No. 35 (February–March 1968), 29–33.

how the media are at all effective except in a limited and rather insignificant manner."[3] Because of the difficulty of reaching people, ideological modernization in Uganda was problematical from the outset.

Communication in Uganda, as in other low income areas, is labor-intensive. Oral means—the "bush phone"—are far more important than written. The scholarly literature suggests that communication is an overriding problem in less developed countries, for the development of modern mass media (and, therefore, by implication, national development) requires a society that is already modern by other measures—geographical and social mobility involving separation of individuals from the family, urbanization, literacy, mass participation, new occupational structures, and sociocompetitive norms. On the basis of data collected in the Middle East, Daniel Lerner argues that the spread of dissatisfaction in developing countries can be attributed to the central role that mass media play as creators of new aspirations.[4] Data collected recently in East Africa, however, indicate that, to the contrary, the degree of exposure to mass media determines neither evaluation of life situation nor effective orientation to the political system in the direct manner Lerner postulates.[5] And Anthony Oberschall suggests that the image of the ignorant African, totally oblivious to national and international affairs, is inconsistent with the data his survey of twenty-one rural areas in Uganda produced. When Oberschall's team of researchers asked rural Ugandans to name the three most important people in the country, 82 percent of the respondents named Obote—and this figure would probably have been higher were it not for the disdain of the Baganda—and 81 percent and 68 percent respectively were able to recall second and third names, most of them national political figures rather than local notables.

3. Dhiru Patel, "Radio and Television in Uganda," *Vidura*, VIII, No. 2 (May 1971), 185–89.
4. Daniel Lerner, *The Passing of Traditional Society: Modernizing the Middle East* (New York: The Free Press, 1958), p. 55; *idem*, "Towards a Communication Theory of Modernization," in Lucian W. Pye, ed., *Communications and Political Development* (Princeton: Princeton University Press, 1963), p. 33.
5. Goran Hyden, *Political Development in Rural Tanzania: TANU Yajenga Nchi* (Nairobi: East African Publishing House, 1969), pp. 204, 205.

The majority of respondents were able to provide the name of the local M.P. as well.[6] According to Oberschall, Uganda had already by the time of his field work, which was conducted in 1966, reached the stage at which people favor more opportunities for themselves and economic and social development for the community.[7]

Despite only intermittent contact, most Ugandans are in touch with the center. In part, the relationship between political cadres and the masses turns on the nature of the linkages—not merely the messages that are communicated, but the way in which transmission belts handle message flows. In other words, the attitudes and positions of middle-level leaders are particularly important. Because of the inability or unwillingness of the center to satisfy the masses, the style and enthusiam of middle-level leaders is critical.[8]

But where were the transmission belts in Uganda in the second phase of ideological modernization? In terms of reaching the masses, the UPC was moribund, and President Obote could not even trust senior officials. Local notables continued to dominate the party, and rural branches were frequently at odds with central headquarters in Kampala. The party did not penetrate to the grass roots; a cell system similar to that of the Tanganyika African National Union (TANU) was never established by the UPC. Moreover, educational institutions in Uganda did not serve as channels for transmitting the regime's political messages. Perhaps the one parallel in Uganda with Tanzania's Kivukoni College, which consciously transmits ideology, was Makerere's short-lived interdisciplinary Development Studies Programme. But to suggest that Makerere's Development Studies Programme served as a channel for ideological diffusion would require a stretch of the imagination; many of the lecturers were American or European, and the Programme was subject to considerable resistance, from within and without.

In terms of informal channels of ideological communication, relatively few government-sponsored measures were attempted. The

6. Anthony Oberschall, "Communications, Information and Aspirations in Rural Uganda," *Journal of Asian and African Studies,* IV, No. 1 (January 1969), 41.
7. *Idem,* "Rising Expectations and Political Turmoil," *Journal of Development Studies,* VI, No. 1 (October 1969), 17.
8. Also see Henry Bienen, *Tanzania: Party Transformation and Economic Development* (Princeton: Princeton University Press, 1967), pp. 250, 251.

Tanzanian technique of organizing mass meetings, seminars, and dance bands for political purposes was not applied in Uganda. In Tanzania, President Nyerere skillfully adapts aspects of traditional culture in rallying the masses for the tasks of nation-building. For example, when he broadcasts in a five-minute program following the news, Nyerere exploits his people's traditional fondness for the clever use of parables to illustrate a speaker's point and usually tells a humorous, earthy story about the relevance of ideology to Tanzania's development goals. But in Uganda these devices were either ineffective or not tried. Having articulated an ideology of modernization, Obote discovered that channels of communication were blocked. Within the party, a business elite rather than peasants or members of the proletariat were the predominant element. Figures for 1970 indicate that 46.3 percent of UPC constituency chairmen were businessmen, while only 16.5 percent were employed as farmers, trade unionists, and professional politicians.[9] In other words, the predominant group in the UPC had most to lose from socialism, and those with occupational interests most consonant with socialist objectives were only a small minority. With an atrophied party, educational institutions that were suffused with Western values, and myriad cultural traditions of hostility, few options were open to Obote.

In large part, the diffusion of ideology was left to discussions and speeches. Since the party was not effective in this regard, the logical alternative would have been the bureaucracy. Unfortunately for Obote, however, the attitudes and behavior of high-level officials in the civil service contributed to the failure to marshal support for the new ideological proposals. The middle and upper levels of the public services are composed predominantly of Baganda, in part because of Ganda ability to adjust to modern norms, in part as a result of the lopsided educational system during the colonial period, which gave the Baganda the greatest access to the schools. In 1964, when Felix Onama discounted charges of nepotism, he quoted figures showing that the civil service included sixty-five Baganda, twenty-seven from the West of Uganda, thirty-five from the East, and twenty-seven from the North.[10] Data compiled by

9. Cohen and Parson, p. 61.
10. "Mr. Onama Denies Nepotism," *Uganda Argus,* December 4, 1964.

Nelson Kasfir confirm the overrepresentation of Baganda in the public services but show them to be underrepresented in the security forces. During the 1959–1967 period, the number of Baganda in the higher civil service posts was two to three times greater than what might have been expected on the basis of their percentage of the total population. Immediately before independence, the Baganda percentage of higher civil service posts was 46.9 percent, but the figure fell to 35.6 in 1967.[11]

Increasingly, Nilotics became identified as the source of ideological diffusion. Obote, of course, was regarded as responsible for the Move to the Left. But evidence is lacking on whether he actually wrote the documents or whether, and to what degree, his assistants participated in drafting the proposals. Unconfirmed rumors circulated that two university lecturers penned the "Common Man's Charter," and it also seems likely that presidential aide Akena Adoko played a major role.

Little information is available on Milton Obote's background. In the early 1950's he left Makerere College without a degree. He spent a number of years working for Argwings Kodhek, a lawyer and politician in Kenya, where the fervor of nationalism surrounding Mau Mau and the uneasy climate of race relations in Nairobi may well have had a radicalizing effect on him. When Obote returned to Uganda, about 1956, he was nominated as the Lango District Council's representative to Uganda's Legislative Council. In the drive toward independence, his attacks on the protectorate government gave him a reputation as a radical, nationalist politician.

Leaders' personal experiences—in Obote's case his period in Kenya and the multitude of problems he faced subsequently as a practical politician—are significant factors conditioning ideological innovation; but the values imbued by traditional culture may be of more fundamental importance. In the African context, traditional belief systems must be regarded as a variable that has considerable explanatory power for indentifying the sources of a modernizing ideology. Obote's republican and socialist persuasions reflect, in large part, the traditional beliefs and values of Nilotic peoples. Com-

11. Nelson Kasfir, "Cultural Sub-Nationalism in Uganda," in Victor A. Olorunsola, ed., *The Politics of Cultural Sub-Nationalism in Africa* (Garden City: Doubleday, 1972), pp. 124–28.

pared with the Baganda, the Nilotics are egalitarian. Unlike the monarchies to the south, Obote's tribe—the Langi—being traditionally acephalous, know neither paramount chiefs nor hierarchical rule. Political organization in Lango is based on an age-set system of highly specialized structures. The clan system is not politically significant. In fact, when Luo colonizers attempted to establish an aristocratic clan there, they met staunch resistance from an indigenous people adamant about maintaining their democratic values. In Lango the criterion for leadership is merit. Traditionally, the Twon Lwak (the Bull of the People, who headed the military) was selected by the group in power; if defeated, he was replaced, by an individual who might represent a different clan altogether.[12]

As Obote sought to spread the values of northern peoples, major structural imbalance in the innovation and diffusion of ideology resulted. Obote would have liked to use the UPC for ideological diffusion, but the party was unreliable. Most of the few officials in the party who could be trusted were lacking in technical skills. Civil servants, on the other hand, were skilled technically but displayed little enthusiasm for the president's proposals. Increasingly, therefore, Nilotic northerners became identified as the source of ideological innovation, while Bantu southerners held the technical posts that could forward ideological diffusion.

Structural problems of innovation and diffusion were compounded by discontinuities in the process of socialization. Rhetoric notwithstanding, few concrete efforts were made to develop curricula that would accord with a "socialist revolutionary society." Uganda's schools are the product of colonialism—in particular of the work of Christian missionaries and, to a lesser extent, Asians concerned with maintaining their own cultures and languages. With an educational system patterned after the British model, syllabi reflect other people's history and needs. Uganda's elitist institutions, most prominently Budo and St. Mary's Kasubi, were designed to replicate public schools in the United Kingdom. Despite the government's stated intentions regarding socialist construction, the

12. Ali A. Mazrui, *Cultural Engineering and Nation-Building in East Africa* (Evanston: Northwestern University Press, 1972), pp. 195–99; Jack Herbert Driberg, *The Lango: A Nilotic Tribe of Uganda* (London: T. F. Unwin, 1923); and Okot P'Bitek, *African Religions in Western Scholarship* (Nairobi: East African Publishing House, 1972).

schools continued to inculcate Britain's hierarchical, prefectorial values. Rather than stressing vocational subjects, such as agriculture, Uganda's schools contributed to the formation of a class of Afro-Saxons bent on individual achievement.

In what spokesmen for the government described as a "socialist revolutionary society," education was, to a significant degree, in the hands of Western, expatriate teachers who did not profess a commitment to socialism. At no time did Ugandan teachers constitute more than 15 percent of the total in government-aided secondary schools. In 1966 the teaching population was about 63 percent European, 23 percent Asian, and 15 percent African. About 60 percent were on contract from overseas, 15 percent on local contract, 15 percent volunteers from various nations, and 10 percent missionaries.[13] The turnover among African teachers has been particularly high. A large proportion of Africans trained as teachers have been drawn into government service, because the reservoir of educated talent is so small. In terms of the regime's intentions for ideological diffusion, the levels of cognitive awareness and affective orientation toward the political system among teachers are instructive. Data on teachers' attitudes indicate that, in comparison with African teachers, expatriate teachers' level of knowledge about Ugandan affairs is quite low. When David Evans asked teachers to name the ministries and their ministers, the average expatriate teacher (not including missionaries) could recall only two.[14] Similarly, in an examination of different teacher groups' disposition, or feeling toward government, the expatriate groups scored lower and local teachers higher.[15]

A large proportion of schools in Uganda are private rather than public, and the Obote regime did little to correct the inconsistency between the values fostered by private education and the desiderata of the "new political culture." Little reliable information is available on the size of the private sector of education in Uganda. Shortly after the coup of 1971, Abu Mayanja, the first minister of education under the Second Republic, mentioned 300 private

13. David R. Evans, *Teachers as Agents of National Development: A Case Study of Uganda* (New York: Praeger, 1971), p. 40.
14. *Ibid.*, pp. 82, 83.
15. *Ibid.*, pp. 74, 75.

schools in Uganda,[16] but this estimate is likely to be low. Probably more accurate are Evans' estimates that, in terms of enrollment, the private sector is roughly half the size of the aided system at the primary level and between a half and two-thirds as large as the government system at the secondary level.[17]

The major problem of ideological innovation and diffusion, however, was much more fundamental. Obote's ideological tracts may have been appropriate for an industrial society, but in Uganda, where there is no common language and the masses are illiterate, these elaborate manifestoes and wordy documents gained little support. For those able to understand them—that is, the elites— socialist goals seemed more of a threat to privilege than a promise of advancement.

Unanswered Questions

The documents and the measures adopted subsequently left a number of questions unanswered, which contributed to an atmosphere of general uncertainty. The ambiguity of the proposals engendered doubts and heightened suspicions about the Move to the Left. The regime's goal was to elicit commitment, but citizens were puzzled by the indeterminate nature of Uganda's "new political culture." The following discussion, while not exhaustive, illustrates the questions and issues that remained unresolved during Uganda's most determined attempt to introduce an ideology of modernization.

The "Common Man's Charter" itself contained little in the way of specific proposals for propelling Uganda toward socialism. Its ideas were expressed at a high level of generality and thus could be interpreted in any number of ways. Who was the "common man"? Can socialism be forged without committed socialists? Should there be a leadership code for those in the vanguard of Ugandan socialism? Should socialist construction begin with reductions in the income of the cabinet members and high-level bureaucrats?

---

16. "Emphasis on Primary Education," *Uganda Argus,* July 7, 1971. Government-aided schools number 2,723 primary, 72 senior secondary, 17 vocational secondary, 5 technical secondary, 25 teacher training, 2 technical and commercial, and 1 university (figures from Statistics Division, Ministry of Planning and Economic Development, Entebbe, 1969).

17. Evans, p. 39.

The Charter does not deal with the agricultural sector, although over 90 percent of Ugandans are peasant farmers or pastoralists. In defense of this omission, it can be argued that Document No. 2 was intended as an expression of concern for the problems of rural development; however, neither the Charter nor any other document tackles the question of rural capitalism. Throughout Africa, the issue of land ownership is highly politicized. The impetus that land alienation provided to Mau Mau is but one case in point. In Uganda, although tribal and clan tenure still predominate, there is a trend toward private freehold and mailos. The most ominous aspects of class formation to accompany the increasing individualization of land ownership may well be the rise of a landed gentry and the associated intensification of social and economic distinctions. A purist view of socialist construction suggests that Obote should have challenged the prerogatives of this group. Clearly a privileged class bent on profiteering in the countryside is inconsistent with the objectives of socialism. But policies of principle are not always well advised politically. In this respect, Tanzania's experience is a useful comparison. That country's program for building socialism, which emphasizes the rural sector, is one of the boldest and most imaginative approaches to modernization anywhere in the Third World. Nyerere, while not a doctrinaire Marxist, is a pragmatic socialist attempting to alleviate class distinctions in Tanzania. Even so, his strategy in the rural sector is one of establishing ujamma (communal) villages; this scheme of villagization carefully avoids confrontation with capitalist modes of production in the countryside. The Ugandan president's ideological linchpin—the "Common Man's Charter"—may be faulted for neglecting the extension of socialism to the agricultural sector; whether Obote should have pursued a more comprehensive strategy is, however, another matter.

The release of Document No. 2 triggered a number of far-reaching questions about the implications of Obote's proposals. How was the national service scheme to be implemented without the social fabric being disrupted inordinately? When young men were serving, who would provide for their families? Some observers wondered whether the national service proposals would create new abuses, for example, forced labor, as in the colonial era. And there was considerable debate about the speed of the Move to the Left: if at first only those who were leaving school or university were required to serve—because they were easier to educate and take away from home—would the result be merely a greater separation between the educated and the masses?

Obote appeared to be seeking to set a prudent pace. An attempt was made to establish a transitional period in which socialism would be launched. Some of the measures were certainly intended to present self-serving capitalists with a fait accompli; however, the general strategy, adopted wittingly or unwittingly, was to ease into socialism. Undoubtedly the Nakivubo Pronouncements' 60 percent nationalization of major industries was the most precipitous act. But even in this case, the scope and intent of the document, which provided implicitly for the coexistence of private industry and the public sector, fell far short of full-fledged socialism. One surprising feature of Document No. 4 was that the nationalization proposals were not used to rationalize the structure of private enterprise. Why the government did not specify areas for joint participation and areas for private investment is unclear. The Nakivubo Pronouncements created a climate of uncertainty concerning Uganda's future attitude toward foreign investment and caused fundamental questions to be asked: Is it possible to develop a socialist sector in partnership with foreign capitalist investors? If foreign investment from capitalist sources were permitted, would this maintain the system of vertical integration that linked local elites and international market forces, thereby perpetuating dependency relations?

Among the enthusiastic supporters of Obote's Labour Day Speech, few appreciated the fact that nationalization is not a panacea. Nationalization does not automatically end exploitation; the act by itself neither severs ties with the forces of international capitalism nor eliminates neocolonialist intrigue. But nationalization can be an effective measure for promoting development. By nationalizing, local leaders attempt to assert their autonomy and gain control. If nationalization is implemented on behalf of the masses, a relationship of dependency can be changed into a more beneficial one of mutual interdependence. More can be expected of nationalized industries than mere profit maximization. In low income countries, they can perform certain socioeconomic functions that contribute to the welfare of the entire society; for example, nationalized industries can follow a policy of strategic investment that will diminish the gap between urban and rural areas. Nationalization may also impose burdens, however. Often the only thing that is changed is the identity of the exploiters—the fruits of exploitation are transferred from expatriates to local elites. Then nationalization only heightens the common man's feeling of deprivation, because the exploitation is being committed by his countrymen. Furthermore, major industries may be nationalized, but lack of a sufficient administrative structure leads to a gross lack of efficiency, causing a diminution of confidence in the government operations generally. Or, partial nationalization, involving partnership agreements between multinational corporations and African statal and parastatal bodies, may be a cover for continued foreign control. Such partnership agreements are, in fact, often welcomed by foreign investors, for state involvement reduces their risks. In other words, a partnership agreement may be a means of ensuring a given rate of return on investment. And partial nationalization usually offers foreign investors the opportunity, through use of advisers and experts, greater technical knowledge and managerial experience, sale of equipment, reliance on capital intensive modes of production, and low rates of reinvestment, to maintain their influence and perpetuate dependency relations.

So short was the period between Obote's May 1970 speech and the military coup of January 1971 that the evidence on whether Uganda's scheme for 60 percent nationalization would have been beneficial to the common man is inconclusive. But there is cause for skepticism. The criteria for drawing up the list of eighty-four major industries to be nationalized were questioned. Some of the firms were either bankrupt or nonexistent, a fact that reinforced the impression that the nationalization project was hastily conceived. Some wondered if Document No. 4 provided only a tentative list and whether other industries would be nationalized as well. The issue of compensation caused further misgivings. What was to be the principle of evaluation? And what would the government do to prevent a major outflow of capital and illegal moves by local capitalists to get money out of the country? There were serious doubts about Uganda's ability to meet the compensation bill. Moreover, economists expressed concern that compensation would absorb surpluses that should be reinvested locally.

Another much debated issue can be termed the dilemma of ownership versus control. Nationalization measures seek, above all, to establish public ownership over the means of production. But is public ownership achieved if the same members of the managerial class occupy their former positions? Low income countries in Africa, Uganda included, suffer from a lack of trained personnel with managerial skills; when a government is seeking to implement socialism, efficiency considerations may, therefore, argue for minimizing dislocation and utilizing the trained people available. A policy of retaining occupants of high-level managerial positions also reduces opposition from the well-to-do. So the optimum strategy may be for the government to appear magnanimous; socialism is being implemented for the good of all, and vengeance will not be taken indiscriminately. On the other hand, if members of the managerial class are allowed to retain their former positions, does this invite willful destruction of the government's policies? Is the effect to license saboteurs to work against policies that are not in their interest? In other words, was Obote's policy of allowing individuals to keep their former positions naive? And with such a policy in effect, how was the Move to the Left regarded by the common man? As empty rhetoric, words without substance?

To astute observers, one fact was clear. Despite the fanfare about nationalization, external market forces would ultimately determine the success or failure of the new measures. If the price of Uganda's three major exports—coffee, cotton, and copper—were to fall seriously, the economy would be crippled and all of the recent proposals for change would be nipped in the bud.

Some members of the local elite, as well as the expatriate community, with their own interests at stake, expressed reservations about the provisions in Documents Nos. 3 and 4 for speeding up Ugandanization. Replacement of qualified Asians and Europeans at the managerial level would, as has been noted, have created at least short term dislocations in the economy. For the Ugandans replacing expatriate managerial talent, there would be relentless requests from the individual's extended family as well as temptation stemming from material expectations of comfort and status. Even those convinced of the merit of rapid localization expressed misgivings about whether the Africans who replaced the noncitizens might be equally as bent on self-seeking profiteering as their predecessors. Further doubts were expressed about the practicality of attempting to rationalize the public service and stamp out graft and corruption in the absence of efforts to correct the misdeeds of the political elite.

A number of questions were also raised about the feasibility of implementing the proposals contained in Document No. 5. Would the government be able to create the administrative and technical machinery necessary to enact the election proposals? Were the proposals too complicated? Only a minority of voters, of course, would have had any formal education; yet they would have to cast separate ballots for president, the basic constituency representative, and three national constituency representatives. How were the campaigns to be organized? Would alliances be forged among candidates in various constituencies? Was there a danger of electoral coalitions? If families entered coalitions in order to strengthen their electoral chances, would female candidates be at a disadvantage?[18] And to what degree would wealth, reputation, and language affect campaigns?

In national constituencies where many of the candidates were not known to the general electorate ability to marshal finances to gain public visibility could have made the difference between victory and defeat. Similarly, the advantage of exposure for incumbent M.P.'s and party officials could have been decisive. What the effect of language would have been is difficult to estimate; but the correlation between the grouping of constituencies, the languages spoken in them, and the linguistic abilities of candidates could have been significant. The president's proposals failed to take adequate account of disparities in population distribution and, thus, the variation in the number of seats allotted to different regions. Presumably the East, being the most populous region, would have most members, while the North, the least populous, would have fewer. If so, the greater number of candidates from basic constituencies in the East would have fewer national constituencies in which to stand in the North. A more serious ethical question was raised by the hypothetical case of the candidate who polled highest in his basic constituency being defeated because he did not do well in the

18. This issue is raised by Mazrui, *Cultural Engineering*, pp. 127–45. Perceptive analysis of the practicality of the election proposals is provided by Peter Willets, "The Proposals for a New Ugandan Electoral System" (mimeo, Department of Political Science and Public Administration, Makerere University, Kampala, 1970).

three national constituencies. Would this amount to denying the electorate in the basic constituency effective representation in parliament?

Dysfunctions

The results of Obote's Move to the Left suggest that the introduction of an ideology of modernization may be dysfunctional in terms both of maintaining a particular political system and of attempting to transform that system. Ideological innovation and diffusion may upset the precarious balance of social forces and precipitate structural change. (Depending on one's normative biases, these dysfunctions may be considered as either desirable or undesirable.)

If the powerful forces of social change unleashed by ideological innovation and diffusion are to be used to promote mobilization and integration, leaders must make sensible calculations as to the likely consequences of their actions; and such calculations require thought about strategies and tactics. The point is so obvious that it may well be overlooked; yet successful ideological innovation and diffusion depend upon its being understood. In contrast to Uganda, Tanzania's efforts to forge development have the great merit that the institutional impact of induced changes in values are carefully assessed in advance. Each measure adopted, whether relating to farming, cooperatives, or industry, is viewed as part of a coherent scheme to redefine values and establish institutions that will promote the new values.

In Uganda at the time of the Move to the Left, contradictions between the goal of socialism and the agents of socialization, and the strains in and between sources of innovation and potential channels of diffusion, heightened feelings of cynicism and skepticism. In most low income countries, there is a predisposition toward social distrust. This tendency is not unique to any one culture but, rather, can be explained as a function of poverty. Particularly in areas of acute economic deprivation, politicians are generally regarded as predators seeking to maximize their own selfish interests; civic projects are viewed with suspicion; and associational sentiment going beyond primordial ties is exceptional.

In Uganda, the predisposition to social distrust was compounded by rhetoric about a "socialist revolutionary society" that was not accompanied by adequate concrete structural change; but Obote's Move to the Left was not ideology-making for its own sake. Obote was a practical politician working within severe economic and political constraints, and he quickly learned that ideology is ultimately linked with economic developments. Ideological modernization necessarily involves investment of scarce resources. Whether ideological initiatives are successful or not frequently hinges on prospects for economic growth: while successful economic policies may invest ideology with an aura of legitimacy, unsuccessful economic policies may well depreciate the value of the ideology. With the introduction of an ideology of modernization, the stakes are higher than in pragmatic, day-to-day politics. The regime encourages its citizenry to think in terms of ultimate goals; ideology becomes the agent responsible for success but, conversely, must bear the brunt of any failure. In this sense, ideological modernization must be regarded as a gamble.

From its inception, the Move to the Left added to Uganda's economic woes. Economists criticized Obote's program for its inconsistencies, poor planning, and hasty implementation. Though in 1967 Ugandans occupied only 210 of the top 540 positions (38 percent) in the private sector, the Move to the Left did not effectively challenge the role of expatriates. The captains of industry continued to be noncitizens. To the degree that localization was achieved in the public services, the effect was merely to widen the gulf between the new elites and the mass of unemployed Africans. The new government payments scale covering professional categories of employment established a lowest level of payment that was five times the average earnings of all Africans; yet the impact of this new scale on income distribution, and the implications for class formation, were largely ignored.[19]

Programs introduced in the second phase tended to have a regressive impact for low income groups. Higher income groups were not taxed heavily, and price movements since mid-1968 also altered the distribution of real income in Kampala in these groups' favor. Relative to income changes, the 22 1/2 percent rise in the

19. [Charles Elliott], *Employment and Income Distribution in Uganda* (Norwich: University of East Anglia Development Studies Discussion Paper, n.d.), pp. 21, 23, 24.

price of food and the increases in costs of household goods and clothing were greater for low income groups than for high. Practices inherited from the colonial era for government officials and civil servants—subsidized or free housing and preferential medical treatment—protected many of the wealthy from the uphill spiral in prices, while those on the bottom rungs of the income ladder continued to feel the pinch.[20] In short, economic policies under the Move to the Left did little to limit the privileges of Uganda's higher income earners. Virtually no attempt was made to regulate salaries in the private sector, and multiple sources of income were not subject to restriction.

Despite the Banking Act of 1969, little change was introduced in loan policies. Short term loans and advances to the commercial sector continued to predominate; loans and advances to the agricultural and industrial sectors actually declined, while the proportion going to the commercial sector increased rapidly. Few personnel changes were made; expatriates, Asians, and Ugandans trained in the colonial tradition retained their former positions in the commercial banks. And none of the banks employed a research staff to investigate how this sector could best contribute to socialism.[21]

Planning and coordination were sadly deficient. In a situation by no means unique to Uganda, ministries and government agencies competed with one another. During the preparation of a third five-year plan, the working parties drawn from private, public, and academic sources, failed to coordinate their efforts. The quality of personnel, expatriate and local, was spotty. Ministries and parastatal bodies were at odds with the Ministry of Planning, which, in turn, was subservient to the Ministry of Finance. A number of loans to Uganda, from private agencies and from governments and intergovernmental organizations, remained unused because of insufficient project planning.[22]

Despite the creation of two official committees to work out de-

20. Michael Tribe, "Uganda 1971: An Economic Background," *Mawazo*, III, No. 1 (June 1971), 19–21.
21. Irving Gershenberg, "Banking in Uganda since Independence," *Economic Development and Cultural Change*, XX, No. 3 (April 1972), 515, 516, 522.
22. *Idem*, "Slouching towards Socialism: Obote's Uganda," *African Studies Review*, XV, No. 1 (April 1972), 86–94.

tails for implementing the Nakivubo Pronouncements, the first few agreements were the result of private negotiations between foreign-owned companies and the president. Large companies were able to breach both the 60 percent-40 percent stipulation and the requirement that compensation be paid out of future profits. Because Uganda lacked qualified personnel and the companies threatened to pull out altogether, external financial interests were able to negotiate lucrative management contracts with the government. When Obote was overthrown, the only firms that had signed partial nationalization agreements were Shell/B.P., Agip, Total, Brooke Bond Tea, Uganda American Insurance, and National and Grindlay's Bank. The oil companies, particularly Shell/B.P. and Agip, settled for accords that forced the government to reduce the percentage of shares to be taken over. Grindlay's agreement gave the government 60 percent ownership of the bank but permitted establishment of a separate international and merchant banking concern in which the government would have only a 40 percent interest. In the case of Shell/B.P., the government compromised on its payment-out-of-profit principle, agreeing to make a 10 percent down payment and to treat the rest as a loan to be repaid at 7.5 percent interest within five years; provisions for management and consultancy services included appointment of four directors each by the company and the government.[23]

To all intents and purposes, the measures designed to effect partial nationalization had little impact on the practices of foreign-controlled business interests. According to the figures compiled by the UN Department of Economic and Social Affairs, direct foreign investment in Uganda by "Development Assistance Countries" (donors of aid) amounted to $48,000,000 at the end of 1967. The main investing countries were the U.K. (48.1 percent), Canada

23. Little information is available on foreign-controlled businesses' negotiations on Obote's partial nationalization scheme; see "Paying the Compensation Bill," *Financial Times* (London), December 18, 1970; "Take-Overs: Uganda Faces Bill," *Standard* (Dar es Salaam), January 6, 1971; Gershenberg, "Slouching towards Socialism," pp. 90, 91; and Selwyn D. Ryan, "Economic Nationalism in Uganda and Ghana" (mimeo, paper delivered to the annual meeting of the Canadian Association of African Studies, Quebec City, February 1970), p. 21. (An abbreviated version of Ryan's paper is available as "Economic Nationalism and Socialism in Uganda," *Journal of Commonwealth Political Studies*, XI, No. 2 [July 1973], 140–58.)

(31.3 percent), and the U.S. (4.2 percent).[24] The government monetary survey for 1969–1970 indicates that net foreign assets in Uganda actually increased during the Move to the Left, rising from Shs. 256,200,000 to Shs. 394,300,000 between September 1969 and December 1969 and to Shs. 557,900,000 by June 1970. In 1969, the most recent year for which data are available, the principal destinations of Ugandan exports were the U.S.A., the U.K., and Japan. While domestic exports to the People's Republic of China declined, from Shs. 34,852,000 in 1968 to Shs. 8,889,000 in 1969, domestic exports to Japan increased, from Shs. 156,525,000 to Shs. 222,588,000. The principal countries from which goods were imported in 1969 were the U.K., Japan, and West Germany. The dollar and sterling areas clearly dominated Uganda's import, domestic export, and re-export trade.[25]

Western technical assistance also perpetuated foreign influence. Experts from the Western countries occupied key positions in such vital government offices as the Ministry of Planning. According to 1969 figures, 242 foreign assistance experts and 197 volunteers were working in Uganda. The greatest number of experts were provided by the United Nations Development Program (65, almost all of them Westerners), the U.S. (54), and Canada (46). Britain supplied almost half (84) of the volunteers. There were no Eastern volunteers, and of the experts only eight were from the People's Republic of China and three from the U.S.S.R.[26] Steps were not taken under the Move to the Left to lessen this heavy reliance on Western technical personnel.

Even after the incorporation of banks, Africans had difficulty

24. By comparison, the Development Assistance countries' investment totaled $60,400,000 in Tanzania at the end of 1967, with the U.K. holding 46.7 percent, Italy 18.2 percent, and Denmark 12.9 percent; and $172,100,000 in Kenya, with the U.K. holding 78.8 percent and the U.S. 8.7 percent (United Nations, Department of Economic and Social Affairs, *Multinational Corporations in World Development,* ST/ECA/190 [New York: United Nations, 1973], p. 182).

25. *1970 Statistical Abstract,* pp. 59 and 21–29; annual trade reports; and Bank of Uganda data.

26. Unpublished paper presented to the World Bank (Pearson Commission) by the Ministry of Planning and Economic Development (Entebbe, 1969), cited in Yashpal Tandon, ed., *Technical Assistance Administration in East Africa* (Stockholm: The Dag Hammarskjold Foundation, 1973), pp. 127–28.

obtaining credit for commercial ventures. Despite the government's official policy of promoting Africans in business, the banks persisted in their conservative and colonial orientation. In addition to the general unavailability of credit, the difficulty of advancing Africans in commercial ventures can be attributed in part to their lack of education and business experience. Moreover, as the Move to the Left opened new opportunities to Ugandan Africans, many took advantage of the situation through embezzlement and fraud. The NTC was singularly ineffective in promoting Africanization; not only did the organization suffer from insufficient funding, but also many M.P.'s and other influential Africans used it for personal gain. Ultimately, in November 1970, the president appointed a commission of inquiry to investigate corruption within the NTC. Nor did the Trade Licensing Act ever fulfill the regime's intentions; by restricting certain geographical areas and sectors of business to Ugandan Africans, it had the immediate effect of touching off a rapid increase in prices and a shortage of goods. Failures in economic planning notwithstanding, the fundamental problem of the localization program was the contradiction between propaganda about socialist revolutionary programs and policies that encouraged private enterprise.

Faulty government policies and the emergence of a self-seeking African national bourgeoisie are not the whole story; the Asian community also contributed to sabotaging the Move to the Left. While it is difficult to go beyond this observation and say just how important Asian opposition was—for noncitizens cannot be lumped together in any meaningful way, and indeed some Asians supported the nationalist cause—the actions of several members of this community certainly impeded economic progress.

The introduction of exchange control in May 1970 had only minimal impact on the export of capital, profits, and assets. Currency could be converted on the black market at 10 or 11 Uganda shillings to the dollar (compared with an official rate of 7.14 shillings to the dollar). Increasingly uncertain about their future in Uganda, Asian businessmen allowed stocks of badly needed supplies to run down, deposited their funds abroad, engaged in double invoicing and inflation of administrative costs, and tempted corrupt public officials with bribes. There were repeated reports of collaboration among Asians to prevent establishment of African business concerns. Many Asians refused to accept African partners; others paid Africans to act as "front men" for businesses that remained under the control of their original owners. Rather than buying goods from the NTC, which was supposed to have a monopoly on the wholesale distribution of many items, Asians continued to make purchases from members of their community residing in urban areas. Since Asian property owners controlled vast amounts of real estate in the towns, they were able to impede aspiring African entrepreneurs' advancement by charging exorbitant rents. Retaining advantages in transport and storage facilities, Asians exercised considerable leverage by hoarding goods, flooding the market with cheap supplies, and smuggling commodities from Zaire and other neighboring countries. The complaint frequently heard was that Asians were purchasing large quantities of food crops from African farmers when prices were low, stimulating demand by restricting supply, and reselling their stocks at inflated prices.[27] Obote must have been aware that his economic policies would cause short-run dislocations. Probably he calculated that the psychic gains from nationalization and localization would offset the inefficiency that resulted. But misguided economic policies do not produce positive political returns. The president's measures, designed to elicit feelings of pride, loyalty, identity, and unity, merely accentuated the prevailing mood of cynicism and skepticism.

The regime advanced abstract ideological notions, but vital intermediary institutions for mediating change were not available. After independence, power was distributed widely; a variety of groups enjoyed constitutional legitimacy in the exercise of power. The crisis of 1966, however, demonstrated that the pull of centrifugal forces was too great for the cause of national development. In the remaining years of the first phase and throughout the second, therefore, Obote relentlessly pursued a strategy of centralization. The situation confronting him was the classic problem bedeviling leaders in many parts of the Third World: If the major tasks are power generation and power management, how is power to be built? How is support to be elicited? When and where should power be distributed? Finding that building central power on a base of

27. On the tactics of Asian businessmen, I am indebted to Ryan, "Economic Nationalism in Uganda and Ghana."

local power was not feasible in Uganda, Obote opted for a strategy of local penetration from a base of central power. The 1967 constitution provided for one officer who would combine the earlier roles of president and prime minister and serve as head of state and government and commander in chief of the armed forces; kingdoms were abolished, the prerogatives of local administration increasingly limited, and the president placed in effective control of the civil service.

With these changes made, Obote also seemed to many observers to turn away from the advice of ministers and to rely increasingly on the General Service Unit (Uganda's intelligence apparatus) and its chief officer, Akena Adoko. The national labor organization remained inactive, and the trade union movement had no political consequence. The report of the Binaisa Commission, established following the 1966 suspension of union activities to make recommendations for reorganizing the labor movement, pointed toward even greater government control over labor. When the national government moved toward centralization, the national executive of the UPC did the same thing. By adopting the revised party constitution of 1968, the UPC leaders seriously undermined the importance of the districts as political units; the party president—Milton Obote—was vested with authority to appoint other national party officers (who had been elected in the past).

Speaking at the inauguration of Makerere University, Kampala, in 1970, Obote posed the issue of devising an appropriate power structure, and his response, in no uncertain terms.

There was a time, immediately after Independence, when many saw Uganda as having three bases of power, to speak nothing of other localised stations of power. There was Entebbe, the seat of Government, and there was Makerere, the centre for higher learning, and thirdly, there was Kampala, the capital, whose role was that of a centre where men of wealth discussed the size of their investments and bank accounts, as well as various ways of exhibiting that wealth. The Government at Entebbe was not considered to have any responsibility at Makerere, and Makerere was considered to be an "island" of higher learning, with no accountability to the "mainland" Uganda. Kampala, on the other hand, stood for the control of the means of production and distribution in the hands of a handful. There was therefore no one indisputable and recognised centre of authority from which the voice and will of the people could be heard and felt and in which they repos-

ited their aspirations, identity and vitality. In eight years of Independence, the situation has dramatically changed. The whole of Uganda
now belongs to the people of Uganda and all the institutions established
by the people must equally belong to and be part of them.[28]

As Obote sought to erect "one indisputable and recognised
centre of authority," the problem became the overcentralization of
what little power did exist. His regime failed to create a judicious
balance between central, elite control and power distributed
throughout the political system.

Paradoxically, when a leader divests himself of some power, he
may not only increase the total power of the system but also, in
the long run, augment his personal power. In Uganda, Obote's
reluctance to delegate power was ultimately responsible for a decline in legitimacy at all levels, a continuing lack of organizational
strength, and the absence of political support that could be
mobilized.

Certainly the need to establish control from the top was clear.
But did this justify Obote's measures to hoard power as his private
reserve? When power is distributed throughout the system, it is
much more difficult to capture. That the military's acquisition of
Obote's reserve should have met with so little challenge is, therefore, in these terms, not surprising; had others been entitled to hold
stock in Obote's private utility, expropriation might have met with
greater resistance.

Power Relations: Obote and the Students

Substance can be given to the ideas advanced in the preceeding
discussion of imbalances in the power structure through examination of a particular case: power relations between the president
and university students.

On the morning of July 22, 1970, 1,000 angry students began a
march from Freedom Square in front of the main building at
Makerere University in Kampala. Brandishing signs protesting
against Britain's announced intention of selling arms to South
Africa, tense and frustrated students tried to force open the main
gate and march to the British High Commission in downtown
Kampala. The police Special Forces Unit provoked the students'

28. "Uganda's Dedication to Africa," *Uganda Argus,* October 9, 1970.

anger by blocking the gate. When the students began to throw rocks, the police dispersed them with tear gas. Ultimately the students had to settle for a letter from the president of the Makerere Students' Guild to the British high commissioner:

At last Britain has shown Black Africa her real colours. Great Britain is as racist as Vorster's regime, and this is how Black Africa should look at her.
The British action signals nothing but a call to arms, an armed strategy by Black Africa. It is no longer a hidden secret that Britain was fully behind Smith's decision to seize power in Rhodesia, and that, by selling arms to South Africa now, Britain is virtually giving both Smith and Vorster power to defend their racialist regimes and crush all liberation movements in Southern Africa. What an accomplice, Mr. High Commissioner![29]

The events of July 22, 1970, represented more than just another incident in the continuing tension between the University and the government; important lessons can be learned from them. In particular, the way in which Obote dealt with the students' demands provides valuable insight into the regime's style of managing power relationships with various groups.

Before exploring the issues at stake, the relationship between the students and their government and such questions as the obligations students should have to their society and the role they play as agents of social change, an essential caveat must be entered. It cannot be assumed that students in any country form a homogeneous group; on the contrary, student politics are marked by intragroup strife. At no time, therefore, can generalizations be assumed to hold for all students.

In 1970, the ire of Ugandan student activists was directed against Britain's statement of intent to lift the arms embargo against South Africa. Some Makerere students adopted the determinist position that an imperialist is an imperialist and there is no reason to expect him to behave otherwise; most, however, expressed disappointment, if not surprise, at the Heath government's statements. A variety of explanations were offered for Britain's behavior: (1) The kith and kin argument holds that white Britons will never turn their backs on white southern Africans and in fact feel mutual solidarity against blacks. (2) The kith and kin argument is rein-

<hr>

29. "Britain Shows Her True Colours," *Uganda Argus,* July 23, 1970.

forced by the upsurge of domestic racism in Britain—Enoch Powell doubled his majority in the 1968 election. (*3*) The quid pro quo hypothesis, again evidencing white racism, sees Britain selling arms to South Africa in return for South Africa's good offices as diplomatic mediator and support against Southern Rhodesia. (*4*) The Tory government, wary of the Soviet presence in the Indian Ocean, is selling arms to South Africa in exchange for the rights and privileges of the Simonstown naval base. (In this explanation, Heath's government, displaying an antiquated political philosophy, is motivated by a belief similar to South Africa's— a communist is around every corner.) (*5*) Britain, facing recurrent balance of payments problems, places economic considerations first, rationalizing that if it does not sell arms to South Africa other powers certainly will. (*6*) Since Heath intends to turn toward the EEC, and the price of his country's membership is preferential trade advantages for Commonwealth countries, the Commonwealth reaction to the arms sales is of little concern. (*7*) Some members of the British cabinet believe that the government must demonstrate that it will not be pushed around by the black Commonwealth.

African students feared that the British arms being sold to South Africa would be used against Africa north of the Zambesi. They believed that Britain had little moral concern about South Africa's apartheid policies and never believed in the liberation of oppressed peoples. The effect of arms sales would be to strengthen South Africa, morally as much as materially, weaken UN efforts in southern Africa, and aid South Africa in its attempt to impose apartheid on Namibia. Obote pointed out the fallacy in the argument that Britain and South Africa had an identity of interests in southern Africa, rejecting the view that Britain had to sell arms to South Africa because of the Soviet presence in the Indian Ocean; a challenge to the Soviet presence would require more power than Britain and South Africa had together.[30]

Makerere students called on black Africa to take diplomatic action against Britain, suggesting that African states sever diplomatic relations, disband the Commonwealth, make every effort to expel Britain from the UN, call back African athletic teams, and

30. "If Britain Resumes Arms Sales to S.A. . . . ," *Uganda Argus,* July 25, 1970.

impose economic sanctions against Britain. And they demanded the right to stage a demonstration at the British High Commission to support their proposals.

The initial issue of Britain lifting the arms embargo against South Africa was quickly superseded by the question of the propriety of the Ugandan government's measures to subdue the Makerere students. As one incredulous Makerere student remarked, "Why are they using tear gas against us instead of against South Africa?"[31]

But why did the government not permit the students to march? One factor was that Obote had not forgotten the previous Makerere demonstration at the British High Commission, in March 1968. On that occasion, when the primary issue was Ian Smith's hanging of three black Rhodesians, the action of three British Teachers for East Africa (TEA's) who attended a meeting of the Makerere Students' Guild and refused to bow their heads in a moment's silence for the deceased fanned the flames of discontent. After throwing stones at the British High Commission, presenting a petition to the high commissioner, and hanging Ian Smith in effigy, Makerere students went on to break store windows, shatter automobile windshields, and beat a few Europeans. The Ugandan government was undoubtedly concerned in 1970 that violence of a similar kind could harm the country's image abroad. Student violence, particularly when it becomes antiwhite, antagonizes influential expatriates and damages tourism. More importantly, if Makerere students were allowed to precipitate a demonstration that turned against whites, a touch of hypocrisy would attend Uganda's accusations of British racism. Apprehension over this scenario was

31. There was irony in the students' choice of costume when they marched to the main gate to protest. Nothing could more symbolize the students' love-hate relationship with English culture than their decision to wear their academic gowns (an Oxbridge tradition) to identify themselves in their intended demonstration at the British High Commission. Although the gowns were worn for identification purposes and as a sign of cherished status, there seemed to be a deeper psychological dimension as well. By exhibiting their gowns, the students—albeit unintentionally—were protesting symbolically against their own heritage.

So far as sustained political commitment at Makerere is concerned, it is instructive to note how quickly deradicalization set in. Very few students appeared for a meeting at the main hall shortly after the teargassing. Moreover, in the wake of these incidents, the president of the Students' Guild was jailed for advocating violence against British citizens resident in Uganda; when he was brought to trial, little was heard from Makerere students.

certainly a major factor in the government's decision not to permit the demonstration. To the president's credit, he invited student leaders to tea to discuss the affair; in his conversation with them, he asked whether it would be possible to protest Britain's anti-African racial policy if anti-European racism were practiced in Uganda.

Another factor influencing the government was the attitude of high ranking officials, who, critical of what they regarded as Makerere's arrogant elite, maintained that it was their role to formulate policy, and students should not try to dictate to them. In the view of these officials, it was not the function of associational groups—in particular, university students—to participate in the formulation of government policies; rather, they were expected to serve the state by putting the government's policies into effect. The role of a university in a developing country, government officials argued, is different from its role in a wealthy Western society that can afford luxuries Uganda must forego; in Uganda the university must play a key role in sustaining modernization and forging integration. Spokesmen for the regime argued that in the introduction of a new ideology students and government must be united. Uganda could not afford to waste scarce human resources by condoning multiple independent sources of power and opposition politics. The decision not to allow the students to demonstrate at the British High Commission—a judgment that came in the wake of the president's Visitation Committee's report recommending that Makerere be placed under national control—reflected these assumptions and represented a refusal to grant any measure of initiative or power to university students.

Obote made it painfully clear that protest outside the University's gates could take place only with the government's countenance. His action was particularly difficult for the students to accept because they were attempting to express solidarity with his foreign policy. Unlike students elsewhere, who usually protest as an anti-government group, Makerere students were seeking permission to demonstrate as a progovernment group.

Obote did not appreciate the students' sense of frustration, which was bound to increase. Not only did the students not have the power to influence the government, but Uganda lacked the power to change Britain's policies. However reprehensible British arms sales to South Africa may have been, the policy options open to Africa were unlikely to have much bearing on Britain's decisions. By comparison, American decision-makers had the power but not the will to change the circumstances of aggression in Indochina and poverty and racism in the U.S. against which students protested. Uganda's decision-makers had the will but not the power to alter the situation to which its students objected. In both cases, the result was government alienation of students. But with a position in international politics very different, in terms of power, from that of the U.S., and facing the arduous tasks of nation-building, could the Ugandan government afford to alienate student activists as the American government did? Would Obote in fact have come to realize that successful experiments in ideological modernization require tolerance and confidence and that forging an alliance between students and government is a step toward building tolerance and confidence, whereby the students serve as active agents of social change?

As this case study of government-student relations has illustrated, fundamental power imbalances and tactical errors complicated the Move to the Left. Uganda's social structure, the questions that were raised but not answered by the government initiatives of 1969 and 1970, and the promotion of measures that antagonized key groups all worked against socialist construction. Not only did Uganda lack the infrastructure for the successful introduction of an ideology of modernization, but also the message was disseminated in the wrong way. Despite the attempt to launch programs of economic nationalism, Obote's ability to bargain politically was impaired by the commanding role that external interests continued to play in the local economy. The president's experience is representative of the exigencies to be met with in ruling new states and the difficulties frequently encountered in making the transition to a new political system. In Uganda, these exigencies and difficulties provided the climate for military intervention in politics.

CHAPTER 7

Military Intervention

On January 25, 1971, Major-General Idi Amin Dada deposed President Obote. While the president was en route from the Singapore Commonwealth Conference to Kampala, troops loyal to Amin defeated the paramilitary General Service Unit and cut off the battalion moving into the capital from Jinja. Speaking on Radio Uganda, General Amin announced: "Matters now prevailing in Uganda force me to take a special task. Mine will be a purely care-taker administration."

Many of the causes of military intervention in Uganda and the events that preceded this, the twenty-seventh coup in nineteen African countries, have been paralleled elsewhere, and doubtless will be again, with the same conclusion. Given the problems of modernization, it is hardly surprising that military intervention in politics is endemic to the Third World.[1]

The scholarly literature on the role of the military in low income areas suffers from both the general weaknesses of modernization theory and an excessive concern with typologies. Rather than offering working hypotheses about the military as rulers, scholars concerned with Africa have tended to regard armed intervention in politics as the terminal point for analysis. Broadly speaking, the literature emphasizes the causes of coups and underplays the consequences. It also tends to be of the status quo ideology type.

1. By emphasizing similarities in military intervention in developing countries, I do not mean to suggest that important differences should be overlooked. To take one example, cross-national comparisons indicate marked differences in the social composition of the military of different states. In most cases, in fact, the army represents a collection of diverse interest groups rather than a homogeneous social unit.

No distinction will be made here among branches of the military or between officers and enlisted men. These distinctions, though vital, are beyond the scope of this book and await further analysis.

Academicians, many of whom strive for value-free theory, have been reluctant to use their tools to pose alternatives for ruling elites.[2]

A variety of propositions accounting for military take-overs have been advanced, but in many cases the conditions that, it is argued, lead to intervention are equally characteristic of situations where intervention has not occurred. Power deflation, corruption, and economic stagnation, for example, have been suggested as determining factors in attempted coups; but these determinants fail to distinguish between countries where coups have taken place and those where they have not. The real test for scholars investigating the role of the military is explaining cases of nonintervention. Typically, however, the "theoretical" studies of military intervention are actually post hoc explanations of accomplished facts. The social scientist's task, therefore, is to assess at what threshold and under what conditions the factors responsible for general social discontent enable the military to displace the civilian politicians. And the first step is to sharpen the theories and concepts by examining the data relating to particular cases.

In looking at the case of Uganda, two fundamental questions must be answered: What were the immediate circumstances and events leading to the coup? And what were the coup's deeper sociopolitical causes? Or, in effect, why did the coup happen on January 25, 1971? And why was there a coup at all? The answers to these questions are relevant to the course of military rule in Uganda, particularly in terms of the options open to the Amin regime and the nature of postcoup cleavages.

Precipitating Factors

In December 1969, a would-be assassin's bullet struck Obote in the lips, tongue, and teeth. This incident, occurring only a few weeks after the sudden death of the kabaka, resulted in an army-imposed reign of terror in Kampala. Army units were reported to be hunting down other army units. Although six men were sentenced to life

2. Robert E. Dowse, "The Military and Political Development," in Colin Leys, ed., *Politics and Change: Studies in the Theory and Practice of Development* (London: Cambridge University Press, 1969), especially pp. 213–32, argues that there has been too much generalization about military intervention in politics; the literature is weak because the events that theorists attempt to lump together are above all diverse.

imprisonment for their part in what was termed a Ganda plot, a number of observers were dissatisfied with the government's case against them.

Attempting to rule without the support of Uganda's largest and most powerful tribe, Obote increasingly worried about the military. He was aware that General Amin had been making conciliatory speeches to the Baganda, going so far as to praise the kabaka. Amin, a devout Moslem, also switched membership from the government-supported National Association for the Advancement of Moslems to the Uganda Muslim Community, Sheikh Islam's Buganda-based organization. Moreover, Amin was implicated in the January 25, 1970, shooting of Brigadier Pierino Okoya, a senior officer in the Uganda army who supported Obote. Despite the inconclusive report of the government inquest, released after the coup, many suspected that Amin was responsible for the murder of the man whom Obote may have wanted to appoint as a replacement for the head of the armed forces. In September 1970, Obote sent Amin to Cairo to attend Nasser's funeral and suggested a pilgrimage to Mecca to follow. Using Nasser's death as an excuse, the president canceled Uganda's Independence Day celebrations (which usually feature a display of military might). Then, while Amin was out of the country, Obote reshuffled the military hierarchy, appointing separate commanders of the army and the air force. On his return from Mecca, Amin seems to have been promptly placed under house arrest; certainly most observers were surprised by his appearance at the inauguration of Makerere University in October.

In his speech at the inauguration, Obote lashed out at students opposing government policies. Having been criticized for his refusal to permit the students to march to the British High Commission to demonstrate against arms sales to South Africa, the president delivered what amounted to a "get tough" speech. Reminding his audience that multiple centers of power had been a feature of Uganda's past, he said that henceforth all power would belong to the people and would be vested in the government.[3] A more tactful statesman might have reminded the country's intellectuals of their vital role in nation-building.

3. For Obote's statement, see above, pp. 161–62.

During the latter half of 1970, Obote appeared to be reluctant to leave Uganda. In October he avoided attending the ceremonies launching China's construction of the Tanzam railway, citing a "national disaster" in Uganda as the reason for his absence—a disaster that turned out to be the death of four students in an automobile accident. In mid-December, however, he was confident enough to spend a few days in Kenya. And the following month he joined Nyerere and Kaunda at the Singapore Commonwealth Conference, threatening there to take Uganda out of the Commonwealth over British arms sales to South Africa.

Obote's usual political acumen finally failed him. Writing several months before the coup, Ali Mazrui summed up Obote's situation in a comment that could serve as Obote's political epitaph:

Faced with a very difficult country, coming from a tribe which had not been specially privileged during the colonial period, battling against a Ganda supremacy which could not be overthrown overnight, bereft of martyrdom in his personal biography, lacking a warm public personality, Milton Obote had to rely on his ability to understand the intricacies of tactical and strategic political calculations.[4]

In 1970, after more than eight years in the forefront of postcolonial African politics, Milton Obote's ability to cope with the dynamics of Ugandan politics finally proved unreliable.

The first statement on the coup broadcast by Radio Uganda gave eighteen reasons for the army's take-over of power, ranging from unwarranted detention and lack of freedom of expression to widespread kondoism (armed robbery) and hypocritical talk about socialism.[5] In the immediate postcoup period, Major-General Idi Amin Dada[6] moved quickly to stabilize the situation and immobilize potential opposition;[7] the airport was closed, a dusk-to-dawn

4. Ali A. Mazrui, "Leadership in Africa: Obote of Uganda," *International Journal*, XXV, No. 3 (Summer 1970), 542.

5. The reasons were published in the "The Army Takes Over—A Message from the Soldiers," *Uganda Argus*, January 26, 1971, and in the *Birth of the Second Republic* (Entebbe: Government Printer, 1971).

6. After the Amin take-over, much play was made by the media of the word Dada, a term used by the northern Madi tribe for grandfather. Doubt surrounds Amin's origins; the majority of his tribe, the Kakwa (a small, northern West Nilotic group), are in fact Sudanese. The term Dada is therefore used to legitimize his Ugandanness.

7. For some relevant comments on the tactics and strategy to be followed in a postcoup situation, see Edward Luttwak, *Coup d'Etat: A Practical*

curfew imposed, and all political activity suspended. Ugandans, however, were assured of an early return to civilian rule, free elections, and an amnesty for political prisoners and exiles.[8]

General Amin followed a strategy of conciliation. The clock would not be turned back to the days of monarchy, he insisted, but the kabaka's body would be returned to Uganda for a proper burial. Pictures of both the kabaka and Obote would be displayed in museums and other public places, for they were part of Uganda's history. And on January 28, amongst cheering Baganda crowds, Amin released fifty-five political detainees.

On February 2, after Amin had dissolved parliament and assumed all executive powers, the names of those who were to comprise the government of Uganda's Second Republic were announced. The appointments were notable in that equitable geographic and ethnic representation evidently served as criteria for selection. A large number of high-level civil servants were given ministerial positions. All but one of the ministers were civilians. But those who had served as ministers under Obote and those placed under detention by the former president were excluded from office.[9]

What happened in the immediate postcoup period can be confirmed; much more controversy surrounds the question of how the coup actually started. There are three versions of events among which to choose: the spontaneity theory, the double coup theory, and the tripartite theory.

In his first press conference after the coup, General Amin

Handbook (Harmondsworth: Penguin Books, 1968), pp. 168–82. According to Luttwak, after targets have been seized, loyal forces and the rest of the bureaucracy isolated, and elements of opposition in the armed forces neutralized, the objective is to freeze the situation. Thus, after the active phase, control must be consolidated among the coup leaders' own forces, within the state bureaucracy, and over the public at large. Always holding the means of coercion as its trump card, a new regime should rely increasingly on political maneuver and allow physical sanctions to decline in importance.

8. The military rarely fails to insist that free elections and civilian rule are forthcoming. Kenneth W. Grundy, *Conflicting Images of the Military in Africa* (Nairobi: East African Publishing House, 1968), pp. 14, 15, 36, and Ruth First, *The Barrel of a Gun: Political Power in Africa and the Coup D'Etat* (London: Penguin Press, 1970), p. 439, present examples of military apologia and promises after seizure of power.

9. Abu Mayanja, the first minister of education under the Second Republic, was the sole exception.

accused Obote and presidential aide Akena Adoko of hatching the "Singapore plot," the alleged purpose of which was to eliminate elements opposed to the Obote regime. The general maintained that when he returned from a hunting trip to Karuma Falls, a tank and a personnel carrier were waiting outside his residence in Kampala. A wounded soldier told him that pro-Obote elements had been instructing soldiers of the Lango and Acholi tribes to arm themselves and arrest members of army units drawn from other tribes. Asked by the soldiers to take control of the government, Amin "could not let them down."[10] He explained: "The soldiers and I did not plan a coup. It happened spontaneously. The Acholi and Lango officers were half-way to victory when the ordinary soldier, seeing the dangers, took the initiative."[11]

Proponents of the double coup theory accept some parts of Amin's story but argue that planning is necessary for a successful coup. According to this theory, Amin got wind of a plan prepared by Akena Adoko before Obote's departure for Singapore, which provided for the arrest and murder of Amin and other leaders during Obote's absence. The Amin-led coup thus headed off the Obote coup.

An alternative version of the double coup theory, advanced by some of Obote's supporters, argues that the former president may have been plotting, but only in response to prior action by Amin. Just before Obote boarded the jet that was to take him home from Singapore, he was handed a statement prepared by C. L. Ntende, permanent secretary of the Ministry of Internal Affairs; this statement, it is suggested, told of a plot to kill the president and take over the government.[12]

The tripartite coup theory goes one step further. The chief villain in this dramatic version was Akena Adoko—a clever English-trained lawyer, Obote's kinsman, and chief of the General Service Unit. Under his plan, the president would return from Singapore only after Amin had been eliminated. Then, when Obote stepped off the plane, he and the ministers waiting at the airport would be

10. "General Amin Tells of Singapore Plot," *Uganda Argus*, January 27, 1971.
11. "The Ugandan Coup: Amin Tells How It Happened," *Daily Nation* (Nairobi), February 15, 1971.
12. "Amin's Treachery Shown by Report," *Standard*, February 16, 1971.

174 IDEOLOGY AND POLITICS IN UGANDA

shot down,[13] whereupon Adoko, using his specially trained troops and loyal henchmen (especially Colonel David Oyike Ojok), would install himself as president.

Any attempt to assess these theories must begin with a candid acknowledgement of the difficulties inherent in the exercise. With many questions still open to debate, historians will undoubtedly probe them for years to come.

It is safe to say that the military acted for personal, punitive, and recreational reasons.[14] The motivation was personal in that Amin believed there was a plot to kill him and moved to protect his own life. Obote had clearly been maneuvering against Amin since the army reshuffle of September 1970. Amin also wanted to punish Obote for his supposed transgressions (related in the army's eighteen complaints).[15] Finally, feeling underemployed and neglected, the army acted for recreational reasons. Since its action against the Baganda in 1966, the army had been relegated to disagreeable routine chores: patrolling Uganda's borders, keeping refugees in check, putting a damper on cattle raids between the seminomadic Karamajong and Kenya's cattle rustling Turkana, and frustrating secessionist movements among the Bakonjo and Baamba tribes.[16] Despite Obote's apparent willingness to appease the military by granting high votes of pay and allowances, several officers feared that he intended to terminate the special privileges that had grown out of the prolonged state of emergency.[17] One

13. In an interview with Colin Legum, Obote indicated that while he was in Singapore the police had uncovered a detailed plan for his murder on his return to Kampala; all ministers waiting to receive him were to be shot as well ("Uganda Coup 'Could Lead to New Congo or Biafra,'" *Observer* [London], January 31, 1971). This testimony, of course, might relate to an Amin rather than an Adoko plot.
14. See William Gutteridge, "Why Does an African Army Take Power?" *Africa Report*, XV, No. 7 (October 1970), 18–21; also Fred Greene, "Toward Understanding Military Coups," *Africa Report*, XI, No. 6 (February 1966), 10, 11, 14.
15. The Amin government offered a reward of Shs. 1,000,000 for the return of Obote; "Obote Wanted: Alive," *Uganda Argus*, May 14, 1971.
16. "The Uganda Army: Nexus of Power," *Africa Report*, XI, No. 9 (December 1966), 37–39.
17. While certain measures were perceived as potentially reducing the perquisites to which the military had become accustomed, there was a countervailing tendency; some officers gained sinecures as a result of the

interpretation of Obote's election proposals, for example, was that they were a move toward restoration of civilian supremacy over military prerogative. And since Obote clearly derived inspiration from Nyerere, elements in the army feared that Tanzania might serve as a model for bringing the military into check in Uganda.

Yet there are inconsistencies in these theories. Shortly after the coup Amin promised to give a full account of Obote's plot and the background to January 25. Why did he go back on this promise and refuse to divulge any further information? Was the affair as spontaneous as the general suggested? Why did Amin's neighbors say they did not see either a tank or a personnel carrier at his residence on January 24–25? How would the general answer the residents of Gulu, a northern town, who insist that he was at the Gulu airbase (which was staffed by Czech and Russian advisors and would therefore have to be neutralized in any coup) on the day he was supposedly hunting?

So far as Obote's plotting is concerned, given his insecure position and his attempts to eclipse Amin, it would not be surprising if he had decided to go one step further and eliminate his rival. But why, being well informed on the volatile and uncertain nature of African politics, would he choose to be out of the country when Amin was to be assassinated? It may be advantageous to be physically distant from an unsavory maneuver, but absence is a flimsy excuse for presidential innocence. Obote's style may provide a more compelling explanation. When the crisis of 1966 erupted, Obote calmly concluded his tour of the north before returning to Kampala to face the serious allegations being leveled against him in the National Assembly; in 1971 he may have planned another Gaullist return to save the nation from domestic collapse.

With regard to the tripartite theory, a careful reading of post-coup political speeches indicates that Amin saw the former head of intelligence operations, Akena Adoko, as his real enemy rather than Obote. However, if Adoko conspired with Obote to eliminate Amin and planned then to have Obote assassinated, why did the military government not release this information? By publicizing

___

Move to the Left—appointments to boards of directors and senior positions in commercial banking. See Irving Gershenberg, "A Further Comment on the Uganda Coup," *Journal of Modern African Studies*, X, No. 4 (December 1972), 638–39.

Adoko's penchant for intrigue, Amin would certainly have but-
tressed his case against corrupt politicians. On the other hand, at
least in the immediate postcoup period, the Amin government may
have been concerned about gaining the support of the civil service;
perhaps it realized that release of further information might impli-
cate and alienate trained personnel whose skills were required for
the technical tasks of nation-building. Amin may have reasoned,
too, despite his personal animosity toward Adoko, that unenlight-
ened individuals had joined the latter's ranks, with or without
knowledge of the final coup de grâce, because they, like Amin,
believed that it was necessary to overthrow the Obote government.

Underlying Sociopolitical Causes

Whatever the immediate factors facilitating the coup in Uganda,
the climate was one favoring military opportunism; and an inventory of underlying sociopolitical causes producing such an atmosphere is not hard to provide. Among the most important items
were the lack of viable institutions, a top-heavy power structure,
the lacuna between the official ideology and political behavior,
ethnic fragmentation, economic instability, the obstacles to recruitment facing the younger generation, and corruption and nepotism
among the elites.

The social basis of military intervention is often the result of, on
the one hand, rapid social change and the recruitment of new
groups into politics and, on the other, an absence of viable institutions to channel political behavior.[18] Without institutions to structure the activities of those recently recruited into the political
system, political participation lacks sustained involvement; what
follows is either detached, sporadic participation or the intense,
rapid intrusion of some group having at least a modicum of
structural coherence—for example, the surgical, allegedly therapeutic intervention of a military elite.

Under Obote, Uganda's traditional sources of legitimacy and
authority were either abolished (as in the case of monarchy) or
increasingly eclipsed (as were local councils). There being neither
a leader with charismatic appeal nor an accepted ideology, the stability of the polity and the longevity of the regime depended on the

18. Samuel P. Huntington, *Political Order in Changing Societies* (New
Haven: Yale University Press, 1968), pp. 5, 12.

strength of the party. But the UPC, Uganda's single party since December 1969, was notoriously weak, both at the center and in terms of links between the center and outlying areas. The only cohesion shown by the UPC was in some of the local branches, and to a certain extent the very strength of these local branches worked against the forging of a strong national party system. The UPC, as Colin Leys demonstrates in his study of Acholi, was really a coalition of local organizations and competing subsystems rather than an integrated national system.[19]

Obote's response to the problems of modernization increasingly took the form of ideological initiatives. And the attempts that were made to introduce an ideology of modernization in Uganda often emulated those of "radical" states elsewhere in Africa. Many observers regarded Obote's actions as imitative of Nyerere's in Tanzania. In terms of ideology, the relationship between the two presidents involved more than affinity or chance resemblance; ideological exchange between them contributed to and reinforced their individual predispositions.

The relationship was not constant but fluctuated. The major shift was from ideological cooperation at the time of independence to ideological emulation when Obote was ousted, though there were were also instances of conflict and, by 1971, a pattern of ideological escalation as well. (While ideological cooperation involves an intended convergence of values, ideological emulation entails the attempt to adopt the same or similar normative values as those derived in another national context. With the increase or spread of ideology in two or more interrelated states, an extreme form of emulation may occur. Escalating ideological relationships arise in situations where one leader perceives that the leader of another state is winning acclaim as an ideologue and from the tendency to employ ideology as a symbolic response to objective problems that remain unresolved at the nonsymbolic level. In other words, ideological escalation is a form of emulative behavior, one-upmanship in an area characterized by the personalization of politics, or a compensatory device.[20])

19. Colin Leys, *Politicians and Policies: An Essay on Politics in Acholi, Uganda 1962–65* (Nairobi: East African Publishing House, 1967), pp. 10, 104. There are no comprehensive studies of the UPC at the national level.
20. Given the complexity of social phenomena, these patterns overlap and

Following independence, Nyerere took the lead in introducing an ideology of modernization. Of the two presidents, Nyerere was the more aware of ideology's potential contribution to nation-building. At least as early as 1958, he had begun planting the seeds of self-reliance, the harvest of which was to be a national program of African socialism.[21] After the army mutiny and the Act of Union of 1964, Nyerere, previously regarded as a moderate leader, demonstrated his leftist inclinations. Industries were nationalized; labor unions became adjuncts of government; the country's single party was blessed with de jure status; a policy of rural mobilization through ujamaa villages was undertaken; Tanzania called increasingly on states with centrally planned market economies for foreign aid; and Eastern countries were also invited to join the Canadians in supplying military advisors. In 1967 the "Arusha Declaration" not only capped the initiatives of the preceding years but also provided an ideological blueprint for the future. The proclaimed purpose of this document was to correct a situation in which "the absence of a generally accepted and easily understood statement of philosophy and policy was causing problems."[22] With the Declaration, "the ideology of the country was made explicit."[23] It placed the accent on public control over the economy, social equality, and rural development through socialism. In subsequent years, self-reliance was to emerge as a major tenet of socialist construction in Tanzania. On many occasions, the president emphasized that a socializing society must shift the emphasis from external to internal resources; only by self-reliance, a strategy for remedying the adverse effects of the world market, does an underdeveloped country redefine its relations with external forces. Since 1967, in part because of the "Arusha Declaration," Nyerere has enjoyed the reputation of a sincere and innovative leader.

Whatever Obote's desires may have been, the options that were open to Nyerere were not available to him. In Tanzania, one

---

coexist. Though the analyst may prefer neatly separable categories, a more realistic but modest objective is to establish broadly identifiable tendencies.

21. Nyerere, *Freedom and Unity*, especially pp. 53–58.

22. *Idem, Freedom and Socialism: Uhuru na Ujamaa* (Dar es Salaam: Oxford University Press, 1968), p. 1.

23. *Ibid.*, p. 231.

language is spoken by over 85 percent of the people, there are a number of small tribes with no one of them able to dominate the political system, and the leader has widespread charismatic appeal; Uganda, by contrast, lacks these facilitating factors. Having to be concerned about his own political survival, Obote must have noted that attempts to challenge established forms of behavior and privilege would jeopardize his position. In the post-independence period, he aspired to match the accomplishments of Nyerere but could not achieve in Uganda what Nyerere was able to do in Tanzania.

Nevertheless Obote's critics continued to question his approach: "Why are the ideological trumpets silent? If leaders such as Nyerere and Kaunda can gain international acclaim (and thereby strengthen their domestic base as well), why does Obote insist on silence?" The Move to the Left was initiated partly in response to this criticism. The "Common Man's Charter," which may be regarded as the ideological step-child of the "Arusha Declaration," was the beginning of the expanding gap between verbal and nonverbal behavior. It does not follow, of course, that the two leaders openly acknowledged the relationship between their ideologies. For the most part, Nyerere assiduously avoided making public statements about affairs in Uganda during the Obote years. He believed that African statesmen should not comment upon, let alone intervene in, the internal affairs of another state.[24] When pressed by a reporter about the effect of his policies on neighboring states, the Tanzanian leader replied: " 'We are not showing other people what to do.' Tanzania was doing what was right for her. Naturally, her actions affected those of others. 'But each country must at every given point judge for itself what is right for itself.' "[25] Obote, for his part, once remarked that Tanzania would not influence Uganda,[26] though in a somewhat more candid statement issued a year later he acknowleged:

24. *Ibid.*, p. 377.
25. "China Gave Inspiration—Nyerere," *Uganda Argus*, February 16, 1967.
26. "Assurance by Dr. Obote—Uganda Retains Public Sector Policy," *Uganda Argus*, February 8, 1967. This statement was made with reference to the nationalization of commercial banks in Tanzania.

I know President Julius Nyerere well. I can say that I have learnt from and hope to continue to learn from him. After all, he is older than myself and his country achieved independence before mine. In the second place, he built a strong party, which is the only party in mainland Tanzania and . . . we in Africa are learning from one another.[27]

Whatever Obote's and Nyerere's perceptions of each other, by 1971 ideological escalation was a major factor in the dynamics of East African politics. Their points of divergence notwithstanding (for example, Tanzania broke diplomatic relations with Britain over Southern Rhodesia's UDI and recognized Biafra, but Uganda did not follow suit), the pattern was that measures introduced in Tanzania presaged adoption of similar steps in Uganda; and the direct correspondence in the official ideologies cannot be passed off as mere coincidence. But for ideological escalation to occur, not just one actor but all parties concerned must contribute. In terms of ideological exchange, the relationship between Obote and Nyerere was asymmetrical—Nyerere had greater influence on Obote than vice versa; nevertheless, each had something to contribute. There is little need to provide further illustration of Nyerere's ideological influence, though mention might be made of Tanzania's lead in the creation of a national service, in using, relatively successfully, elections to forge integration, and in introducing measures to nationalize major industries. A major area in which Obote led was in attitudes to foreign aid, toward which Uganda, from the early years after independence, displayed consistent skepticism. When Nyerere was attempting to attract foreign assistance without the more contemporary emphasis on its consequences and implications, Obote was actualizing such reservations in government policy. Uganda voiced its concern that those who supplied aid were reaping political concessions and maintaining instability in the Third World; the prime minister warned that while foreign assistance could be a helpful supplement to local programs it could never be a substitute. Uganda, accordingly, made a less concerted effort to secure aid than did its East African neighbors.[28] In 1964,

27. Obote, *Myths and Realities*, p. 32.
28. Yashpal Tandon, "East African Attitudes to Foreign Aid" (paper presented to the Universities of East Africa Social Science Conference, Dar es Salaam, December 1970), pp. 10, 11.
Yet there is no doubt that Nyerere was aware of the dangers of economic dependence even before independence. In a 1961 speech delivered to the

Uganda received 1.9 percent of the U.S. economic aid going to 32 African countries and Tanzania 4.6 percent; in 1968, Uganda received 0.89 percent (which amounted to 30¢ per capita) and Tanzania 2.02 percent (44¢ per capita). By 1968, Uganda had drawn a total of $30,000,000 in economic aid from the U.S., while Tanzania had accepted $60,000,000. Eastern bloc aid between 1958 and 1965 amounted to $30,000,000 for Uganda and $51,000,000 for Tanzania.[29] Later, Nyerere continued to attempt to attract aid, but only as a supplement to local initiatives; Tanzania's official policy emphasizing self-reliance and admonishing outside powers against a "second scramble for Africa" was a note Obote had sounded earlier. It seems likely that Tanzania's modified position was at least partly the result of Obote's policy in Uganda.

By the time Obote was deposed in 1971, the association of ideological partners had an institutional dimension. In August 1967, Nyerere, Obote, and Zambia's increasingly radical head of state, Kenneth Kaunda, formed a fraternal order called the Mulungushi Club. As part of the club arrangements, the three presidents agreed to attend the annual meetings of one another's political parties. The way in which these three leaders influenced each other cannot be delineated with any precision. It is interesting nonetheless to note that one of Obote's few public comments about about Nyerere was made at a Mulungushi meeting; in an address to the TANU delegation in October 1967 Obote remarked: "The UPC is using in its policies part of the policies of its neighboring countries."[30] And it was at an annual meeting of the UPC, with Nyerere and Kaunda in attendance, that the "Common Man's Charter" was adopted as Uganda's official ideology. Obote did not

---

UN, Nyerere commented (*Freedom and Unity*, p. 152): "The word 'neo-colonialism' is one which I believe has some danger, but there is also a reality: the replacement of political domination by economic domination."

29. Data on foreign aid are derived from Donald George Morrison *et al.*, eds., *Black Africa: A Comparative Handbook* (New York: The Free Press, 1972), pp. 134–38. Their data on British aid relate only to 1967 and 1969, when the U.K. cut its aid program to Tanzania as a result of a dispute about pensions and compensation to ex-colonial civil servants; these figures shed no light, therefore, on the issue posed in the text and are not cited. In view of the December 1965 break in diplomatic relations over UDI, to use the figures for the mid-sixties would also be misleading.

30. "President Obote Addresses TANU Conference," *Uganda Argus*, October 18, 1967.

deliver his "get tough" speech to the students, concerning the events of July 1970, until the inauguration ceremony of the following October—an occasion at which the other East African presidents were present. Obote's "last stand"—adamant opposition to the sale of arms to South Africa—was common cause among the presidents of Uganda, Tanzania, and Zambia; a careful reading of the speeches delivered at the Commonwealth Conference in Singapore suggests that Obote was attempting to outdo Nyerere and Kaunda in militancy. And when Obote was removed from office, he immediately visited his erstwhile Mulungushi partners. In search of refuge, the former president was granted sanctuary at State House in Dar es Salaam.

It must be emphasized that there are many causes for the overthrow of a government (as well as many consequences). The argument being advanced here is not that patterns of ideological exchange produced a coup in Uganda but that those patterns which have been examined—ideological cooperation, ideological emulation, and ideological escalation—contributed importantly to the political violence that followed.

Obote's ideological pronouncements, because they were at such an abstract level, precluded the formation of specific goals. The government's excessive concern for symbolic or prestige projects (for example, the $70,000 spent on the Makerere University inauguration ceremony and the more than $10,000,000 allotted to the construction of an OAU conference building) added to widespread cynicism and skepticism. Increasingly, talk was heard about the "Rhetoric to the Left." And as this rhetoric became more and more a subject of discourse among the elites rather than a system of beliefs and values embraced by the common man, the figure of Milton Obote grew in importance. Some saw the beginning of a personality cult in Uganda; the specter of Obote-ism was a pervasive cause of concern. Others regarded Obote's professed socialism not as ideological conviction but as a display of tribal politics; since the Baganda were the wealthiest ethnic group in Uganda, equalizing privilege and spreading domestic economic opportunity would have the effect of leveling Ganda pre-eminence.[31]

31. Of course, any policy that has the effect of reducing the power of a predominant tribe is likely to be interpreted in terms of antitribal politics.

As in Nigeria, Ghana, and a host of other African states that have known military intervention, the coup in Uganda took place against a background of economic disorder. During the final months of the Obote regime, private capital outflow increased considerably and private capital inflow declined. The outflow of capital from the private sector, particularly acute toward the end of April 1970, when exchange control was introduced against Kenya and Tanzania, resulted from "the absence of a clear policy statement about the role of private initiative and the *de facto* indecisiveness about the question of non-citizens."[32] After the establishment of the Export Import Corporation, the announcement of partial nationalization of major industries, and the imposition of controls on capital transfers to the rest of East Africa, the balance of payments, having peaked in September, registered a large deficit in the final quarter of 1970. Between the end of September and the end of December 1970, there was a significant expansion in domestic credit extended to the government to meet the growing deficit. During this period, the net foreign assets of the banking system declined by 21.5 percent. Total domestic credit increased by 44.8 percent, the onus of financing falling upon the Central Bank.[33]

Thus it is not surprising that the army's eighteen complaints should have included a number focusing on economic grievances: unemployment, the government's failure to provide the basic amenities of life, proliferating taxes (including development tax, graduated tax, sales tax, and social security fund tax), falling prices for cotton and coffee, and the creation of a wealthy ruling class. In a country with an average per capita income of slightly less than $100 per year, the conspicuous consumption of self-serving elites and construction of the extravagant OAU conference hall were bound to exacerbate grievances.

Sources in Kampala report that in order to meet the Yugoslav loan for the OAU building, Obote instructed all ministries to reduce expenses by 20 percent and to cut back on the hiring of new

32. *Bank of Uganda Quarterly Bulletin*, III, No. 1 (December 1970), 3. After the coup, Amin announced that a 49 percent–51 percent formula would replace Obote's 60 percent–40 percent policy and that the government intended to be flexible in determining the minimum amount of capital for incorporation ("President Scraps 60%–40% Formula," *Uganda Argus*, May 3, 1971).

33. *Bank of Uganda*, pp. 12–14.

personnel. The result was one more instance of the younger generation feeling excluded from a share of the gains being enjoyed by older and perhaps less qualified leaders.

The older generation displayed little reluctance to take advantage of the expansion of government authority and the creation of new sources of wealth and power. The auditor-general's report for the year ending June 30, 1969, revealed that unauthorized expenditures in that year totaled Shs. 45,355,067, of which Shs. 23,828,995 was attributed to the Ministry of Defence.[34] In an undoubted understatement, attention was drawn to the fact that "This report makes reference to a disturbing increase in the number of instances of abuse of public funds" (for example, costs incurred for private bills pending recovery, personal and social journeys, air fares for children and wives in excess of entitlement, increasing instances of unauthorized advances in salary, illegitimate allocation of houses additional to an official residence, apparently unjustified entertainment, and payment of mileage claims beyond provision of hired transport or government vehicles).[35]

It would be a mistake to suggest that Obote was responsible for Uganda's widespread corruption.[36] Indeed in his last year of office he tried to stem corruption (through, for example, civil service reforms and legislation enabling the government to examine private bank accounts). In retrospect, then, did Obote suffer the tragic misfortune of being a leader isolated—not merely politically but also ideologically? Or does leadership, by definition, preclude isolation? The task of leadership is to provide guidance, direction, persuasion; but isolation involves detachment, insularity, separation. Surely one of the primary objectives of effective leadership is to avoid isolation. If Milton Obote became isolated, he failed to lead.

Military Permanence?

In the wake of military intervention, what are the alternatives for a society as problem-ridden as Uganda? What courses of action

34. *The Public Accounts of the Republic of Uganda for the Year Ended 30th June, 1969* (Entebbe: Government Printer, 1970), p. 3.
35. *Ibid.*, p. 1.
36. I am indebted to Professor Locksley G. Edmondson for raising this essential point and provoking the comments that follow.

are open to a new regime lacking cohesion and legitimacy? Are viable options available?

Events in Uganda in the period immediately after the coup could have followed a number of paths.[37] Given the personalized nature of politics in Africa, a first consideration was: what role might Obote or Amin play? With the military remaining in power, three types of postcoup coalition seemed possible: a progressive Nasserite junta led by a military head of state, an alliance between the army and the bureaucracy, and a tutelary democracy with a vanguard party at the forefront.

At the time of the coup, political commentators pointed out parallels between the overthrow of Obote and the deposition of two other African leaders. Just as Obote was overthrown on a diplomatic mission to Singapore, Nkrumah was unseated while attending to foreign relations in Peking. Just as the Ugandan coup took place while Obote was constructing a multimillion dollar OAU conference hall, in Algeria Boumedienne took control while Ben Bella was making preparations for an extravagant conference hall for a meeting of neutralist and nonaligned heads of state. Intentionally or unintentionally, political observers failed to draw attention to another incident: in 1960, a coup was on the verge of success in Ethiopia while Haile Selassie was outside the country and was only quashed when the emperor returned to rally local forces. Obote, who did more than any other Ugandan to unify his country, stifle the remnants of monarchy, and stand firm against ethnic separatism, had supporters, both at home and abroad. Although few deposed African presidents return to power, the possibility of Obote's doing so could not be ruled out altogether.

But Amin held the key to Uganda's immediate future. The general's background was that of an up-from-the ranks soldier who joined the King's African Rifles just after World War II. Fighting with the British colonial forces against Mau Mau in the 1950's, Amin developed a reputation for brutality. After independence, although he survived the gold scandal, his excessive use of violence on patrol almost brought an end to his military career. Limited in

37. The following discussion focuses on the most likely paths; it does not claim to exhaust the possible alternatives.

formal education and command of the metropolitan language, Amin was known as an avid sportsman—an accomplished hunter and swimmer as well as heavyweight boxing champion of Uganda. Indeed Amin might have been the Platonic timarchic personality incarnate:

rather more self-willed, and rather less well-read, though not without intelligent interests: ready to listen, but quite incapable of expressing himself. He will be harsh to his slaves, because his imperfect education has left him uncertain of his superiority over them. . . . He will be ambitious to hold office himself, regarding as qualifications for it not the ability to speak or anything like that, but military qualities, and he'll be fond of exercise and hunting.[38]

Like the Platonic timarchy, Uganda's postcoup regime was spawned by social change rooted in civil strife; but Amin came to power possessing one virtue that the timarchic Guardians lack—popular appeal, even if the appeal was, to a certain degree, limited by ethnic and regional lines. This advantage (indeed a rare trait in Ugandan politics) gave the general an opportunity to prove his mettle as a politician. He had the chance to play kingmaker in forging a viable postcoup coalition.

Amin could have taken the initiative in utilizing to maximum effect such assets possessed by the military as its near monopoly of the means of coercion, absence of political debts, corporate identity (partly as a result of separation from the primordial community), and ingrained notions of leadership. Such a combination could produce a government with the kind of modernizing and re-forming ability that the military provided in the Middle East (routinization of personal authority plus military skill equals a progressive Nasserite junta). Equally, however, it could lead to the weaknesses of the military as a ruling body becoming manifest: lack of legitimacy, difficulties in establishing public confidence because of continued reliance on coercion, absence of the political skills of bargaining and negotiation. In Uganda, because of recurring internal strife and the undisciplined nature of the armed forces, attempts to forge an enlightened junta merely aggravated military factionalism.

Generally in postcoup situations, the army, lacking expertise and

38. Plato, *The Republic,* trans. H. D. P. Lee (London: Penguin Books, 1955), p. 319.

numbers to rule the country effectively, seeks to forge an alliance with another elite. The bureaucracy, having little or no control over the means of coercion, is a logical partner. Both the military elite and the bureaucracy are potential agents of development with long-term associations with modern norms as well as relatively ordered hierarchies that are formally committed to growth, unity, and stability.[39] Rule by the coercion-administration axis may be fragile, however, and with the vacuum left by a no-party system, provides a dubious base on which to launch a governing coalition.

The factors that impel the military to intervene, and enable it to do so, are superseded by heightened fragmentation within the army. Wielding political power promotes internal antagonisms. No longer the cohesive force whose intention it was to cleanse the body politic of its corrupt civilians, the military regime is beset by divisiveness within. Whatever solidarity may have been associated with a formerly detached martial role ceases to be a weapon in the arsenal of military resources. The onset of decay is apparent when the army devotes more political and monetary capital to sustaining its own position than to rectifying those ineptitudes that were the justification for intervention.

In various low income countries under military rule, given the deficiencies of the alternatives, increasing strife within the armed forces, and the inevitable civilian pressure for the soldiers' return to the barracks, the most viable course of action is establishment of a vanguard party, the initial objective of which is to exercise strong control at the top while gradually expanding the base of power throughout the system. This step follows logically from the fact that a party lends itself more readily to certain functions than does the military—for example, the mobilization of new groups into the political system, the representation and integration of diverse ethnic groups, communication from the center to outlying social units, and the expansion of power from central bodies to interstitial elements of the system. During a period of "tutelary democracy" the leaders strive to realize "the institutional apparatus of political democracy but . . . attempt to keep the system going more or less democratically through very strong initiative and a continuous pressure from the top."[40] The tutelary approach entails

39. Dowse, "The Military and Political Development," pp. 239–42.
40. Edward Shils, "The Military in the Political Development of New

curtailing democratic liberties in the short run while the regime establishes authority structures for control; at the second stage, these liberties are extended across a society that has already experienced social and economic reforms. In attempting to generate support, the tutelary regime must seek ideological consensus. Shared values, particularly when attached to interests, are required if confidence and a sense of societal purpose are to be generated. And this is one of the foremost reasons why civilians are needed. As Edward Feit so aptly puts it, "Even though power came to them by force, soldiers have to legitimate themselves by means other than force."[41] The deficiencies that have been noted, however, leave the military ill-equipped to establish a sense of national purpose.

History provides relatively few examples of voluntary military disengagement from politics. Hence it is not surprising that while the scholarly literature abounds with studies of intervention disengagement is not a topic of concern. Similarly, rigorous analysis of political recruitment has been conducted in most areas of the world, but political withdrawal is a neglected subject.[42] Although three military regimes in West Africa (in Dahomey, Ghana, and Sierra Leone) voluntarily restored civilian rule, these cases are the exception rather than the rule. Moreover, little time has passed since independence in Africa; it may, therefore, be premature to attempt to discern any long-term trend in intervention and disengagement in this area of the world. Certain non-African cases of military disengagement—in particular, early twentieth century Turkey and Mexico—may offer the most instructive examples to

---

States," in John J. Johnson, ed., *The Role of the Military in Underdeveloped Countries* (Princeton: Princeton University Press, 1962), p. 59.

41. Edward Feit, "Pen, Sword, and People: Military Regimes in the Formation of Political Institutions," *World Politics,* XXV, No. 2 (January 1973), 255. Feit cites a range of examples to indicate that the military, along with the bureaucracy, has considerable difficulty in formulating coherent ideologies: Burma under Ne Win (from 1962), Egypt under Gamal Abdel Nasser (1952–1970), Pakistan under Ayub Khan (1958–1969), and Spain under Primo de Rivera (1923–1931).

42. Exploratory work has been undertaken by Claude E. Welch, Jr., "Cincinnatus in Africa: The Possibility of Military Withdrawal from Politics," in Michael F. Lofchie, ed., *The State of the Nations: Constraints on Development in Independent Africa* (Berkeley: University of California Press, 1971), pp. 215–37; and Frederick W. Frey, *The Turkish Political Elite* (Cambridge, Mass.: Massachusetts Institute of Technology Press, 1965), especially p. 392.

African countries in which rapid social change is blocked by ineffective military rule. This is not to imply that the experiences of
these early modernizers are directly applicable to Uganda in the
second half of the twentieth century, but, rather, that they can
provide instructive lessons.

The developmental experiences of Turkey, Mexico, and Uganda
are marked, of course, by numerous historical and cultural differences. Most important, perhaps, Turkey and Mexico were not new
states and attained their political independence in a period very
different from the early 1960's. When Turkey's General Mustafa
Kemal came to power at the beginning of the second decade of this
century, he assumed the mantle of leadership in a state whose
identity, despite territorial redefinitions, could be traced back over
600 years. Then, too, although early twentieth century Turkey and
Mexico had to contend with imperial expansion, the techniques of
dominance were less advanced than those of present-day industrial
concentration and monopolization. Finally, it is difficult to imagine
a Ugandan head of state assuming an autocratic Kemalist posture
without facing concerted pressure for an extension of equality. In
the contemporary world, modernizing impulses that embrace the
egalitarian ethos are a motivating force for social change; at the
same time, the spread of the egalitarian ethos contributes to the
problems of modernization.

Despite these differences, and others, the obstacles to development experienced in the three countries have many similarities. Just
as Uganda displays a variety of social cleavages, nineteenth and
early twentieth century Ottoman Turkey was characterized by
racial, linguistic, and religious differences. The strategic locations
of Turkey and Uganda—one at the crossroads of three continents,
the other at the headwaters of the Nile—placed both directly in the
line of imperial expansion. Each gained its independence, too, at a
time when the great powers were weakened by fighting world wars.
The modernizing elites of both countries had to deal with the
problems posed by monarchies—the sultanate and the kabakaship—
not easily adaptable to change. To forge new identities, the elites
experimented with attempts to establish loyalties at the transnational level through pan-Islam and pan-Africanism. Ethnic separatism or secessionist movements were complicating factors in both
situations. In Turkey, the challenge to national unity came from the

secession of such non-Turkish Moslems as the Albanians and the Arabs, discontent among Turkey's Greeks (which ultimately led to a population exchange), and recurring problems, at least until the 1930's with the Kurds. Both Turkey and Uganda launched programs of economic nationalism to take trade and commerce out of the hands of alien minorities (in the one case, Armenians, Jews, Greeks, and other non-Turks; in the other, non-Ugandan laborers from neighboring African countries and noncitizen Asians). Finally, leadership styles in both Turkey and Uganda have tended to be highly personalized.[43]

A great hero in the war for independence, General Mustafa Kemal resigned from the Ottoman army in July 1919. In order to serve the nation better, he devoted himself to giving direction to the Assembly and forming the Progressive Republican Party. Using his guiding influence in the Assembly adroitly, he secured legislation whereby military officers could stand for political office only if they resigned their commissions. In 1923–1924 ranking military officers and civilian leaders concluded an agreement under which two of the most prestigious generals would leave the military to assume high-level governmental posts while a third maintained control of the military without interference. Gradually, Ataturk and his successor, Ismet Inönü, were able to separate political and military functions. By means of benevolent authoritarianism, these military men-cum-politicians forged social and national unity in the tutelary manner. As civilians replaced the officers, the latter guided the transition and retained considerable influence. Late in the 1950's, to be sure, the civilian Menderes regime succeeded in alienating both the officers and the urban population, and the military re-entered the political arena. Following the coup of 1960, however, the military—heir to the Kemalist legacy—gracefully retired from office, paving the way for another civilian regime. Just over a decade later, intervention was triggered again, this time by leftist agitation; in the wake of a series of political assassinations, kidnapings, bank robberies, and highjackings, the army forced the resignation of Premier Suleyman Demirel and imposed martial law.

43. Some of my information on Turkey is derived from Robert E. Ward and Dankwart A. Rustow, eds., *Political Modernization in Japan and Turkey* (Princeton: Princeton University Press, 1964).

The vicissitudes of recent years do not necessarily detract, however, from the relevance of the Kemalist model of military disengagement from politics. Further examination of Ataturk's role in forging a modern society may well provide inspiration for later modernizers.

In Mexico, a much more socially homogeneous society than either Turkey or Uganda, an astute military elite skillfully employed a combination of Machiavellian tactics, clever political engineering, and efficiency in administration to civilianize and institutionalize the politcal process. After the revolution of 1910, military power in Mexico was divided between regulars and the revolutionary forces. Military power was dispersed among small fiefdoms maintained by strongmen or regional caudillos, chiefs who commanded their separate, semiautonomous bands, mostly for personal enrichment. An enlightened elite resourcefully met the challenge of the caudillos by crushing the less powerful and buying off the stronger; some were "promoted" to high government or civil service posts, while others, retaining their military commands, were rotated or balanced against the jurisdiction of civilian leaders. But tactical shifts alone were insufficient. The generals in power sought to consolidate the revolution, and this entailed military disengagement. If social and national unity were to be realized, a decentralized and unprincipled army would have to be modernized. The ruling elite pursued the tactics of expediency as well as the more long-range strategy of building support from the bottom up. Military reforms included the introduction of new training schools for officers, increased opportunity for promotion, competitive examinations, recreational facilities, better living conditions, and educational programs designed to inculcate patriotism and loyalty. In the political realm, the early military presidents attempted to shift the basis of their support from personalismo to institutional politics. Accordingly, they formed a single party system to serve as the mechanism for transferring power. The Partido Nacional Revolucionario (later reconstituted as the Partido Revolucionario Institucional) was sectorally organized to include all major interests—labor, agrarian, and "popular"—within the party. Standing in the wings, the generals paved the way for the civilians to assume power. At the end of Avila Camacho's tenure of office, civilian presidents took over political power. Mexico's ruling elites under Obregón, Calles, and Cárdenas were effective in promoting economic growth, forging national consciousness, and building viable institutions for the politicians to direct.[44]

In both Turkey and Mexico, then, the generals established parties, civilianized the political process, and institutionalized revolution and stability. With the shift in the locus of power from the military to the civilians, the soldiers' chief role was to serve as watchdog over politics. Despite their continued control over the means of coercion, the trump card was rarely played. Rather, military regimes acted as agents of social change by shaping new values that were pragmatically linked to coalitions of interests; and the introduction of new values thus linked played a major part in achieving social transformation. Ideology provided a framework in which new social groups and organizations were harmonized with values and beliefs advanced by modernizing elites.

In applying these lessons to Uganda, two major considerations should be kept in mind. The first provides the key to calculating the prospects for military disengagement or perpetuation and analyzing ideological patterns. If military disengagement from politics means a transfer of power by which the balance of social forces is fundamentally altered, the soldiers' material interests must be gauged. Once in control of the state, the men on horseback normally adopt policies consonant with their class identities and corporate loyalties.[45] Soldiers, like others, are unlikely to act purely on the basis of ideals or altruism. If the military is viewed in the context of social structure, the paramount questions become: Whose interests are being served or contravened by the armed forces? To what degree are class interests maintained or eroded by military rulers? And do the soldiers' actions support or work against world market forces?[46]

44. Huntington, *Political Order in Changing Societies,* pp. 255–58; Edwin Lieuwen, *Arms and Politics in Latin America* (New York: Praeger, 1961), pp. 101–21; Martin C. Needler, "The Political Development of Mexico," *American Political Science Review,* LV, No. 2 (June 1961), 308–12.

45. Eric A. Nordlinger, "Soldiers in Mufti: The Impact of Military Rule upon Economic and Social Change in Non-Western States," *American Political Science Review,* LXIV, No. 4 (December 1970), 1131–48.

46. Preliminary assessments of class standings in the Ugandan army differ in the emphasis they place on economic privilege and social background; see Michael Lofchie, "Uganda Coup: Class Action by the Military," *Journal of*

For the officers, the disincentives to civilianizing the power base may also include fear of civilian political opponents, the likelihood of intervention again later at the behest of another group of soldiers, and the desire to maintain a given set of principles. Under certain conditions, however, relinquishing an overt political role may be seen as advantageous. If they can be assured that class and corporate interests will be protected, officers prefer in some cases to retain leverage over those installed in office. In such cases, while continuing to exercise influence, the military gives up its official political positions.

The second consideration is that any recommendation to induce social change through a military-backed juggernaut must be made with an appreciation of the need for astute tactical engineering. As indicated in Chapter 9, postcoup Uganda was fraught with fragmentation. Societal cleavages were reflected, if not accentuated, in the army. Although many Ugandans shared a common opposition to Milton Obote, they agreed on little else.

Obote's contribution to a severely divided society was to concentrate power. Having built a hierarchy, albeit with foundations weakened by corruption and nepotism, his failure was not to include diverse participant groups. The legacy of the Obote regime was the dilemma of how to provide firm control from the top and at the same time spread the prerogatives of participation in government through the political system without increasing the potential for disruption.

In 1971, Uganda's problem was not the need for a seizure of power but the necessity to create power at the systemic level. Nonetheless, the intervention of the military in Ugandan politics should not be regarded as a pathological condition developing in response to a malevolent regime. General Amin, neither sycophant nor savior, came to power as a seasoned soldier with a rare opportunity to speed the dialectics of consensus through dissension, order through disorder, and stability through instability.

Modern African Studies, X, No. 1 (May 1972), 19–35, and Ali A. Mazrui, "The Lumpen Proletariat and the Lumpen Militariat: African Soldiers as a New Middle Class," *Political Studies,* XXI, No. 1 (March 1973), 1–12.

CHAPTER 8

The Internationalization
of Political Violence

In his *Myths and Realities: Letter to a London Friend,* Milton Obote claimed, "As regards the position of the Uganda army, I am perhaps the only African leader who is not afraid of a military takeover."[1] The then president's self-confident assertion that he could not be overthrown by a coup is reminiscent of Julius Nyerere's boast that his country would not suffer an army mutiny; speaking in 1960, Nyerere maintained, "There is not the slightest chance that the forces of law and order in Tanganyika will mutiny."[2]

Both prophecies proved inaccurate. Just over two years after Obote's statement was made, it was disproved by a military coup d'état. Three and a half years after Nyerere's boast, the First Battalion of the Tanganyikan Rifles, stationed near Dar es Salaam, mutinied; and a day later, on January 21, 1964, the Second Battalion at Tabora followed suit.

It was more than coincidence that in the two days following these events in Tanganyika two companies of Uganda's African Rifles and the Eleventh Battalion of the Kenya African Rifles should also have engaged in mutinous activities.[3] As events in Uganda after the coup of January 25, 1971, indicate, the extranational consequences of political violence can be the most momentous aspect of rapid political change. The political significance of civil strife extends far beyond the scene of the strife itself. The interplay of subnational, national, and international politics in Uganda illustrates a set of evolving *norms* that characterize African international relations—integration, integrity, and nonintervention.

1. Obote, *Myths and Realities,* p. 16.
2. *Inside East Africa* (August–September 1960), pp. 13, 14.
3. "The Brushfire in East Africa," *Africa Report,* IX, No. 2 (February 1964), 21–25.

In Uganda, when Obote was deposed, these norms, the internal struggle for power, and the national interests of foreign powers all had immediate international *implications* with regard to (*1*) the importance of recognition as an act of legitimation, (*2*) Uganda's relations with neighboring states, (*3*) cleavages within the OAU, (*4*) the demonstration effect in African politics, and (*5*) great power involvement. The long-term *consequences* in Africa of internationalizing political violence may be (*1*) a major shift in the East African balance of interests, (*2*) a movement toward fluctuating alignments and counteralignments in Africa, (*3*) a summons to reorder African international organization, and (*4*) clarification of African diplomatic norms.

In a world in which 700 million colonized peoples have gained their independence since World War II, the significance of the Uganda case extends well beyond this immediate set of norms, implications, and consequences. The effect of changes in traditional patterns of behavior, uncertain efforts to involve new groups in national politics, relentless increases in population, and the ever widening gap between rich and poor is to heighten the potential for international instability.

When military intervention in domestic politics occurs, generals claim that armed action is the result of politicians' inability to provide solutions to the problems of modernization. Once the army enters politics, a precedent is set; a process has begun; a countercoup is likely. Like virginity, once the original condition of the polity in its relationship with the military is violated it can never be restored.[4]

Military intervention in politics may assume a variety of forms and employ a range of techniques: threat, ultimatum, armed insurrection, mutiny, assassination, and coup d'état. Each technique is a manifestation of political violence. If violence refers to the legal or illegal use of force, political violence is the utilization of force to maintain or upset the prevailing mode of allocating values authoritatively. Of course, not all violence is political; the indiscriminate use of force may be personal, anomic, and politically inconsequential. Acts of violence are deemed political when the

4. See First, pp. 20 and 437: "Once shattered, the sanction against a military seizure of power is broken forever."

violence has an impact, intended or unintended, upon the authorita-
tive allocation of values.[5]

Coups occur not only within a national system but also within an
international system; and political violence frequently originates as
antigovernmental behavior and results in intergovernmental discord.[6] In writing about military intervention, academicians tend to
focus on antigovernmental behavior and to neglect the intergovernmental discord that results. Concentrating almost exclusively on the
domestic aspects, scholars largely ignore (except in cases of overt
armed incursion or subversion from abroad) the international
dimensions of military intervention in Third World politics.[7]

The term "internationalization" refers to a process whereby a
discrete series of events within a nation-state is generalized and
externalized, either existentially or potentially, to become part of
interstate and transnational relations. Conversely, interstate and
transnational relations impinge upon domestic politics, thus further
adding to the process of internationalization of the initial phenomenon. The phrase "internationalization of political violence" is
employed in analyzing the impact of one coup on interstate relations and in political relations among individuals and groups at the
transnational level. It should be emphasized that account must be
taken not only of the acts of political violence that actually occur
but also of the extent to which political violence bears the potential
for internationalization. And the analysis of potential, as well as
actual, internationalization entails examination of the role of extranational actors, their reactions and/or contributions to the series of

5. For useful discussion of political violence, see Kenneth W. Grundy,
Guerrilla Struggle in Africa: An Analysis and Preview (New York: Gross-
man Publishers, 1971), pp. 7–40; Victor T. LeVine, "The Course of Political
Violence," in William H. Lewis, ed., *French-Speaking Africa: The Search for
Identity* (New York: Walker and Company, 1965), pp. 59–79; and James
N. Rosenau, "Internal War as an International Event," in Rosenau, ed.,
International Aspects of Civil Strife (Princeton: Princeton University Press,
1964), pp. 45–91.
6. For the distinction between antigovernmental and intergovernmental
violence, I draw on Samuel P. Huntington, "Patterns of Violence in World
Politics," in Huntington, ed., *Changing Patterns of Military Politics* (New
York: The Free Press, 1962), pp. 22, 23.
7. Yashpal Tandon, "Military Coups and Inter-African Diplomacy,"
Africa Quarterly, VI, No. 4 (January–March 1967), 278–84, provides exploratory work.

events in question, and the nature of the links between national and extranational actors.

One of the reasons why scholars find it difficult to explain or make predictions about the phenomenon of political violence in general, and the coup in Africa in particular, is that they fail to note the links—and the nature of these links—between myriad individuals and groups transcending national boundaries. In order to specify linkage patterns, it is necessary to go beyond statecentric models of international relations and to analyze, in addition to the behavior of nation-states (the conventional unit of analysis for the student of international relations), the kaleidoscopic pattern of interaction among a variety of actors—individuals, groups, governments, and international and transnational organizations.[8]

For the student of international relations, the Uganda coup and the internationalization of political violence provide an opportunity for analyzing variegated linkage patterns in a highly fluid subsystem of international relations. For the student of African affairs, the Uganda coup and the internationalization of political violence offer a case study of the impact of military intervention on inter-African diplomacy and the international system at large.

Evolving Norms

Since the onrush to independence, more than a decade ago, two sets of principles have been employed to define permissible behavior in inter-African diplomacy. The first, general international law, has been criticized as having sanctioned colonialism, being based on European standards of behavior, and using as its foundation a unit of organization (the nation-state) foreign to African tradition. Thus, African statesmen have developed a supplementary set of standards, pan-African law, to govern relations between African states.[9]

Pan-African law, as codified in the OAU Charter and as de-

8. For relevant theoretical inquiry into the relationship between internal and international politics, see James N. Rosenau, ed., *Linkage Politics: Essays on the Convergence of National and International Systems* (New York: The Free Press, 1969); also sections of Robert O. Keohane and Joseph S. Nye, Jr., eds., "Transnational Relations and World Politics," *International Organization*, XXV, No. 3 (Summer 1971).

9. Mazrui, *On Heroes and Uhuru-Worship*, pp. 36, 37.

veloped in practice, includes an evolving set of African ethics as well as specifically African notions of legitimacy. An example of African ethics is to be found in the requirements for membership in the OAU. In principle, membership is open to all African states.[10] In practice, however, all African states do not have an equal right to join. For according to African notions of legitimacy, African states must not only be in effective control of their territory but must also recognize the right of all people to self-determination and call for the complete eradication of colonialism.[11]

One of the most important determinants shaping the evolution of inter-African ethics and principles of legitimacy is the coup d'état.[12] The first ethical principle to have been influenced by this phenomenon is pan-African integration. Few would argue with Legum's definition of pan-Africanism as "a movement of ideas and emotions";[13] however, there is a great deal of disagreement as to the exact nature of pan-African norms for inter-African diplomacy.

At a high level of abstraction, African statesmen recognize the right of territorial integrity. The principle of integrity—that each state has the unimpaired right to exercise sovereignty and self-determination—is endorsed in the UN Charter. The symbol of national integrity is diplomacy, that is, the conduct of foreign relations by a sovereign state, and its badge is the right to a seat in regional and global organizations. The foremost threat to national integrity is extranational intervention. One of the most ambiguous and controversial principles to be analyzed in general international law, intervention can be defined as physical coercion directed against a state from outside.[14]

10. Article IV, "Charter of the Organization of African Unity," in *Basic Documents of the Organization of African Unity* (Addis Ababa: Secretariat of the Organization of African Unity, n.d.), p. 8.
11. Boutros Boutros-Ghali, "The Addis Ababa Charter," *International Conciliation,* No. 54 (January 1964), pp. 38, 39.
12. See Tandon, "Military Coups and Inter-African Diplomacy."
13. Colin Legum, *Pan-Africanism: A Short Political Guide* (London: Pall Mall Press, 1965), p. 24.
14. Some authors give broader definitions of intervention and nonintervention. See Richard A. Falk, *Legal Order in a Violent World* (Princeton: Princeton University Press, 1968), especially pp. 143–80; and Oran R. Young, "Intervention and International Systems," *Journal of International Affairs,* XXII, No. 2 (1968), 183. According to Falk, a state that has the capacity to intervene directly but chooses restraint has an impact on the

In pan-African law, there are indications that intervention is regarded as impermissible. When the OAU was founded, in May 1963, the Summit Conference of Independent African States adopted a Charter that reflected the dominant position of the Brazzaville-Monrovia group. In contradistinction to the proposals of the more radical Casablanca group, the Brazzaville-Monrovia group succeeded in writing into the Charter a conventional interpretation of state sovereignty and only minimal functions for a supranational organization. (As a concession, the Casablanca group was granted the inclusion of strong anticolonial provisions.) Following the January 1963 assassination of President Sylvanus Olympio of Togo and subsequent reports of Ghanaian complicity, the OAU repudiated political assassination and subversion as techniques in inter-African diplomacy.[15] (And the Ghanaian coup of 1966 brought an end to Nkrumah's allegedly subversive tactics against the governments of neighboring states.)

Despite the normative and historical rationale for the proscription of intervention in inter-African diplomacy, however, intervention is not necessarily regarded as either moral or immoral, legal or illegal. Many Africans condemned external intervention in the Congo but condone intervention in South Africa. Others pronounced foreign powers to be guilty of intervention in Nigeria but called for humanitarian aid to Biafra or regarded military support of the federal government as legitimate.

Immediate International Implications

In Uganda, the internal struggle for power that followed Obote's overthrow was complicated by the ethics of inter-African diplomacy. Uganda's new head of state was quick to appreciate the importance of recognition by foreign governments as a means of establishing legitimacy. Immediately after the coup, the new government sent delegates to secure the recognition of neighboring states, while

---

affairs of another state and is, therefore, intervening. If state X intervenes in the domestic affairs of state Y, the failure of state Z to counterintervene can be considered as a form of interventionary diplomacy. This definition, failing to distinguish between intervention and interference, is too general. Under such a definition, as Kenneth W. Grundy has pointed out (in a personal communication to the author), the U.S. always intervenes because it has the capacity to do so.

15. Article III, "Charter of the Organization of African Unity," p. 5.

former President Obote, insisting on the illegality of the new regime, lobbied with Kenyan, Tanzanian, Zambian, Ethiopian, and Congolese officials.

On February 5 the diplomatic scales tipped in favor of the Amin government. Britain, followed by Liberia, recognized Uganda's military regime. A few other states—Ghana, Malawi, Zaire, and Nigeria—were quick to follow. Others let it be known that, irrespective of how a government comes to power, recognition does not necessarily require a formal act; de facto recognition can be assumed. Others still, aware of the possibility of a countercoup, as in Nigeria, adopted a wait-and-see policy.

Wary of the stigma of neocolonialism, General Amin would have preferred an African state to have been the first to bestow recognition on his government. African states, however, were hesitant and appeared to be waiting for a big power to take the lead. London's calculated diplomatic gesture of being the first government to recognize the new regime in Kampala can be attributed to a variety of interrelated factors: Britain's historical ties with Uganda, Obote's policy of partial nationalization of foreign companies, the plight of Asians carrying British passports, the disappointment expressed by the former president over the electoral victory of the Conservative party in England, the Tory government's obvious pleasure at the overthrow of the increasingly radical Obote, and the expressed wish of the new head of state for close ties with the former metropole.

One of Uganda's East African neighbors was initially apprehensive, the other hostile. Kenya, with a moderate and capitalist-oriented government, although probably pleased by the coup, refused to take a public stand for a month. Then Foreign Minister Njoroge Mungai announced, on February 26, that Kenya's policy was to recognize states rather than governments; by implication, Kenya had recognized the Amin government. Tanzania, however, alarmed by the overthrow of a president who aspired to be a fellow social revolutionary, expressed undisguised hostility.[16] Nyerere asked how he could sit at a conference table with a murderer who had seized power by force. General Amin's supporters argued in

16. See, for example, "We Will Never Recognize Amin—Nyerere," *Daily Nation,* February 22, 1971.

reply that not only had Obote become president through a coup d'état[17] but also Sheik Abeid Karume, Tanzania's first vice-president (until his death by assassination in April 1972) became the leader of Zanzibar in a revolutionary coup in which thousands were slaughtered.

As early as January 27, 1971, the Ugandan press reported that the Tanzanian military was being mobilized to invade Uganda. In response to the alleged mobilization, the Ugandan army and air force announced military maneuvers with live bombing, strafing, and rocketing near the Tanzanian border. For several months, the Ugandan press published accounts of clashes between the Ugandan army and Tanzanian forces, their Chinese advisors, and dissident Acholi and Lango guerrillas loyal to Obote. Newspaper accounts acknowledged that at least 1,000 Ugandan soldiers had died, but relatively few Tanzanian deaths were reported; clearly the killing— mostly of Acholi and Langi—was taking place within the Ugandan army. Of the continuous but unverified reports of intraarmy ethnic strife, the most serious were of the July 1971 killings (acknowledged by Amin as an attempted coup), which took place at Mbarara in the south, Moroto in the north, and Magamaga and Jinja in the east, and the alleged mass murders at Mutukula prison in January and February 1972.[18] In order to validate his claim that foreign advisors were involved in the "battles" between Uganda and Tanzania, General Amin publicly displayed the corpse of an alleged Chinese colonel serving with the Tanzanian army. The Tanzanian government identified the body as that of Hans Poppe, a senior police officer of German-African descent.

In addition to Tanzania, the governments of Zambia, Somalia, and Sudan expressed hostility to the new regime. Less than one week after Amin's coup, the Ugandan press first reported that the leftist military government in the Sudan was preparing to attack from the north. Obote's earlier willingness to harbor southern Sudanese refugees had led to strained relations between Sudan and

17. The Uganda crisis of 1966 was not, of course, a typical coup d'état. Obote, as prime minister, was the effective political leader before the crisis, and the presidency then was not an executive presidency.
18. See, for example, "Ovonji-Ocima Plan to Stage Coup," *Uganda Argus,* October 14, 1971; "Uganda Tribal Strife Seen Disrupting Army," *Los Angeles Times,* August 9, 1971; "Uganda Soldiers in Tribal Pogrom," *Observer,* February 13, 1972.

Uganda. Immediately before the coup in Uganda, however, there were indications of a move toward rapprochement. As a result of the Sudanese government's relaxation of its efforts at forced Arabization, the policy by which Khartoum attempted to erase southern identity, Obote began to repatriate refugees settled in Uganda's northern district. He also turned over the German mercenary, Rolf Steiner, who was accused of having worked with the Anyanya, and after June 1967 took steps to amend his government's earlier pro-Israeli stance. Sudan was, therefore, not likely to welcome the change of government in Uganda. Under these circumstances, General Amin claimed, in April 1972, that 500 pro-Obote guerrillas had crossed from southern Sudan and clashed with Ugandan troops;[19] and, because of President Jaafar al-Nimeiry's continued support of the Obote cause, he also expelled the Sudanese ambassador from Kampala.

Stories of would-be invasions were intended to perform domestic functions. In an attempt to stir up a nationalist response to external enemies, Amin sought to unify the citizens of Uganda behind him. The threat of armed invasion was also used to legitimize military rule and justify Uganda's rapidly rising defense expenditures.

In emphasizing the illegality of government change by force in neighboring Uganda, the Tanzanian president too was playing a domestic card. While he genuinely grieved for a close personal friend and ideological ally, destabilizing factors in Tanzania probably also contributed to Nyerere's insistence on the propriety of adherence to constitutional procedures. At the very time of the coup d'état in Uganda, seven individuals were on trial for treason in Dar es Salaam. (Another treason trial was being conducted in Zanzibar.) The Dar es Salaam trials came to an end in February 1971; of the group of seven accused which included Oscar Kambona (formerly general secretary of TANU and foreign minister) and was alleged to have plotted to overthrow the government and assassinate the president, six were found guilty. Moreover, Nyerere was subject to increasing criticism from the left and the moderates. His former first vice-president and president of Zanzibar's Revolutionary Council, Sheik Abeid Karume, criticized the government's

19. "Sudanese Invade Uganda Says New Ruler," *Observer,* January 31, 1971; and *African Recorder,* X, No. 11 (May 21–June 4, 1971), 2820.

policy of barring office holders from owning remunerative property, pointing out that private citizens—mostly Asians—had been permitted to do so. Hinting that Nyerere was not radical enough, Karume argued that citizenship should be restricted to black Africans and that all foreigners should leave the country by 1972. At the other end of the political spectrum, those with entrenched interests inevitably resented socialist attempts to curtail privilege and prerogative (for example, through nationalization of housing).

Nyerere's reaction to the Amin-led coup had a psychological aspect to it also. The president's hostility to military intervention in politics is related to the humiliation he suffered when, in 1964, he went into hiding and called in British troops to put down the army mutiny. Although this mutiny was not an attempt to take over the government, the army's action revealed the fragility of Tanzania's political institutions. Having previously considered the possibility of having no army in Tanzania, in 1964 Nyerere expressed his attitude to the military thus: "Those who brought this shame upon us are those who tried to intimidate our nation at the point of a gun."[20] Aware of the dangers of military intimidation, Nyerere may well have proposed a people's militia as a potential competitive source of power that could block armed intervention in politics.[21] Furthermore, dispatching Tanzanian troops to the Ugandan border removed the military from the capital at a dangerous time.

Although there is little doubt that troops were mobilized, the reports of a Tanzanian invasion lacked credibility. Military, geographical, logistical, and political factors all restricted Dar es Salaam's options. According to Booth's 1970 estimates of military strength in Africa,[22] Uganda's defense expenditure in 1968 was Shs. 143,000,000, Tanzania's Shs. 78,000,000; Uganda's military

20. Quoted by Ali A. Mazrui, "Anti-Militarism and Political Militancy in Tanzania," *Journal of Conflict Resolution*, XII, No. 3 (September 1968), 273. Mazrui, pointing to the many military idioms used in Tanzanian politics, argues that Tanzania has displayed, on the one hand, increasing militancy toward international problems of colonialism and racism and, on the other, a fundamental distrust of military solutions to domestic problems.

21. First, p. 429, indicates that similar attempts to create countervailing forces to neutralize the army have not been successful. Resort to special military formations in Ghana, Mali, Algeria, and Congo-Brazzaville, provoked the army to protect itself from other centers of armed autonomy.

22. Richard Booth, *The Armed Forces of African States, 1970* (London: Institute for Strategic Studies, 1970).

manpower consisted of 6,700 armed forces and 7,000 police, Tanzania's of 7,900 armed forces, 8,500 police, 100 naval men, and 4,000 reserves; Uganda's air force was composed of 450 men and 19 combat aircraft, Tanzania's of 300 men and no combat aircraft (Soviet MIG-17 interceptors expected).

Tanzania and Uganda share a common border only across Lake Victoria and in the remote area west of the lake. With Tanzania wanting in air power, possessed of a navy of only 100 men and four patrol boats (stationed on the Indian Ocean, not Lake Victoria), lacking a bridge or ferry across the Kagera River, and not able to contemplate a land invasion through Karagwe or Bukoba's rough terrain (this being next to impossible, particularly in terms of supply lines), how an invasion of Uganda was to be mounted is not clear.

With the exception of the Algerian-Moroccan war of 1963, which lasted only one month, there have been virtually no conventional international wars in Africa.[23] The ideological theme of pan-Africanism, as embodied in the OAU Charter, makes interference by one African state in the affairs of another difficult to justify. Nyerere has often asserted that African unity should have higher priority than support for ideological allies. In 1966, after Sekou Touré's announcement that Guinean troops would march on Ghana to reinstate Nkrumah, Nyerere advised: "Whether a Government is popular or unpopular or brought in by constitutional or unconstitutional means, it remains only the duty of citizens of that country to accept or change that Government. It does not justify any interference."[24]

But perhaps the most important political factor deterring Tanzania from invading Uganda was the prospect of the damaging and probably irreparable impact such an action would have on the East African Community. In the struggle for independence, Nyerere had been a symbol of East African unity. Having offered to postpone Tanganyika's independence for a few months, he warned: "To

23. Border skirmishes hardly qualify; in the Somalia-Ethiopia and Somalia-Kenya cases, the governments did not commit troops to full-scale battles. Scholars agree that the conflict potential of border skirmishes is minimal. Ravi L. Kapil, "On the Conflict Potential of Inherited Boundaries in Africa," *World Politics*, XVIII, No. 4 (July 1966), 656–73.
24. "Tanzanian Viewpoint," *Reporter* (Nairobi), March 25, 1966.

those who would wait [for federation] until the countries are separately independent I say that they do not know human nature. You must rule out the question of federation after we take our seats as sovereign states in the United Nations."[25] His prophecy was correct. The centrifugal tendencies of competing nationalisms had a divisive impact on attempts to forge pan-African unity. While Nyerere could offer to delay independence in 1960, a year later his attention was necessarily turned to Tanganyika's plethora of national problems. "In this sense," Nyerere said, "independence made us less free." Resigning his position as head of government (for two months) in order to reorganize TANU, and diverging increasingly from the policies of Uganda and Kenya, Nyerere proceeded to initiate policies in Tanzania that his East African neighbors were either unwilling or unable to pursue. The Tanzanian reaction to the coup in Uganda marks the fulfillment of Nyerere's prophecy. The evidence indicates that Tanzanian hostility provoked an initial rightist reaction within Uganda. While the first foreign policy pronouncements of the Amin government reaffirmed Obote's "progressive" foreign policy, subsequent statements called for close ties with the former colonial metropole, reversed Obote's militant stance on arms sales to South Africa, and endorsed the need for a dialogue with South Africa. Although a causal relationship cannot be established, the identification of Tanzania (as well as other "radical" states opposed to the Amin regime) with socialism undoubtedly also contributed to Uganda's move to the right in domestic affairs. Speaking at Lira stadium in June 1971, Amin said that Tanzania's socialist policy of nationalization of churches, mosques, and housing—property built out of people's sweat—"is wrong and should be condemned." He added that his government did not intend to construct empty theories on the lines of the "Common Man's Charter" and the "Arusha Declaration"; "We are not interested in political ideologies and slogans to deceive people."[26]

In a political, nonfunctional sense, the East African Community appeared doomed to collapse unless a face-saving solution could be found. Tanzanian officials accused Amin of sabotaging the Com-

25. Thomas M. Franck, *East African Unity through Law* (New Haven: Yale University Press, 1964), quoting the *Times* (London), November 5, 1960, p. 6.
26. "President Amin Condemns Nationalisation," *People,* June 21, 1971.

munity by usurping power, not only in Uganda but in East Africa as well. While the Amin regime assailed the Tanzanian government for preventing the new director-general of harbours, Mr. Disamunyo, from entering his office, officials in Dar es Salaam insisted that Amin had violated Articles 74 and 76 of the Treaty for East African Cooperation by appointing two directors-general (for airways and harbours) to his entourage of ministers and replacing the chairman of the East African Railways Corporation. The Treaty of Cooperation stipulates that the appointment of chairmen and directors-general to Community corporations is the responsibility of the East African Authority, composed of the legal heads of state of the three member states. Since Amin's nominations had not been approved by the Authority, Nyerere insisted that they were illegal.[27] Amin's initial reaction was something less than conciliatory. Uganda, he said, must have assurance that Community property located in Tanzania would not be nationalized like other buildings.[28] Having accused Tanzania of preventing the East African minister for communications, research, and social services—Z. H. K. Bigirwenkya, a Ugandan—from performing his duties, the Amin government declared the East African Community minister—John Malecela, a Tanzanian—persona non grata; the director-general of the East African Development Bank—Idi Simba, another Tanzanian—was also ordered to leave Uganda. Uganda's borders with Tanzania and Rwanda were closed, East African Airlines flights connecting Uganda and Tanzania were discontinued, and all movement of vessels on Lake Victoria between Tanzania and Uganda was brought to a halt. Amin indicated that he would not sign the East African Community appropriations bill unless Tanzania demonstrated that it wanted the Community to continue; he also advanced strong objections to the Community secretary-general's decision, made with the tacit approval of Kenya and Tanzania, to appropriate the Shs. 303,000,000 budget and to cover the salaries of 15,000 Community officials.

As the polemics continued, the positions of the two leaders appeared increasingly irreconcilable. Nyerere maintained that there was a distinction between "necessary compromises" to avert col-

27. "Comment," *Standard,* February 19, 1971.
28. *Africa Research Bulletin* (Economic, Financial and Technical Series), VIII, No. 6 (July 15, 1971), 2065A.

lapse of the Community and recognition of an illegal regime; however, in tacitly acknowledging Amin as the man whose signature was needed on the appropriations bill, Nyerere was offering a form of de facto recognition. Amin insisted that if Uganda was to cooperate in the Community, Nyerere must state in writing his "commitment" to the "letter and spirit" of the Community; in effect, he was demanding de jure recognition.[29]

Within Uganda, manifestations of ethnic divisions were increasing, becoming particularly apparent in intraarmy strife. His efforts to use external threats to forge internal unity having had little success, Amin realized that normalization of relations with neighboring states would be a more viable strategy in the quest for legitimacy. With President Kenyatta serving as mediator, a compromise between Uganda and Tanzania was reached in November; Nyerere approved Uganda's nominees for various posts in the East African Community, and Amin signed the appropriations bill and lifted the ban on Tanzanian Community officials entering Uganda. Before the accord, in June, a new secretary-general, Charles Maina of Kenya, was named to succeed Z. Bigirwenkya. This appointment was significant in that it demonstrated the Community's flexibility in establishing means to make crucial decisions in the face of acrimonious relations between two member states; although the Treaty of Cooperation vests power to appoint secretaries-general in the Authority, the announcement of Maina's appointment referred not to the Authority but to the Community. Paradoxically, a situation that almost brought about the demise of the organization may instead have rendered the Community stronger for having weathered the storm.

The internationalization of Uganda's political violence extended beyond the subregion to the regional (continental) realm. In response to Nyerere's hostility, the Uganda government sent a telegram to the executive secretary of the Liberation Committee of the OAU in Dar es Salaam informing members that, because of Tanzania's posture, Uganda would not be represented at the Liberation Committee meeting. Subsequently, General Amin announced that continuing border skirmishes with guerrillas were leading

29. *Africa Research Bulletin* (Economic, Financial and Technical Series), VII, No. 7 (August 15, 1971), 2093B; "East African Community: Amin Sticks to His Guns," *Financial Times*, July 29, 1971.

Uganda to discontinue its Shs. 500,000 annual contribution to the financing of guerrilla training in Tanzania. Already operating with a meager budget (and with many contributions outstanding), badly divided over the issues of dialogue with South Africa and rivalries among liberation movements, and handicapped by member states' lack of commitment,[30] the OAU was presented with another knotty problem.

Before the coup of January 25, 1971, the next meeting of the Assembly of Heads of State and Government had been scheduled to be held in Kampala in June 1971. With Yugoslav workers laboring day and night to complete the extravagant conference hall, and with the structure itself having become an important symbol in Amin's quest for recognition, the OAU Council of Ministers was stalemated over whether to seat the Amin or the Obote delegation in Addis Ababa. Unable to agree on this issue, the February session of the ministerial council adjourned sine die on March 1.

Leaders of many of the countries that opposed Uganda's military government argued that to convene the meeting of heads of state in Kampala would be to provide the new regime with a form of de facto recognition. And had the June meeting been held in Kampala, there is little doubt that Guinea, Somalia, Tanzania, Zambia (whose president, Kenneth Kaunda, was due to chair the meeting), and the Sudan would have refused to attend. President Kaunda, who had expressed solidarity with the militant position of Obote and Nyerere at Singapore, and established a reputation for making Zambia the southern frontier of black power in Africa, lobbied to change the meeting place from Kampala to Lusaka, Addis Ababa, or Kinshasa. Accusing OAU officials of prejudice and discriminatory behavior,[31] Amin's delegation to the ministerial conference issued an ultimatum, then withdrew it, and finally threatened to pull out of the organization altogether. Ultimately, the venue for the conference was changed to the OAU's headquarters in Addis Ababa. General Amin argued that the Charter had been violated

30. For commentary on these problems, see my, "The Development of Post-Colonial African Regionalism and the Formation of the OAU," *Kroniek van Afrika,* XI, No. 2 (June 1971), 83–105.
31. Amin referred to the fact that Zambia's Kenneth Kaunda led the summit meeting, Somalia's Omar Arteh chaired the ministerial conference, and Guinea's Diallo Telli served as administrative secretary-general of the OAU.

and boycotted the meeting; Uganda's new minister of foreign affairs, Wanume Kibedi, contending that already half of the forty members of the OAU had governments that had come to power through a coup d'état asked whether Zambia and some of the other anti-Amin states could be sure of not experiencing a coup before June.

In asking such a question, Kibedi, aware of Zambia's domestic problems—particularly heightened tribal sentiment and charges of widespread corruption in government—may have been thinking of the well-known demonstration effect in African politics, whereby political violence in one country sets off a reaction in others. Insofar as grievances are generalized, a climate favoring military opportunism is pandemic to Africa; thus, any coup is a potential catalyst for emulative behavior. Boumedienne's Algerian coup of June 19, 1965, heralded a rash of coups in Zaire, Dahomey, the Central African Republic, Upper Volta, Nigeria, Ghana, and Burundi. In early 1971 it remained to be seen whether the first military coup to have occurred in Africa in more than a year, and the first ever in East Africa, would trigger the aspirations of generals in other African states.

Although a causal relationship between the Uganda coup and later subversive behavior in Kenya cannot be established, the events of January 25, 1971, did not pass unnoticed by those who plotted to unseat the Kenyatta government. Just how much Nyerere's stand against Amin contributed to the perceptions and motivations of the conspirators in Kenya is difficult to say; however, a Kenyan group was said to have dispatched a Kenyan senior lecturer from Makerere University to Tanzania to seek aid from the president. Asked to provide thirty-nine machine guns, moral support, and a military presence on the Kenya-Tanzania border, Nyerere categorically refused. He is quoted as having replied: "Not against Mzee's Government. If it was Malawi, I would think about it. But not Kenya and definitely not when Mzee is alive."[32] One of the conspirators testified that the Kenyan chief of defense staff was also approached; another indicated that a Kenyan M.P. was helping to recruit Kalenjin-speaking tribesmen in the armed forces to the cause of removing the government.[33] Thus, while the links between the Uganda coup

32. "Nyerere Shocked, Plot Trial Told," *Uganda Argus,* June 5, 1971.
33. "Plotters Had Links in High Places," *Ibid.,* June 8, 1971.

and subsequent political violence in Kenya are tenuous at best, those convicted of plotting the overthrow of the Kenya government clearly did think that Nyerere would be willing to consider providing support for action against a neighboring government.

Finally, beyond the region, the potential internationalization of Ugandan political violence had extraregional dimensions. In view of Obote's militant stance at Singapore on the issue of British arms sales to South Africa, London and Pretoria were delighted with the change of government in Kampala. Just a week before the coup, 700 British troops were dispatched to the coast of Kenya. The reasons for this move, and why it took place when it did, remain matters of controversy. British government officials explain that the troops were posted to East Africa for regular joint exercises with Kenyan forces; quite probably, however, they were sent to protect British lives in the event of violence following Heath's announcement of arms sales to South Africa. (According to another interpretation, the dispatch of these troops indicates British involvement in the Uganda coup. However, there is simply no evidence to support this view.)

In the British press, the ouster of Obote was a cause célèbre. The *Times* of London commented: "The news of a coup d'état comes as a surprise only because it has been so long delayed," while the *Daily Express* editorialized: "It would be absurd for Britain to base her policy on the shrill cries of leaders who are here today and gone tomorrow." In an article entitled "Good Riddance to Obote," the *Daily Telegraph* described the Obote regime as "corrupt, racist and cruel." In Johannesburg, the political correspondent of the *Star* concluded his account of the Uganda coup with the gratuitous suggestion that the events of January 25 "underlined the tremendous role South Africa could play in helping Africa towards economic, social and political stability."[34]

Opinion among some members of Britain's Conservative party and South Africa's Nationalist party veered toward the argument that Africans cannot govern themselves and, in such circumstances, could hardly proffer advice on matters of British foreign policy. The Tories and Afrikaners had good reason to be pleased with

34. "The New Men in Uganda," *Times*, January 26, 1971; "His Exit Cheered in the U.K.," and "Obote, The Cool Tyrant," *Star* (Johannesburg), January 30, 1971.

Amin's early statements on Britain and South Africa. After announcing that he would not leave the Commonwealth over the issue of arms sales, Amin said that some African leaders, such as Obote, could not solve their problems at home, and continued: "How can they, therefore, start talking about solving the problems of South Africa or Rhodesia?"[35] In a similar vein, just two days before the opening of the ministerial conference in Addis Ababa he issued a statement that had a major impact on many delegates' views of the new regime in Uganda: "Everybody is talking of South Africa but we have another South Africa in Southern Sudan where Catholics and Protestants are not allowed to go to Church. When worshippers went to Church in Southern Sudan, people with machine guns killed them and burned their houses. This must be solved first before arms to South Africa."[36] Coming out in favor of dialogue with South Africa, Amin said that he would be willing to visit Pretoria if the OAU approved. Subsequently he offered to send a ten-man fact-finding mission to South Africa, an offer Prime Minister Vorster rejected. In less conciliatory gestures, the general suggested that Uganda should serve as a training base for land and air forces for the defense of Africa, and extended an invitation to ten young South African and five Namibian students to study in Uganda; whether these overtures represented merely the impulsive moves of a military leader unschooled in diplomacy or a coherent strategy—well advised or ill advised—for bringing an end to Pretoria's racist policies remained to be seen.

The events of January 25, 1971, also produced theories concerning the involvement of one (directly) or both (indirectly) parties to the Middle East dispute in relations with Uganda. Obote's supporters accused Israel of duplicity, if not complicity, in the ouster of the former president. There are five pieces of evidence, all of them circumstantial, unsubstantiated, and unconfirmed, bearing on the question of Israeli involvement. First, General Amin and

35. *Africa Research Bulletin* (Political, Social and Cultural Series), VIII, No. 2 (March 15, 1971), 2027C. In June, Amin thanked the British colonial government for establishing sound administration in Uganda and for working hard to educate "our children." " 'Political' Civil Servants Face the Axe," *Sunday Nation* (Nairobi), June 20, 1971.

36. "We Won't Quit Commonwealth over Arms," *Uganda Argus*, February 24, 1971.

Colonel Bar-Lev, former head of Israel's military mission in Uganda, were close personal friends. In addition to its military functions, the Israeli mission in Uganda advised on the intelligence operations of Obote's aide, Akena Adoko. Colin Legum reported that in the months immediately preceding the coup the relationship between Adoko and the Israelis cooled noticeably, while Amin and the Israelis drew closer together.[37] Second, just after the coup Uganda's Moslem head of state showed little reluctance in displaying his pro-Israeli posture. On at least one occasion, General Amin, driving his jeep around Kampala without a bodyguard, was accompanied by only one companion—identified as an Israeli. Third, in a display of military might following the mobilization of the Tanzanian army, five French-designed, Israeli-built aircraft flew in neat formation over Kampala; sources in the capital insisted that the pilots were Israeli. Fourth, at the February 5 swearing-in of ministers, Israeli officials were prominently seated in the front ranks. Fifth, Obote's delegates to the OAU ministerial council meeting in Addis Ababa accused the Amin delegates of relying on six Israeli advisors.[38]

Did Israel in fact participate in the ouster of the pro-Khartoum Obote government, in order to further her strategy of keeping the Sudanese army tied down by aiding the southern rebels?[39] Was Israel trying to establish Uganda as the southern front of its Middle East campaign? Did Israel hope to locate a striking force at the source of the Nile?

Undoubtedly Israel was initially pleased about the coup. But while it is easy to hypothesize about possible Israeli motives for

37. "Sudanese Invade Uganda Says New Ruler," *Observer*, January 31, 1971.

38. The Israeli Foreign Ministry viewed Obote's allegations as an attempt to dissuade African states, particularly North African states, from recognizing the new regime. "Plot against Kenya Says General Amin," *Uganda Argus*, March 4, 1971; "Israeli Aid to African Nations," *Uganda Argus*, March 5, 1971.

39. For discussion of Israeli aid to the Anyanya, via Uganda, see Arthur Jay Klinghoffer, "Israel in Africa: The Strategy of Aid," *Africa Report*, XVII, No. 4 (April 1972), 14. According to Abel Jacob, "Israel's Military Aid to Africa, 1960–66," *Journal of Modern African Studies*, IX, No. 2 (August 1971), 170–72, wherever political structures are weak in Africa and the future political role of the army cannot be underestimated, Israel follows a strategy of attempting to befriend those with the greatest potential influence.

involvement, there are no hard facts implicating the Israelis. General Amin, facing the pressing tasks of postcoup consolidation needed advisors. Since the Israelis were pleased about the coup, could provide expertise, and lacked ethnic ties to existing political forces in Uganda, the new government turned to them as potentially valuable allies. This does not mean, however, that the Israelis had a hand in planning the coup.

Fourteen months after the coup, Ugandan-Israeli relations changed suddenly. Amin left little doubt about the future role of Israeli advisors in Uganda: the Israeli Embassy in Kampala was closed, and all Israeli advisors were asked to leave. The official story was that an Israeli newspaper, *Davar*, spoke of Amin canceling a trip to Egypt because of mounting opposition at home and that for Amin—since, in his view, the newspaper account was obviously based on intelligence reports coming from the Israeli Embassy in Kampala—this confirmed that the Israelis were planning subversive activities. But other explanations have been advanced for the expulsion of the Israelis. One suggestion is that, on a trip to Israel, the Ugandan president—a devout Moslem—asked to be flown to Mecca and was offended by the refusal of his Israeli pilots. Certainly the inconsistency between General Amin's genuine devotion to Islam and desire to establish himself as a Moslem leader on the one hand, and his reliance on the Israelis on the other, contributed to the rupture; clearly Israel's considerable influence in Uganda undermined Amin's credibility in the Moslem world. A further factor was the monetary crisis. Uganda's debt to Israel was increasing, while her foreign exchange reserves were already badly depleted; at the same time, there was the prospect of receiving aid from oil-rich Libya. When Amin visited Libya in February 1972, he joined Colonel Mummar El Qaddafi in condemning Israel as the aggressor in the Middle East and supporting the Arab "struggle against Zionism and imperialism."[40] Finally, the change in the political climate in the Sudan, which removed a binding force from Ugandan-Israeli relations and provided additional rationale for a shift in Uganda's foreign policy, was a key element in Amin's volte

40. "Eban Sees Plot in Ugandan Break," *New York Times,* April 11, 1972; "Ugandan Expulsion Seen a Setback for Israel," *New York Times,* April 22, 1972; and *Africa Research Bulletin* (Political, Social and Cultural Series), IX, No. 2 (March 15, 1972), 2369C.

face. As long as the civil conflict in the Sudan continued, Amin and the Israelis had common objectives; once it was settled, Uganda's national interests were best served by improving relations with neighbors to the north.

The potential for the internationalization of Ugandan political violence extended a step further, to include the superpowers. Israeli decision-makers were aware of the danger of the extension of Egyptian influence through southern Sudan and East Africa to the Indian Ocean, and uneasiness over the increasing Soviet presence in the Indian Ocean, coupled with Obote's pro-Arab stance after June 1967, served to enhance the importance Israel attached to keeping the Sudanese army tied down. Tel Aviv deemed it advantageous to have a neighbor of the Sudan friendly to the Israeli-assisted Anyanya rebels, particularly in view of the fact that Egypt and Libya were supplying aircraft to Khartoum. Since much of Israel's weaponry has been purchased in the U.S. and Egyptian arms were largely supplied by the U.S.S.R., the situation was, for a period, one in which Uganda's political violence had been internationalized to the point of providing an invitation to great power involvement.[41]

In the second half of the twentieth century, protracted political violence between major powers characteristically takes place within a single nation, most typically through surrogates in the Third World.[42] Injecting an added element of instability into international relations, political violence in Uganda displayed the potential to escalate well beyond East Africa.

Political Prognosis

The consequences of the internationalization of political violence in Uganda must be viewed within the context of the fluidity of African international relations. Inter-African diplomacy is conducted among relative equals, and the distribution of power within Africa is diffuse rather than hierarchical or polar.[43] The fluidity of

41. The U.S. became more directly involved when an American newspaper reporter and an American university lecturer disappeared. Investigating a story about a massacre at an army barracks near Mbarara, the two Americans are said to have been tortured and murdered on the orders of Lieutenant-Colonel W. F. Ali, commander of the Simba Battalion.

42. Falk, p. 70.

43. I. William Zartman, "Africa as a Subordinate State System in Inter-

inter-African relations is shown in the shifts that occur in the balance of interests and forces in East Africa. The Amin-led coup represented the completion of one full rotation during which each of the three East African countries took its turn at being the one to diverge most from the others. (Noting that the differences between states alter according to the variables selected, we can rely on certain indices that appear to be the most salient for international integration at a given time.) In the immediate postcolonial period, Uganda was the most divergent state: the least Swahili, away from the coast, smallest in size, and most opposed to federation.[44] When Obote created a unitary form of government, established a one-party state, and directed the Move to the Left via socialist construction, Kenya—the least centralized, wealthiest, and most capitalist of the three—became the exception. With the take-over by a moderate regime in Uganda, radical Tanzania assumed the role of odd-man-out.

Uganda shares a common border with Zaire, also ruled by the military. When Uganda was moving to the right, Tanzania cast its diplomatic nets toward the only other remaining member of the Mulungushi club, Zambia, and Somalia to the north. (But not the Sudan: for although the ideological proclivities of the Sudanese leaders were toward the radical states, nonideological criteria of national interests included avoidance of subversive actions from the territory to the south. Normalization of relations with Uganda thus tended to take precedence over an alignment with a Tanzania-Zambia-Somalia grouping.) This picture of fluctuating alignments bears a resemblance to Africa's protobalance of power period (roughly 1959–1963), characterized by a mobile pattern of alliances and counteralliances in which no one group of states was able to dominate the system.[45] Although such realignments are unlikely

national Relations," *International Organization*, XIII, No. 3 (Summer 1967), 550.

44. Nye, p. 192.

45. The "protobalance of power" period, during which two competitive alliance systems (the Casablanca and Brazzaville-Monrovia groups) vied for hegemony, is described by I. William Zartman, *International Relations in the New Africa* (Englewood Cliffs: Prentice Hall, 1966).

Only five weeks after the coup, reports of increased functional cooperation between Uganda and Kenya, as well as between Uganda and Zaire, began to appear in the press. See, for example, "500m/- Pipe Project," *Uganda Argus*, to ossify into formal alliance systems, the contagion effect could spill over to the continent at large and contribute to a polarization of moderate and radical states. The desideratum for African states opposed to counterrevolutionary trends is to institutionalize progressive change.[46] The institutionalization of progressive change requires a realization that: (1) certain problems are the by-products of modernization (and the structural relationships between industrial states and the Third World), and not merely the doing of corrupt, misguided politicians; (2) as a consequence of these problems, political violence will characterize Africa for years to come; and (3) if political violence is to be localized, rather than internationalized as protracted insurrection, the right of national governments to recognize other governments—one of the prerogatives of a state system superimposed on Africa from without—must not be allowed to develop into a system of opportunism.

Political violence in Africa can be institutionalized either as in Latin America (plus ça change, plus c'est la même chose) or by organizing progressive change. Insofar as the latter is the more desirable alternative, there is an overwhelming need for a reordering of African international organization. The imbroglio produced

March 5, 1971, and "Uganda-Congo Tours Link," *Uganda Argus*, March 3, 1971. In a subsequent meeting between Presidents Mobutu and Amin, proposals were put forward on establishing a joint technical commission or study of the proposed trans-African highway, embarking on a hydroelectric project on their common border near the northern end of Lake Albert (later renamed Lake Mobutu Sese Seko) and taking steps to improve cooperation in commerce, communication, and tourism. See *Africa Research Bulletin* (Economic, Financial and Technical Series), IX, No. 1 (February 15, 1972), 2265B, C.

46. Contributing to the counterrevolutionary trend in the year before the Uganda coup were such factors as: Portugal's escape from retribution after employing Guinean exiles and hiring mercenaries to attempt to overthrow a black sovereign state; the decision of two powerful Western states (Britain and the U.S.), who claimed to be champions of human rights and self-determination, to withdraw from the UN Special Committee on Decolonization; Britain's announcement, using the pretext of honoring the Simonstown Agreement, of its decision to sell arms to South Africa; endorsement of the need for dialogue with South Africa by some of the conservative Francophone states (with fluctuating support from Busia's Ghana and encouragement from France, a seller of arms to Vorster's government); and South Africa's action, while attempting to seduce African states into engaging in diplomatic relations, in offering a plebiscite in Namibia.

by the Ugandan coup suggests an initial step that should be taken: questions of recognition should be institutionalized as a collective responsibility of the OAU. In view of the subtle ambiguity surrounding intervention and nonintervention, the OAU should use its moral influence to proscribe intraregional intervention—whether diplomatic or military—by national actors; specific acts of intervention should be identified and condemned as impermissible.[47]

Although the legality of the interventionary practices of a group of states acting in concert is a matter of considerable controversy in jurisprudence, sheer numbers clearly do not confer legality on an act that would otherwise be illegal. If a group of states commits an act of intervention, that act can scarcely be deemed to have greater legality than when performed by one state. However, several states may organize to form an international juridical community and accede to a multilateral treaty; if the treaty stipulates that each state agrees to accord the right of intervention to the juridical community, in certain situations and under specified circumstances, intracommunity intervention can be legal.[48]

As a form of interventionary diplomacy, recognition is not so much a question of jurisprudential principle as of political discretion. In the absence of a competent international organ to determine the existence of a duly constituted government, the prevailing practice is for each government to perform this function for itself, and hence to grant or refuse recognition according to its perception of its national interests. But if progressive change is to be institutionalized in Africa, it is in the best interests of the states concerned to find a new method to replace the individualized, decentralized, and uncoordinated practice of recognition.

But is inter-African diplomacy consensual to the extent that recognition could be collectivized? Does collectivization presuppose a high degree of political integration? Would an unsuccessful attempt at international institution-building weaken the foundations of pan-African unity? Rather than inducing stability, might efforts toward collectivization come to symbolize the absence of international order? If an OAU organ for collective recognition were

47. For a discussion of collective recognition, see Falk, p. 138.
48. Ann Wynen Thomas and A. J. Thomas, Jr., *Non-Intervention: The Law and Its Import in the Americas* (Dallas: Southern Methodist University Press, 1956), pp. 98, 99.

created, might a situation arise in which OAU policy was at odds
with Chapter VIII of the UN Charter, which stipulates that regional
arrangements, agencies, and their activities must be consistent with
the purposes and principles of the global organization? Given the
counterrevolutionary trends to be perceived in African international
relations and the numerical predominance of moderate states,
would the chances of institutionalizing progressive change be better
if recognition were collectivized under the auspices of a global
international organization? Finally, is there a possibility that a
pan-African organ vested with the power of recognition might have
an interventionary impact such that it became a coup-maker in its
own right?

These potentially negative considerations must be balanced
against the possible advantages of a change. Collectivization of
recognition would prevent the delictual situation in which states
grant premature recognition and thereby practice diplomatic intervention. Conversely, it would preclude states from denying the
legitimate right of international personality to other states. Hence
the anomalous case of a community existing as a state in relation
to some states but not others could not arise.[49] Thus, collectivization
is a technique that can be employed to avoid the weakening of
international order caused by the individualized use of state power.

Realpolitik suggests that the collectivization of recognition should
be regarded as a desirable but unlikely course. History demonstrates
that drastic structural change in international affairs is precipitated
by shock treatment, and more often than not, for the shock treatment
to be strong enough it must be of the magnitude of an international
or world war.[50] Although it did not have the physical impact of an
international war, the Amin coup may have had a sufficiently de-
structive effect, in an already badly divided state system, for debate
on restructuring inter-African diplomacy to be initiated. Whether, in
view of the ideological differences and recurring cleavages that have
marked the history of the OAU, attempts at restructuring could go
beyond mere debate is, however, open to question. And, even as a
modest first step, is the recommendation for collective recognition
realistic?

49. H. Lauterpacht, *Recognition in International Law* (Cambridge, Eng.:
Cambridge University Press, 1947), pp. 8, 9, 66, 68, and 142–44.
50. Falk, pp. 8, 35.

At first glance, it would appear that the Ugandan coup and the internationalization of political violence contributed to the OAU's decline as a viable force in inter-African affairs. Closer inspection of the implications indicates, however, that the crisis in Uganda may have created a fleeting opportunity to reform the OAU to the satisfaction of both radical and moderate member states. Such an opportunity must be grasped at a moment reasonably close to the events that stimulated debate on issues of long-term importance and at the same time sufficiently distant from those events that a modicum of detachment from the immediate crisis has developed. The balance is delicate. Taking the Uganda coup and the internationalization of political violence as the issues underlining the need to collectivize recognition practices in the OAU, the long-term implications of such a reordering would be consistent with the ideological interests of the radical states, which have long demanded stepped-up functions for the OAU; the moderate states, for their part, could agree to at least the short-term implications of greater OAU authority in Uganda-type situations so long as the organization was bound by the will of the majority.

African statesmen have a choice. They can allow similar crises to occur and divisive tendencies to remain unchecked. Or they can capitalize upon converging interests in a postcoup situation to affirm and encourage integrative behavior. Heretofore, unless tension has erupted into outright conflict and a member state has brought a complaint to the OAU, the organization has tended to refrain from searching for fundamental answers to the problems that caused tensions.[51] Insofar as the OAU has been effective in the management of conflict, success has been achieved in normalizing relations among African states; its performance in finding durable solutions rather than short-term settlements has not been good, however.[52] Berhanykun Andemicael notes that by failing to deal with the underlying issues, the OAU may be missing opportunities to solve problems that give rise to crises.[53] In good part, the reluctance of the OAU to expand its functions can be explained by

51. Berhanykun Andemicael, *Peaceful Settlement among African States: United Nations and the Organization of African Unity* (New York: United Nations Institute for Training and Research, 1972), p. 50.
52. *Ibid.*, pp. 50, 54.
53. *Ibid.*, p. 50.

the classic dilemma of international organizations: If sufficient consensus exists for the performance of conflict-management functions, is there any need for an international organization? On the other hand, if consensus does not exist, is the international organization rendered ineffective?

Yet this is too rigid an argument. As Ernst Haas suggests, crises that create tension between organizational objectives and hostile or competing environmental pressures can be manipulated into having an integrative impact. Politics being the art of the possible, leaders can manage the stress between international organization and the challenges posed by disagreements in such a way as to further the growth of international community.[54] In the tension between the aspiration to build political pan-Africanism and the internationalization of political violence arising from the Ugandan coup, the creation of an OAU committee on collective recognition might be a modest step toward "upgrading the common interest" and encouraging "creative leadership," thereby serving as a catalyst for integrative behavior. If compliance on recognition practices were secured, the OAU might perform additional integrative functions. In this sense, the coup in Uganda cannot be said to have initiated "the politics of destruction,"[55] but can be seen as having provided an opportunity for the construction of more resolute pan-African unity.

But why should this coup provide such an opportunity? Given the frequency of changes of government in Africa through coups d'état, what makes the Uganda coup different from others? Did not the Togolese coup of 1963, the Ghanaian coup of 1966, and the

54. Ernst B. Haas, *Beyond the Nation-State: Functionalism and International Organization* (Stanford: Stanford University Press, 1964), pp. 101–13, and *idem, The Uniting of Europe: Political, Social and Economic Forces 1950–1957* (Stanford: Stanford University Press, 1958), p. xiv. Community formation is directed by individuals and groups who turn toward supranational unity and "upgrade the common interest" when such a course appears profitable.

55. Semakula Kiwanuka, one of Amin's delegates to the ministerial con-ference, warned that what was happening Addis Ababa in February 1971 could destroy the OAU; the organization could be crippled, he said, by the determined politics of destruction and brinksmanship that dispense with the Charter when it is convenient to do so ("The Politics of Destruction and the Organization of African Unity," a lecture delivered at Makerere University, Kampala, March 8, 1971).

Nigerian coups of 1966 raise many of the same issues? The Ugandan coup became a contentious issue in African international relations because of its timing (that is, it took place immediately after Obote's forceful stand at Singapore) and the consequent ramifications in terms of pan-Africanism. The sudden ouster of one of Africa's militant leaders brought the practicality of the radical cause into question. The very doubt cast on the ability of the radicals to maintain momentum helps to explain the intransigent reaction of other radical statesmen. Yet it was not merely the ouster of a leader who advanced principled stands on issues of foreign policy that caused deep concern throughout Africa—after all, many senior statesmen in Africa disagreed with Obote's foreign policies; the Ugandan president's overthrow also caused dismay because Obote had succeeded in holding the reins of power for over eight years in an African state suffering from serious ethnic differences. Insofar as this latter problem is pandemic to Africa, the Amin coup precipitated a crisis that assumed generalized international significance.

Irrespective of whether the suggested reordering of recognition practices takes place, the Ugandan coup constitutes an additional precedent for African diplomatic norms. Compared with relations between "established" nations, those between African states are characterized by normative ambiguity. Relations between the superpowers generally follow codified rules of international law and are governed by tacit understandings necessitated by the ominous specter of nuclear war. In 1956, the sympathy of the American public was overwhelmingly on the side of the Hungarian rebels; American decision-makers realized, however, that the Soviet Union saw its vital interests as being involved in this sphere of influence and little serious consideration was given, therefore, to dispatching American troops. Similarly, in 1962, decision-makers in Moscow recognized that Washington would go to war over Cuba and therefore withdrew the Soviet missiles. At times the boundaries of tolerance are fuzzy—Khrushchev installed the missiles —but the threshold exists. In the African subsystem of international relations few clear-cut norms exist. The internationalization of political violence generated by the Ugandan coup represents one more precedent-setting step in inter-African diplomacy. In the Ugandan case, the potential manifestations of internationalized political violence were of far greater significance than the expressions of interstate physical violence actually occurring. The impact of the coup on inter-African diplomacy indicates that while nonintervention and respect for a state's territorial integrity may be desirable norms, these doctrines are simply too ambiguous. The collectivization of recognition practices, under the auspices of the OAU, could represent a first step in promoting international order and progressive change.

The creation of viable structures of international cooperation cannot, of course, be equated with progressive change. Since the majority of African states are "moderate," international organs in Africa, even if "progressive" in terms of the development of international law, could be "counterprogressive" in terms of promoting social change in Africa. Nor can it be supposed that the collectivization of recognition would automatically or necessarily spill over to promote integrative behavior. "Spill-over" must be demonstrated rather than asserted. Nevertheless, there does appear to be a reciprocal relationship between the two desiderata for African international relations, international organs for cooperation and progressive change. In view of the balkanization of Africa, progressive change is unlikely to develop on a piecemeal basis; its promotion presupposes the creation and utilization of more viable structures for international cooperation. Thus, it is to be hoped that the ultimate significance of the Ugandan coup lies in its contribution to international integration through seemingly disintegrative national behavior.

CHAPTER 9

Ideology and

Black Nationalism

When General Amin seized power, he seemed about to usher in Uganda's Thermidor. Just as after the coup that ousted Robespierre and the French revolutionaries, in postcoup Uganda the previous regime's programs for radical change were, it appeared, about to be reversed. Ironically, however, the man responsible for unseating Obote accomplished many of the former president's goals, albeit by very different means. Under Amin, Ugandans asserted local control, speeded indigenization, and challenged foreign enterprise. While canceling Obote's principal programs, Amin brought about many of their desired ends. As compared with the ideological fervor that marked the late Obote years, ideology became less important and certainly less calculated under Amin. Nevertheless, measures introduced by the new regime had far-reaching repercussions in terms of normative values.

In the 1971–1974 period, black nationalism was the emerging orientation, with anti-imperialism an important concomitant theme. Amin's "war of economic liberation" resulted in the appropriation of large amounts of wealth and, with the uprooting of great numbers of Israelis, Asians, non-Ugandan Africans, Britons, American Peace Corps volunteers, and foreign missionaries, the ouster of almost the entire expatriate community. Whatever the human suffering caused by these dislocations, Amin can be said to have taken the preliminary steps toward placing Ugandan Africans in control of their own affairs.

In an analysis of ideology in Uganda in the early 1970's, the emphasis shifts from the societal level to the psychological and, to a lesser degree, cultural. As a result of the change of regime and the personality of the new president, ideology was expressed in terms of individualized appeal and rustic values rather than institutionalized norms. The emergence of black nationalism in Uganda, and its relationship to social structure, can be explored by reviewing the major events of the postcoup period in the areas of intramilitary affairs, civil-military relations, and foreign policy. This examination will permit an assessment of the ideological implications, in terms of how the regime sought to adjust or neglected to adjust normative values to changes in the sociopolitical system.

Intramilitary Affairs[1]

Before the coup, the Ugandan army was already well paid in comparison with the military elsewhere in Africa. In addition to their regular salaries, the soldiers enjoyed extra perquisites because of the extended emergency regulations in Buganda. When Amin became president, one of his first steps was to enlarge the armed forces. While reliable figures are difficult to obtain, one observer has estimated that the size of the army increased from 9,000 in 1971 to about 20,000 three years later.[2]

Within a year of the coup, the military's share of the development budget had soared from Shs. 51,000,000 to Shs. 160,000,000, or 27 percent of the total; military expenditures represented 64 percent of the increase in the total recurrent budget.[3] After education, defense was Uganda's greatest expense. Added to this enormous bill was the cost of a new naval base on Lake Victoria. Yet, despite the jump in postcoup military spending, Uganda's third development plan called for a "temporary deceleration in the expansion of social services" on the grounds that cutbacks were necessary because of the stringent financial situation facing the country.[4]

1. This discussion stresses the consequences of military intervention and the demands imposed by a governing role in terms of heightened fragmentation among the soldiers; but, as in Chapter 7, no systematic attempt is made to identify competing interests among branches of the armed forces or between commissioned and noncommissioned officers. Vital information is lacking, and there is no way to confirm some of the reports coming from Uganda.
2. "Hired Guns and Fear Keep Amin in Power," *Observer,* March 31, 1974.
3. J. C. Howard Elliott, "The Uganda Budget 1971–72: An Economic Evaluation," *The Uganda Economic Journal,* I, No. 1 (December 1971), 25.
4. *Uganda's Third Five Year Development Plan 1971/2–1975/6* (Entebbe: Government Printer, 1972), p. 16.

As president, Amin employed three techniques to control the military. First, he purged the army of particular ethnic groups and liquidated rival power formations. Second, in order to stymie the development of effective opposition, he initiated a process of constant shuffling within the command structure, continually promoting and demoting officers so that younger, less experienced men replaced their predecessors. Third, he created countervailing sources of armed force, accountable directly to himself: a special bodyguard, the Public Safety Unit, and the State Research Department. Directed by Major L. M. Ozi (until he fell into disfavor), the State Research Department was the most dreaded group; many Ugandans regarded it as responsible for the abduction and killing of both military personnel and prominent civilians.

When the purges began in 1971, northerners, who, because of their ethnic affiliations, had been identified as allies of Obote, were the first to suffer. Early statements by government spokesmen about the activities of dissident Acholi and Lango tribesmen inflamed ethnic antagonisms; in particular, publication of the Lango "master plan," the alleged purpose of which was to keep particular groups in power, caused intense resentment.[5] Numerous reports chronicled "mopping up operations": Acholi and Lango soldiers responded to guarantees of safe conduct only to face cruel and sometimes perverse execution.[6] Amin's frequent visits to various army barracks represented an attempt to resolve intraarmy conflict; however, the violence that had erupted at several barracks in July 1971 recurred thereafter.

In September 1972, 1,500 Obote supporters invaded Uganda from neighboring Tanzania. The former president calculated that his troops would upset the fragile military balance. Under the command of Colonel David Oyike Ojok, Obote's forces planned to combine a land invasion with an air attack. However, the airdrop and the attempt to prompt a mutiny among Amin's troops failed,

5. See "Lango Development Master Plan," *Uganda Argus,* March 5, 1971.
6. See, for example, "Curious Calm Marks Uganda Today," *Standard,* February 16, 1971; "Uganda on the Bridge of Shame, Executions in the Night," *Sunday Post* (Nairobi), March 7, 1971; "Uganda's Busy Bridge of Death," *Observer,* March 4, 1971; and "Uganda's Silent Evidence," *Observer,* March 21, 1971.

the masses did not rebel, and Obote's forces were killed, captured, or driven back.

Late in 1972, another dissident group, a guerrilla organization calling itself the Front for National Salvation (FRONASA) emerged. Led by a young Ugandan graduate of Dar es Salaam University, Yoweri Musebeni, FRONASA thought in terms of mass struggle rather than conventional warfare and was composed largely of young radicals. Its main objective was to depose Amin, though not necessarily to restore Obote. About 200 of its members infiltrated Uganda and launched clandestine operations, but the group's impact was small, especially after the discovery of one of their camps in January 1973.[7]

Amin's base of military support continually narrowed. When he turned against the Acholi and Langi, he calculated that he could rely on the major Western Nilotic groups—the Alur, Kakwa, Lugbara, and Madi. However, beginning in 1972, each of these groups had their differences with the president, and Amin took measures to undercut their power. The Alur were the first; the general's ill-feeling toward them became evident when their most senior officer and the former chief of staff, Lieutenant-Colonel Valentine Ocima, was arrested and murdered. Subsequently, several senior Lugbara officers, including Colonel Obitre-Gama, were either demoted or killed. The best known Madi politician and former minister of defense, Felix Onama, was placed under house arrest, while the Madi soldiers were denounced by Amin in public speeches for their lack of discipline and shameful conduct.[8] Antagonism between Amin and the Western Nilotic groups continued to grow, culminating in March 1974 in an abortive coup and the shootings that resulted in the death of Uganda's chief of staff, Brigadier Charles Arube. This coup, led by Arube—a Christian member of Amin's Kakwa tribe—and several Christian Lugbara officers, triggered further purges in the army.

Both Arube and the former foreign minister, Michael Ondoga, whose body was found floating in the Nile a month before the abortive coup, had recently returned from a course in the U.S.S.R.

7. "Guerrillas against Amin," Observer, February 4, 1973; Colin Legum, ed., Africa Contemporary Record: Annual Survey and Documents 1972–1973 (London: Rex Collings, 1973), V, B278–79.
8. For further details, see ibid., pp. B272–73.

Though some observers claimed that Amin was concerned about Moscow's role in the March fighting, the general denied that Arube and Ondoga's overseas training had anything to do with the coup.[9] Officers continued to plot against Amin. In November 1974 he withstood the attempt of a group of commandos to overthrow him. At Kampala's Mbuya barracks, rebellious soldiers complained of not receiving their pay checks for three months and of shortages in food rations. However, troops loyal to the government put down the uprising.

Civil-Military Relations

Amin's political campaign aimed at civilians consisted primarily of a series of conferences with the masses and councils of elders, an emphasis on authenticity, the reorganization of district administration, and a program of mass mobilization. His most momentous acts affecting groups residing in Uganda were the expulsion of the Asians, the "war of economic liberation," and new policies in the realm of civil liberties.

Shortly after the coup, the military government sought to meet directly with the people. Extolling a Rousseauian notion of political participation, Amin showed little confidence in intermediary institutions. He therefore began traveling extensively throughout the country to elicit personal support and explain his government's objectives. Military officers and civilian officials encouraged citizens to state their views and to engage in discourse with the new regime. Conferences were held with chiefs and religious leaders of all faiths. "Councils of elders" were designated to replace district councils, though the government repeatedly warned the elders that Uganda would not turn the clock back.

Although the Baganda initially expressed enthusiastic support for Amin, a marriage between Buganda and the military could only be regarded as a tenuous affair. Ganda support was generally available for any regime sympathetic to their complaints about Obote. Yet while fulfillment of Buganda's traditional aspirations demands, above all, greater decentralization and increased autonomy, the army officially represented a centralizing rather than a decentralizing force in political affairs. After the army had gained

9. *Africa Research Bulletin* (Political, Social and Cultural Series), XI, No. 3 (April 15, 1974), 3176A–78A.

considerable grass-roots support in Buganda by returning the kabaka's body for burial, military spokesmen insisted on Uganda's republican status. Amin publicly advised Ronald Mutebi, the son of the deceased kabaka, that he would not occupy his father's throne. Instead, General Amin suggested that the prince should serve in the army. It should not be forgotten that the military has always been unpopular in Buganda; less than five years before the coup, Deputy Commander Amin led the national army against Buganda.

In an effort to remove the residues of colonialism, Amin changed the names of many of Uganda's major streets, parks, mountains, lakes, and rivers. Street signs reading Ali Visram, Borup, Harcourt, Hunter, Queens, Rosebury, Salisbury, and Stanley came down. Sites in Uganda were retitled Kabarega, Lumumba, Malcolm X, Nasser, Nkrumah, and Sukarno. Lakes Albert and Edward became known as Lakes Mobutu Sese Seko and Idi Amin.

In 1974 the government divided the eighteen districts established by the Obote government as the basis of administration into thirty-eight new districts in ten provinces. Of the ten provincial governors appointed, eight were recruited from the military, one from the prisons service, and one from the police. With the introduction of a mass mobilization program in February 1974, the former chiefs of every village, county, and subcounty were replaced by individuals designated by the military, many of them soldiers. At the same time, all people in Uganda were ordered to carry identity cards.

General Amin's decree announcing the expulsion of noncitizen Asians—one of the most notable events in Uganda's history—was to have vital ideological repercussions. In October 1971, Amin called for verification of the official census data on the Asian community; irrespective of citizenship,[10] all Asians (as well as those of Asian-African parentage) were required to report for

10. When Uganda became independent, Asians were given two years in which to opt for local citizenship. The largest number preferred to carry British passports; fewer chose local citizenship; some retained their Indian, Pakistani, or Portuguese passports; and still others—because of technicalities —became stateless persons. According to 1969 census figures, in a total population of 9,548,847, the Asians numbered 74,308—25,657 citizens and 48,651 noncitizens (*1971 Statistical Abstract* [Entebbe: Government Printer, 1971], p. 13).

enumeration, and subsequently to carry census receipts at all times. On December 7 and 8, he assembled the Asian community at an "Indian Conference," where a series of complaints about the Asians were catalogued. In his message to the nation on Cooperative International Day, August 5, 1972, Amin announced that Uganda had no place "for the over 80,000 [sic] Asians holding British passports who are sabotaging Uganda's economy and encouraging corruption."[11] Claiming divine intervention, the president ordered the Asians to leave within ninety days; he said that a dream dictated the decision: "I . . . had a dream that the Asian problem was becoming extremely explosive and that God was directing me to act immediately to save the situation."[12]

This summary expulsion order must be viewed in the light of the legacy of British paternalism. The imperial power assembled in Uganda diverse groups between whom the social divisions were clear and strong. Asians and Africans interacted in the market place, but relations rarely extended beyond those of buyer-seller and master-servant. Their culture made the Asians a separate community; they were an exclusive and an excluded minority. Their traditions of endogamy, restrictive social networks, and family firms sustained by loyalties of kinship contributed to intercommunal rivalries. The Asians' greatest liability may well have been their visibility. As a mercantile class dealing with African peasants, often as the representatives of foreign capital, they played an all too conspicuous role in the local economy; when Africans were faced with falling prices for their crops or rising costs in the towns, the agents whom they confronted were the Asian middlemen.

To question why the international community castigated General Amin for his decision is not to be callous about the fate of the Ugandan Asians. Certainly the Asians suffered the tragic denouement of historical, economic, and political forces rooted in the colonial era. But, to put the issue in perspective, uprooted minori-

11. Embassy of the Republic of Uganda, Washington, D.C., *Uganda Newsletter,* IV, No. 8 (August 1972), 1; and "The Future of Asians in Uganda," *Uganda Argus,* August 5, 1972.
12. "Message to the Nation on British Citizens of Asian Origin and Citizens of India, Pakistan and Bangla Desh on 12th/13th August, 1972," *Speeches by His Excellency The President General Idi Amin Dada* (Entebbe: Government Printer, 1972), p. 5.

ties are not new or even unusual in the annals of history.[13] Nor is a sovereign state legally obligated to host aliens. Noncitizen Asians were Britain's responsibility, not Uganda's; a debt to imperial expansion bound Britain to fulfill an obligation to those whom she had colonized.

The unintended but major impact of the expulsion of the Asians was to accelerate the formation of classes in Uganda. When an alien group forms a distinct class, its precipitous ouster creates a gap in the social hierarchy. The gap does not persist, however; others seek to assume vacated positions of privilege. But which would-be upwardly mobile group fills the void? When economic nationalism is a major motivating force in the removal of advantaged aliens, local entrepreneurs replace them. Indigenous aspirants compete with one another for occupational mobility. Ultimately, this competition contributes to a society with winners and losers.

While the bourgeoisie may have been a central driving force in Western development, it does not necessarily perform the same role elsewhere. If non-Western societies need not follow a path identical to that of the European class struggle, measures that encourage class differentiation are likely to be counterproductive. An indigenous petty bourgeoisie is bound to be more powerful than a politically effete alien class.

A long-run perspective may argue for a higher priority being assigned to egalitarianism among citizens than to short-term ideological capital. This argument is not intended as counseling tolerance of a parasitic bourgeoisie. Rather, the point is that alien

13. After World War II, East European states ousted Germans; and in 1948 Palestinians were required to settle in neighboring countries. Before independence came to the states of Africa, the Ivory Coast repatriated Togolese, Dahomeyans, and Nigerians. Under duress, Ghanaians left Nigeria, the Ivory Coast, and, more recently, Sierra Leone and Guinea. In the last decade, Niger ejected Dahomeyans; Senegal its Guineans; and Cameroun, Ivory Coast, and Zaire their Nigerians. In 1968, Ghana dislodged over 100,000 non-Ghanaian Africans. Similarly, there was a purge of Chinese in Indonesia after the abortive coup of 1965, of Vietnamese in Cambodia after the overthrow of Sihanouk, of Iranians in Iraq, and of Iraqis in Iran. Among a long list of enforced transfers of population, Turks and Greeks have been exchanged and Han Chinese forcibly relocated internally. Even in Uganda itself, expulsion has precedent: former President Obote swept non-Ugandan laborers out to Kenya. Finally, settlers from the Indian subcontinent (in Aden, Burma, Mozambique, and Sri Lanka) have been displaced on previous occasions.

pariahs can be politically useful in their host countries. If muting class struggle is a long-range goal, the alien petty bourgeoisie represents the stopgap layer. Properly handled, it can be molded or manipulated to serve national objectives. In time, as the value of the aliens to their adopted society diminishes, their fate can be negotiated in a humane and dignified manner.

In Uganda, the Baganda were the most likely candidates to replace the Asians. They have been the best educated, wealthiest, and most commercially advanced of the indigenous peoples; moreover, nearly 60 percent of the Asian population had resided in Buganda. Though unintended, the potential danger of the expulsion was, then, that ethnic conflict and economic class antagonisms would be reinforced. However, though for motives different from those suggested by this line of reasoning, the military blocked a coincidence of ethnic and economic class divisions that would have put the Baganda supporters of the military on one side and the rest on the other. The military sequestered Asian capital for its own use and redistributed property as a form of patronage, largely to selected northern Ugandans and Sudanic peoples.

The military, lacking legitimacy and hoping to civilianize its power base, actively sought the support of a middle class. Though it is dangerous to impute rationality where purposive behavior may be lacking, it was important that both the decision to expel the Asians and subsequent acts of nationalization released large amounts of capital, making wealth and property suddenly available to Ugandan aspirants to the bourgeoisie. For their newfound class status, the successful were indebted to the military regime. Many who profited from the government's action assumed an abiding interest in preserving the system.

In Uganda, the army did not, as it did in other developing countries that have experienced "middle class coups" (for example, Argentina and Brazil), intervene on behalf of a middle class.[14]

14. Cf. Lofchie, "Uganda Coup"; and José Nun, "The Middle Class Coup," in Claudio Veliz, ed., *The Politics of Conformity in Latin America* (London: Oxford University Press, 1967), pp. 66–118.

To explain the coup d'état of January 25, 1971, primarily in class terms is to misinterpret social stratification in Uganda. The economic explanation ignores the failure in class solidarity. The Ugandan army is deeply divided, not united around common interests; and military intervention exacerbated intraarmy fragmentation, as the mass killings of soldiers from particular

Rather, the class factor became salient when the military attempted to consolidate its coup d'état. The effect of the army's postcoup strategy was to establish an emergent, indigenous bourgeoisie that owed its existence to the ruling elite. And insofar as their memberships overlapped, the indigenous bourgeoisie and the ruling elite increasingly became one.

The economic consequences of the expulsion of the Asians included a greater concentration of capital and a decrease in the flow of nonessential goods into Uganda. The property of departing Asians became the government's, and the elimination of a privileged merchant class resulted in a cutback of consumer imports. At the same time, the expulsion led to a decline in revenues from taxation on profits and import duties, while, according to official accounts, the government incurred large bills for transportation and other relocation costs of departing Asians. Shortages of trained manpower were acute. The disruption was felt immediately in social services, hospitals, and schools.

Amin's "war of economic liberation" created an uncertain climate for foreign investors. Despite such incentives as liberal terms for the repatriation of profits and capital allowances, those in control of foreign capital were generally put off by the volatility of political conditions in Uganda and the capricious behavior of the country's president. The economic war harmed the tourist industry, previously Uganda's third most important source of foreign exchange, while within Uganda the dislocations were felt directly in terms of increased unemployment in urban centers and a decline in the flow of credit from urban to rural areas. Such essential commodities as soap, milk, sugar, and matches became increasingly scarce. Prices of basic foodstuffs, such as matooke, maizemeal, groundnuts, sweet potatoes, beans, and fish rose sharply; and low income groups suffered most severely from the record-high prices. According to the Kampala cost of living indexes for 1972 and 1973, the prices of the goods consumed by high, middle, and low income groups rose by 11.3 percent, 12.2 percent, and 24.3 percent respectively.[15]

---

ethnic groups demonstrated beyond any doubt. Moreover, the perquisites granted to the army and the promotion of officers to high-level positions in banks and corporations meant that Obote's Move to the Left did not necessarily threaten the soldiers' economic interests.

15. *Budget Speech Delivered at Uganda International Conference Centre,*

While some of these difficulties can be attributed to worldwide inflation, the energy crisis of the early 1970's, and dry weather, these factors were not responsible for all of Uganda's economic woes. Because Uganda's industrial activity was at a relatively low level, while an increasing number of vehicles were immobilized by a lack of repair services and spare parts, fuel represented a smaller portion of the country's imports than in many other countries. The petroleum products bill amounted to Shs. 112,000,000 in 1973; it had been Shs. 98,000,000 in 1972 and was estimated at Shs. 150,000,000 in 1974.[16]

The Ugandan economy had been in a weak state when Amin came to power, but it deteriorated further under military rule. After limited growth in 1971 and 1972 (3.1 percent for both years), Uganda experienced a negative growth rate of 1.2 percent in 1973. Population was increasing at a rate of 3.3 percent per annum; so that per capita GDP declined by over 5 percent in 1973.[17] Total exports increased by 9 percent per year in the two years 1971–1973, while net imports fell by 40.3 percent between 1971 and 1972 and by 49.4 percent in the first six months of 1973.[18] Despite this striking improvement in the balance of trade, however, the balance of payments still registered a large overall deficit—the result of prepayment requirements by foreign suppliers and a reduction in capital inflow. By late 1972, foreign reserves had dropped to an all-time low of Shs. 81,000,000, an amount that would cover only three weeks' imports.[19]

In order to cope with these ills, Amin invoked harsh measures to deal with local evaders of regulations; promoted a number of women and university students to high-level jobs; and passed a decree requiring university graduates to spend their first five working years in the public sector. In addition, teams of recruiters were sent overseas to invite skilled personnel to Uganda; in early 1973, representatives, led by Apolo Kironde, traveled abroad seeking to

Kampala, on Wednesday, 12th Day of June, 1974 by the Minister of State for Finance, Hon. M. S. Kiingi (Entebbe: Government Printer, 1974), p. 5.
    16. Quarterly Economic Review (London), No. 2 (1974), p. 7.
    17. Budget Speech . . . 1974, pp. 1, 3.
    18. Ibid., p. 6; Michael J. Schultheis, "Economics and Economic Research in Uganda during the Amin Period" (paper presented to the annual meeting of the African Studies Association, Chicago, November 1974), p. 16.
    19. Colin Legum, ed., Africa Contemporary Record: Annual Survey and Documents 1973–1974 (London: Rex Collings, 1974), VI, B314.

persuade foreign experts and Ugandan students to fill manpower vacancies and another mission, headed by Professor Kibuka Musoke of Makerere's Department of Medicine, visited Britain to attract Ugandan professionals back to the University.[20]

In an attempt to raise additional revenue, the government imposed tighter controls and heavy taxation. Government investment centered on public corporations, especially the Uganda Development Corporation (UDC). The president abolished the State Trading Corporation and replaced it with the Uganda Advisory Board of Trade, an agency established to supervise eight new companies dealing in particular areas of foreign trade. While attempting to centralize trade, the government relied increasingly on deficit spending and a heavy growth in credit, extended by the banking system. During 1973, the volume of money (currency in circulation and private bank deposits) rose by Shs. 770,500,000, or 37.4 percent. This rapid expansion of the money supply put a strain on prices and hence on foreign exchange.[21] In an effort to reverse these trends, several additional tax measures were introduced; the development tax was reintroduced, the commercial transactions levy extended, and the special business levy continued. While the proportion of total government expenditures going to defense increased by over 250 percent under the military, the common man was called upon to join in an effort to counteract massive deficit spending, mounting inflation, and a severe liquidity crisis by tightening his belt.

Civil liberties became increasingly precarious, and Uganda was soon notorious for gross violations of human rights. In November 1973, Amin ordered a census of all foreign religious personnel working in Uganda and inspection of their papers. In some cases where applications for renewal of entry and work permits were pending or irregularities found, the persons concerned were declared illegal immigrants or spies. While the decision to expel white missionaries contributed to the indigenization of the Church, the government's demonstrated willingness to intervene in religious affairs caused dismay among many African clergymen.

The Moslem-Christian cleavage became increasingly pronounced

20. "Uganda: An Inside View," *Africa* (London), No. 23 (July 1973), p. 16.
21. *Budget Speech . . . 1974*, p. 8.

under Amin. With the ascendancy of Islam in national politics, a variety of affronts were offered the country's Catholic population; Uganda's first prime minister, Bendicto Kiwanuka was killed, and the archbishop of Kampala, His Grace Emmanuel Nsubuga, was placed under house arrest. Similarly, the erstwhile Protestant establishment wielded less power than ever before, as was illustrated by the refusal to allow the archbishop of Uganda, Rwanda, and Burundi, The Reverend E. Sabiti, to participate in services at Namirembe Cathedral. The Catholic and Anglican Churches both angered Amin by publicly expressing reservations concerning the president's announced intention to create a Ministry of Religious Affairs. Ultimately the government created a less comprehensive Department for Religious Affairs, an office that nevertheless was placed directly under the president's jurisdiction.

Social malaise as reflected in widespread crime (kondoism) represented a serious problem under Uganda's First and Second Republics. Amin acted forcibly to crack down on kondos; however, the primary act adopted—the Armed Forces Power of Arrest— was aimed at political dissidents as well as criminals. The Robbery Suspects Decree, No. 7 of 1972, gave a security officer the right to use "any force he may deem necessary." In effect, the government's directives exacerbated the problem of lawlessness by members of the armed forces.

A variety of decrees gave the government broad powers to detain individuals without trial. Another extension of government prerogative involved the imposition of tight controls over newspapers. The Ministry of Information and Broadcasting, and later Amin himself, assumed responsibility for the *Voice of Uganda* (previously the *Uganda Argus*). Foreign journalists were ordered out of the country, and *The People* stopped its presses. In July 1974, the president banned all "imperialist" newspapers, including six British and four Kenyan papers.

After reprimanding university students for the high incidence of venereal disease among them, Amin suspended the National Union of Students of Uganda on the grounds that it was "dangerous to peace and order." As a result of the army's intimidation of students and teachers, over one-third of Makerere's instructional staff left during 1973; several departments experienced serious teaching difficulties, and a few shut down temporarily.

What have euphemistically been called "disappearances" have been a serious problem in Uganda. When a government-appointed commission completed its investigation into the deaths of the two Americans slain while investigating reports of killing and torture at Mbarara army barracks in July 1971, the head of the inquiry, Mr. Justice David Jeffrey-Jones, fled the country before his report was filed. After extensively examining the circumstances surrounding the deaths of Nicholas Stroh and Robert Siedle, Judge Jones concluded: "There was positive evidence disclosed in Lt. Silver Tibihika's affidavit which I have accepted as true. . . . It is obvious that the two Americans died an unnatural death. They were in fact murdered by personnel of the Simba Battalion of the Uganda Armed Forces."[22] Estimates of the number who have lost their lives vary widely. Ex-President Obote presented a letter to the OAU heads of state claiming that between 80,000 and 90,000 people had been killed during Amin's first two years in power and providing evidence of "mass murder and human degradation of the most heinous type." In a 63-page document identifying many who "disappeared," the International Commission of Jurists placed the figure for those who had died at between 25,000 and 250,000.[23]

Ugandan Africans experienced the greatest suffering.[24] Eyewit-

22. *Commission of Inquiry into the Missing Americans Messrs. Stroh and Siedle Held at the Conference Room, Parliament House, Kampala* (Entebbe: Government Printer, 1972).

23. *Violations of Human Rights and the Rule of Law in Uganda* (Geneva: International Commission of Jurists, May 1974), p. 61.

24. It is not my purpose to provide an inventory of the human tragedy, the types of torture, or the atrocities committed in Uganda. Reports on these matters are referred to elsewhere in the text. The facts are often wrongly used by critics of black Africa, among them whites in South Africa and others, who invoke the evidence from Uganda to support their argument that Africans cannot govern themselves. Similarly, opponents of Third World initiatives at the UN have accused Africans of having double standards, in that African delegates use their aggregate voting power to push through resolutions condemning racial discrimination in southern Africa while closing their eyes to gross violations of human rights in Uganda. Those who take this line fail to realize that the apartheid regime is unique in being the only government in the world that seeks to legalize racial discrimination, the only government to adopt racism as an official ideology. While transgressions have occurred in Uganda, the offending regime is not a racial oligarchy supported by the wealthy industrial nations. The government of Uganda does not pose a threat to international peace and security by refusing to relinquish control over a neighboring territory. Nor are its policies likely to

ness accounts of the kidnaping or death of former Minister of Internal Affairs Basil Bataringaya, barrister Michael Kaggwa, Minister of Agriculture and Cooperatives John Kakonge, Vice Chancellor Frank Kalimuzo of Makerere University, Mayor Francis Walugembe of Masaka, and others are readily available. Those who fled the country seeking voluntary exile include Ambassador to the Federal Republic of Germany John Barigye, Permanent Representative to the UN Grace Ibingira, Foreign Minister Wanume Kibedi (Amin's brother-in-law), and Minister of Education Edward Rugumayo. Barigye attributed his departure to "the reign of terror that has . . . shocked all men of goodwill"; Kibedi deplored "the large-scale liquidation of innocent people in Uganda."[25]

Ministers' resignations were handed in with increasing frequency. After dissolving the National Assembly and imposing his Suspension of Political Activities Decree, Amin expressed his anger with members of the cabinet. At first he scolded ministers and embarrassed them publicly. Subsequently, he retired some of Uganda's most senior officials, dismissed the entire cabinet for two months, and replaced several civilian members with soldiers; for the civilians retained, the defense minister was instructed to provide daily weapons training. Following the resignation of Kibedi as minister of foreign affairs and the death of Lieutenant-Colonel Ondoga, Amin appointed Princess Elizabeth Bagaya of Toro, a former actress and fashion model, as the new minister and first woman to occupy a cabinet post. Responsibility for this portfolio was assumed by the president himself, however, when he sacked Bagaya for "making love to an unknown European in a toilet" at Orly airport in Paris and accused her of having contacts with British and American intelligence.[26]

Although the military became the dominant element within the

lead to racial warfare throughout a subcontinent whose people are demanding self-determination.

25. "Open Letter to General Idi Amin from Wanume Kibedi, Former Uganda Foreign Minister (1971–1973), Dated June 21, 1974" and "Addendum to Open Letter to General Idi Amin" (Supplement to *Violations of Human Rights and the Rule of Law in Uganda*), p. 1.

26. "Amin Ousts High Aide, Charging Misbehavior," *New York Times,* November 29, 1974; and "Woman Amin Accuses Has Champions at U.N.," *New York Times,* November 30, 1974.

cabinet, the Defence Council was where Amin preferred to make most policy decisions. The composition of this council was never revealed in full, but its members included the commander in chief as chairman, the army chief of staff, the chief of the air staff, and other military personnel appointed by Amin. With the diminution of civilian influence, the Defence Council appeared to be the only functioning decision-making body in Uganda. However, there is no reason to believe that its proceedings provided more than an institutionalized ratification of one-man rule.

Foreign Policy

Amin's policies had a divisive impact on African international relations. Presidents Nyerere and Kaunda, as well as other African leaders, deplored the Ugandan head of state's decision to remove the Asians. Zaire's Mobutu Sese Seko traveled to Kampala in an attempt to reverse or mitigate the terms of the expulsion order. The official Zairian communiqué submitted to UN Secretary-General Kurt Waldheim reported that Amin had agreed to extend by three months the time allowed for the Asians' departure. But Amin did not in fact permit such an extension, and Ugandan officials insisted that the Western press had fabricated the story of his agreement in order to vilify him. The minister of state for foreign affairs, Paul Etiang, maintained that he had attended all meetings between the two heads of state and that Amin never wavered from his original position;[27] but Mobutu Sese Seko was said to have been highly indignant that Uganda should have reneged on the agreement.[28]

In response to Tanzanian opposition, Amin sent a telegram to Nyerere that was to receive much publicity; his message read: "I want to assure you that I love you very much, and if you had been a woman I would have considered marrying you, although your head is full of gray hairs, but as you are a man that possibility does not arise."[29] Associating courage with masculinity, Amin chided Tanzania's president for his alleged feminine traits.

27. Related by Paul Etiang to the author, New York, October 21, 1973.
28. See, for example, "Names May Change, But Amin's Deadline Doesn't," *Economist* (London), October 11, 1972. A copy of the personal communication between Zaire's permanent representative to the UN, Ipoto Eyebu Bakand'Asi, and Secretary-General Kurt Waldheim, dated October 6, 1972, is in my possession.
29. *Africa Research Bulletin* (Political, Social and Cultural Series), IX,

Seeing the East African Community to be near collapse, and responding to pressure from other African statesmen, Uganda and Tanzania moderated their positions. The Mogadishu Agreement, concluded in 1972, led to a temporary halt in hostilities. Subsequently, at a meeting of the OAU heads of state in May 1973, Amin approached Nyerere publicly and grasped his hand. Under the good offices of Somalia and Ethiopia, the two leaders agreed to normalize relations. Despite Nyerere's disdain for Uganda's military head of state, Tanzania was prepared to recognize the exigencies of the situation. Amin agreed to pay compensation for Tanzanians murdered in Uganda, and high-level government officials from Dar es Salaam visited Kampala. Nevertheless, as Amin's base of domestic support continued to narrow, he returned to the tactics of using external enemies as scapegoats. Violations of the Mogadishu and Addis Ababa reconciliation agreements recurred, and Amin threatened to invade Tanzania, warning that his armies would capture Tanga, in northeast Tanzania, as a Ugandan outlet to the sea. Moreover, he announced his intention to extend Uganda's border twenty miles to the south in the region of the Kagera River.

Despite conciliatory gestures by Kenya's Vice-President Moi, Ugandan soldiers mistreated Kenyan workers; several "disappeared," and others fled to safety. Since Kenya remained open to foreign capital and continued to impose relatively few restrictions on overseas investment, its economy remained vulnerable to political fluctuations within East Africa. Moreover, since Kenya too relied heavily on the tourist industry, the country suffered from the convulsions in Uganda. As a result of the ouster of the Asians, Community services (railroads, telephones, and so on) lost revenue. In addition, many Kenyan capitalists dependent upon Asian shopkeepers regarded Amin's expulsion order as a threat to their own future.

In a search for allies, Amin turned to his Moslem brethren in North Africa. Largely because of mounting financial difficulties and the growing debt to Israel, Amin looked to the oil-rich Arab states for aid. According to the general, Uganda received promises of technical assistance from Algeria, Egypt, Libya, Mauritania, and

No. 9 (October 15, 1972), 2599B; Christopher Munnion, "If Idi Amin of Uganda Is a Madman, He's a Ruthless and Cunning One," *New York Times Magazine,* November 12, 1972.

240 IDEOLOGY AND POLITICS IN UGANDA

Syria, as well as financial assistance from Libya, Morocco, and Saudi Arabia. King Feisal of Saudi Arabia made an official state visit to Uganda, and a small contingent of Libyan troops arrived in Kampala. The Libyan people donated funds "to help the Muslims in Uganda," and a Libyan Arab Uganda Bank for Foreign Trade and Development was opened in Kampala. Amin and Qaddafi pledged their "support for the Arab peoples rights and struggle against Zionism and imperialism."[30] Uganda's head of state applauded Hitler's persecution of the Jews: "Germany is the right place, when Hitler was the Prime Minister and supreme commander, he burnt over six million Jews."[31] With the outbreak of the Yom Kippur War, Ugandan volunteers were called upon to sign up for the campaign against Israel. Speaking in Damascus, Amin volunteered to fight with his troops; he added: "It remains for Golda Meir to pack up her knickers and minis with General Dayan and the rest of the Zionist Israelis to run to Washington and New York."[32] Subsequently, in 1974, although the Moslem community is a small minority in Uganda, Amin attended the second Islamic summit conference in Lahore, Pakistan, joining the representatives of thirty-six other countries in setting forth the views of the Islamic nations on issues of international economics.

From one perspective, North African (primarily Libyan) participation in Uganda's economic war could be viewed as an expression of pan-African unity. From another perspective, however, the Libya-Uganda link seems pernicious. Previously, Africa's proto-alliance systems—the Casablanca and Brazzaville-Monrovia groups—reflected ideological solidarity based on common political commitments. The mainstay of the Libyan-Ugandan affair, by contrast, was financial considerations; Libya had the funds to buy support south of the Sahara, and Uganda was desperate for assistance.

At the 1973 OAU meeting, Amin publicly criticized the Libyans' proposal to move the organization's headquarters from Addis Ababa—the first indication that this relationship was one of short-term convenience to two fickle partners. Despite generous

30. *Africa Research Bulletin* (Political, Social and Cultural Series), IX, No. 1 (February 15, 1972), 2369C; *Uganda: The Second Year of the Second Republic* (Entebbe: Government Printer, 1973), pp. 23–26, 91–99.
31. "President Amin to the U.N. Chief," *Voice of Uganda,* September 12, 1972.
32. Legum, *Africa Contemporary Record . . . 1973–1974,* p. B314.

offers of aid, a financial institution supported by Libya withheld credits from Ugandan traders and farmers on the grounds that many borrowers did not pay back their loans. Amin claimed that only a small portion of Libyan aid was in fact delivered. Then, in May 1973, he announced that Uganda would not accept loans from Libya. This decision reflected the general's growing disillusionment with various North African and Middle Eastern states over their failure to offer ample financial assistance to Africa south of the Sahara. After initial attempts by Third World leaders to concert their appeals to oil exporters for development aid, Amin was one of the first African leaders to express disenchantment. In a telegram to the heads of state of oil-rich nations, he explained that countries like Uganda had suffered greatly; the oil weapon, he complained, although intended for use against Israel's allies, had hurt faithful supporters of the Arab cause.[33]

As regards relations with the West, in early 1972 Amin invited the British to establish a training school in Uganda, a request to which they agreed. However, when Whitehall refused the general's application for jets, armored cars, and a special aircraft to fly him to the 1973 Ottawa Commonwealth Conference, the British training team was ordered to leave. Amin accused the U.K. of interfering in the exodus of Asians, expelled the British high commissioner, declared on December 18 that British citizens must either depart within twelve days or remain on local terms, and announced that Uganda would nationalize 500 foreign firms including 87 British-owned companies. In May 1973 what remained of British investments were seized. And at the Commonwealth Conference in Ottawa, where an amicable climate prevailed, Amin's representative attacked the U.K. in no uncertain terms: "Now that Britain appears to be devoid of any principles, of any moral strength, can we repos [sic] any moral confidence in her for guidance of Commonwealth matters and as a rallying point for Commonwealth cooperation?"[34]

Responding to the U.K.'s economic woes, at the end of Decem-

33. *Africa Research Bulletin* (Political, Social and Cultural Series), XI, No. 5 (June 15, 1974), 3225C; *ibid.* (Economic, Financial and Technical Series), XI, No. 3 (April 30, 1974), 3064B.
34. "General Amin's Ottawa Commonwealth Speech," *Voice of Uganda*, August 4, 1973.

ber, 1973, the general launched a Save Britain Fund, initiating it on Old Kampala Hill, where, eighty years before, Lord Lugard had first raised the Union Jack in Uganda. Explaining that the purpose of the fund was "to save and assist our former colonial masters from economic catastrophe," Amin appealed to Ugandans to contribute generously: "We have duly assisted financially and materially in various disaster stricken areas all over the world."[35] Replacing his cynical and ironical approach with a more conciliatory manner, in 1974 Amin indicated his willingness to discuss compensation for British interests taken over by the Ugandan government. This change in attitude can be attributed to Uganda's difficulties in securing external credit and aid; the pressure exerted by creditors who demanded prepayment in cash impelled Amin to reach a settlement with London.

Other Western nations supported Britain's attempts to secure compensation from Uganda. The West Germans and the Italians discussed such payments with Ugandan officials; the French offered to sell Amin's regime a large quantity of arms—though the weapons were never delivered. French-Ugandan relations cooled when Amin threatened to take strong measures over a documentary film about him produced by a French firm; although he had agreed to the production and had prescreened the film, he was enraged that audiences in Paris found it hilariously funny.

In relations with America, Uganda's head of state became well known for his unorthodox style and disregard of the conventions of international diplomacy. In view of "Uganda's internal security problems," the Peace Corps withdrew volunteers and Washington recalled its ambassador. Subsequently, in July 1973, Amin delayed 112 members of the U.S. Peace Corps, in transit at the Entebbe airport, on the grounds of suspected "imperialist" or "Zionist" subversion. After dispatching a telegram to then President Nixon wishing him a "speedy recovery from Watergate," Amin sent a cable to Cambodian Chief of State Lon Nol criticizing American bombing in Southeast Asia; yet he praised Nixon's foreign policy in general and referred to the American president as a "brother and colleague." When Nixon resigned, Amin asked his foreign minister to invite the former president to come to Uganda for a rest. In

35. Ministry of Foreign Affairs, *Uganda Quarterly Bulletin,* I, No. 1 (January 1974), 1, 22.

other gratuitous gestures, he suggested that the UN should be moved from New York to Kampala and urged Nixon's successor, President Ford, to nominate a black American to the office of vice-president.

The American Congress of Racial Equality (CORE), an Afro-American group that espouses separatism and the Garveyite tradition, supported Amin enthusiastically. Its national director, Roy Innis, praised him for having done more than any other African to further the cause of black nationalism. Innis visited Kampala in 1973, attended the OAU as a member of Uganda's delegation, and pledged to bring black Americans to aid Uganda. Subsequently, another Afro-American leader, Stokely Carmichael, traveled to Kampala and was granted Ugandan citizenship. After Innis' program had received considerable publicity, the Ugandan government decided to reassess the situation. Innis explained that CORE's efforts to fill Uganda's manpower needs had generated considerable publicity, leading many Ugandans studying abroad to return home; Amin had therefore postponed the program.[36] However, Grace Ibingira, formerly Uganda's permanent representative to the UN, has attributed cancellation of the CORE operation to "certain internal difficulties at home."[37]

The U.S., Norway, and Canada terminated aid programs to Uganda. Britian cancelled a £10 million loan. The World Bank and the International Development Association advised Amin to honor Uganda's debts. Israeli creditors invoked arbitration clauses and obtained court orders in New York and elsewhere to attach Ugandan assets held in foreign banks. But although overseas interests reacted strongly against Amin, they had no immediate success in either upsetting him or deterring him from his audacious policies.

Amin countered Western opposition by reversing some of his earlier foreign policies and by exploring other options. Despite his professed dislike of socialism, he concluded an agreement with the Soviet Union under which the latter provided a squadron of fighter planes and a shipment of tanks, armored personnel carriers, and antiaircraft guns. Yugoslavia and Czechoslovakia provided techni-

36. Personal conversation with Roy Innis, New York, October 9, 1973.
37. Personal conversation with Grace Ibingira, New York, October 9, 1973.

cal assistance. Though Amin had accused the Chinese of playing a part in the Tanzanian-backed invasion of Uganda, diplomatic relations were resumed in 1973. Uganda and Cuba exchanged ambassadors in 1974, and relations improved with North Korea and East Germany. Less than two years after the expulsion of the Asians, Amin sent a team of officials to India to recruit technicians to work in Uganda. An economic and cultural delegation from Pakistan visited Uganda in 1974, and measures were taken to strengthen ties between the two countries.

Black Nationalism

If one attempts to sum up the situation after the military had been in power for four years, it is clear that, in terms of principles, Amin had moved neither to the left nor to the right. Consistency and a guiding ideology had not been the distinguishing traits of Uganda's Second Republic. Rather than devising a coherent ideology, Amin preferred to act impulsively, make decisions arbitrarily, distribute unsolicited advice, exercise an uninhibited sense of humor, and engage in clowning. Major government policies were beset with innumerable contradictions. Nevertheless, even if no ideological clarity can be discerned, the theme of black nationalism emerged as a significant stage in the development of a Ugandan ideology.

Measures introduced by Amin challenged the asymmetry of dependency relations. Under his leadership, Uganda acted to change three cardinal features of dependence: the expatriate role in the public and private sectors, foreign ownership of productive enterprises, and the ties between trade and aid and local economic performance. His means may be disputed, but the general took more concerted action than most leaders in the Third World to dislodge external control. Whatever his frailties, Amin demonstrated that meaningful action begins with self-help.

Uganda's moves against foreign interests and the expatriate community suggest that the poor need not be helpless in dealing with the rich. In a sense, General Amin improved the bargaining power of many new nations. The West was forced to take notice of the extreme policies that can be pursued. Amin's actions to remove the vestiges of colonialism symbolized the limitations of great power attempts to work their political will in the Third World.

Despite its defiance of dependency relations, the regime continued to rely on outside suppliers for military hardware and willfully entered into transitory alliances. Although Uganda's relations with the world economic order changed, the military failed to introduce a program for constructing a just society. An egalitarian redistribution did not follow the attack on structures of dependency. Within Uganda, as a result of a lack of political consciousness on the part of the masses and the self-serving behavior of officers, Amin's campaign against international finance gained little support. Rather, the growing authoritarianism, the abandonment of constitutional procedures, and the arbitrary use of intimidation were the characteristics of military rule that most impressed themselves on the citizenry.

While some of the principal policies designed to forward black nationalism—for example, the expulsion of noncitizen Asians and the adoption of Swahili as an official language—were well received by many Ugandans, the military undermined, if not totally impaired, the instruments for transmitting normative values. In terms of ideological innovation, Amin's chief inspirations were his peasant origins, his countrified values, and his identification and rapport with the common man—a quality that the author of the "Common Man's Charter" sorely lacked. Hence, insofar as this ideology fulfilled any of the functions of an operative ideology, it scored best on communications with the masses and lowest on legitimation. On any level other than that of the most direct personal appeal, however, the military destroyed the mechanisms for disseminating an ideology. Brute force was used to dissolve all would-be competing institutions. Politicians were arrested, deported, or liquidated, political parties banned, and such interest groups as students and the Church harassed. If Obote discovered that the channels for ideological diffusion were blocked, Amin sought to destroy them. Under the military, nearly all of the major institutions for mediating social change were eliminated.

In order to secure compliance, Amin relied on the military's trump card—its monopoly of the means of coercion. But coercion is a dubious way to forge a national identity. The skills and training of a soldier are usually better suited to commanding troops and armor than to mobilizing political support; in the final analysis Amin resorted to the former, since it was what he knew best.

The evidence suggests that the military was ill equipped to introduce an ideology of modernization. The officers' experience and
background were not such as to promote the skills required for the
tasks of generating new norms to restructure a society and attach-
ing motives in a concrete way to the political system. Ironically,
Obote's poorly planned introduction of an ambiguous ideology in
a malintegrated society was one of the primary reasons for military
intervention in Uganda; yet the military's incursion into politics
dramatically demonstrated the need for establishing a viable ideological consensus and a semblance of national purpose.

CHAPTER 10

Conclusions

This study set out to examine ideology as it relates to social structure and to specify the links between ideas and action. The position that argues the primacy of ideas has been rejected, emphasis being placed on the centrality of modernizing norms to social change. The attempt to introduce socialism in Uganda was unsuccessful. The crucial question is, why did ideology fail?

At the outset, it was noted that Fanon and Nkrumah had warned that the absence of a viable ideology produced social disequilibria in Africa. In fact, ideologies there have had a problematic and far from straightforward impact. I have tried to show the subtleties, dilemmas, and paradoxes which attended Obote's attempt to introduce a modernizing ideology in Uganda. This chapter summarizes the findings of this book and assesses the implications for theory-building and African politics.

The models constructed by political scientists are inadequate for explaining major issues of social change in Africa. The criticism of the development literature has become so familiar to political science that it has been incorporated into the stock and trade itself. Not only does political science have a standard literature on development, but standard criticisms are regarded as standard companion pieces to the standard literature. Development theorists are so well versed in the inadequacies of the literature that they expect their students to be thoroughly acquainted with those inadequacies too. Assigned readings on the models usually include lessons in the generally accepted criticism as well. Students are expected to recite these conventional orthodoxies and to find fault as dictated by major disciplinary trends at any given time. The critique becomes canonized, and the problems are dismissed with some banality— "Oh, the constraints under which we labor in this imperfect discipline!" Yet political scientists continue to teach these models. Some defend this practice on the grounds that social science is a cumulative enterprise; whatever the limitations of existing theory, knowledge must be built on what has preceded. Others ask: Where do we go from here? What alternatives present themselves? Do we merely turn to a Babel of case studies? Many are reluctant to accept new approaches. With good reason, they are suspicious of trends that come into vogue quickly and may die out just as suddenly. In the world of academic fashion, scholarly fads come and go; new catchwords are in one day and out the next. Most scholars would agree that, while new departures are sorely needed, better constructs are not appearing.

One major limitation of the existing literature is that the propositions advanced by theorists working in the dominant Western tradition are too broad to be usefully applied to the burning social issues at hand. While theoreticians may have a scholarly interest in devising long-term criteria of development and modernization, or in working with indexes of these processes, African politicians are primarily concerned with insuring their political survival and forging unity in fragmented countries. A single decision—for example, to shuffle the command structure in the armed forces—may determine the fate of a leader and is likely to have a profound impact on the country's future. The fifty-year package models fail to deal with the mundane but nevertheless critical questions of strategy and tactics that face leaders in the Third World.

Given these problems, I do not advocate a general theory of development in this book; rather, an analytic framework is suggested that focuses on ideology as values-in-action. The analysis began with definitions and propositions about ideology in general and, more specifically, about ideology in Africa. Ideology is a syndrome of functionally interrelated beliefs and values linked to interests. In an operative ideology, beliefs and values tend to be resilient, so that individual themes provide support for the general ideological syndrome. Ideology's components include a judgment as to prior social malaise, a program for proceeding, and a vision of the future. The orientation may be in the direction either of constructing an entirely new social system or of recapturing a previous state of affairs.

But ideology cannot be explored merely by examining cognitive factors. Analysis must go beyond social ideas. The contribution of the Marxist approach is that the existential base of knowledge is emphasized. Focusing on the social genesis of thought, Marxists and other proponents of the sociology of knowledge stress the relevance of extracognitive factors. While Marx et al. are correct in drawing attention to the intimate relationship between ideology and group interests, the task for analysis is to specify the ways in which ideologies correspond to interests. The complexity of the relationships suggests interdependence between ideas and interests, and the patterns of interaction can only be delineated empirically. To argue merely that one is the independent variable and the other the dependent is to oversimplify the realities and does not contribute to understanding political behavior.

A particular variant is characteristic of ideology in developing countries in the second half of the twentieth century. The compulsion toward an ideology of modernization develops with the desire to transform a political system that is not supported by existing beliefs and values. Ruling elites may also feel impelled to introduce a new ideology when they already have support but want to propel a society toward national development goals. As societies increase in complexity, the emergence of specialized institutions multiplies the options open to individuals in their relationship to values. With greater diversity, there are more choices. But more choices can give rise to intolerance or, at least, uncertainty about the future. Hence a new paradigm is introduced to fill the void and harmonize beliefs and values. The process of ideological modernization uses beliefs and values as a major driving force to bring about social change. Ideological modernization entails a widening of perspective and the building of associational sentiment in the movement from parochial toward more universal categories of thought.

In countries whose economies are dependent and subordinate, however, the availability of agents to effect social transformation is limited. Few options present themselves. Insofar as world market forces play a preponderant role in low income countries, the possibility, in most of the Third World, of successfully challenging those who determine the use and movement of capital is slight. Hence in cases where local leaders rely primarily on ideology to transform society, the chosen strategy merely testifies to the weakness of the national bourgeoisie; a turning to change at the normative level, when coordinated measures for implementation are lacking, demonstrates the inability or the unwillingness of the ruling elite to confront dominant concentrations of wealth and privilege.

If ideology is seen as an aspect of political culture, the observation that regimes which emphasize ideological modernization are generally incapable of adopting more fundamental economic and political development strategies is valid. But given the staying power of traditional cultures, strategies adopted at the cultural level can also signal the serious intention of a ruling elite to concern itself with basic socioeconomic formations. And, as was indicated in the discussion of levels of analysis, an ideology of modernization need not be merely a cultural response; it may also be programed at the societal (institutional) and individual (psychological) levels. Clearly a modernizing ideology that is pitched at any one level—that is, without supportive institutional, psychological, or cultural measures—is likely to be inadequate.

Nonetheless, in increasingly complex societies governmental leaders frequently look to ideology to play a critical role. Ideology may be expected to perform the six functions of legitimation, rationalization, interpretation, solidification, communication, and mobilization. As an ideology becomes operative, these functions can increasingly be said to be performed. Because modernizing ideologies have the potential for playing these roles, ruling elites attempt to stimulate behavior that is ideologically inspired. By lending coherence to social change, eliciting commitment to the political system, and encouraging sustained participation rather than anomic or idiosyncratic behavior, ideology can be a vital instrument for a regime engaged in transforming society.

Innovation and Diffusion

Where does ideology come from? How does it spread? These questions have long puzzled students of social science. The literature indicates that social values are generated in certain groups; but interpretations vary as to the affinity between ideology and social structure.

In the Ugandan experience, transnational and continental sources of identification were of primary importance during the early stage of ideological innovation. Following independence, Obote derived much of his inspiration from ideological initiatives undertaken elsewhere in Africa. Because a domestic consensus and a national ethos were lacking in Uganda, efforts to build a sense of solidarity on a national base failed miserably; any attempt to forge a specifically Ugandan identity only served to resurrect old rivalries among traditional peoples. To avoid activating existing antagonisms, Obote's early appeals were made, therefore, in broad, abstract terms.

A second source of ideological innovation in Uganda was traditional culture. Although it is not easily demonstrated in any empirical fashion, clearly an important factor conditioning Obote's attempt to effect socialist construction was the egalitarian norms with which he was imbued as a Lango. Obote embraced the values of northern peoples and espoused them as part and parcel of a modernizing ideology.

The introduction of a modernizing ideology in Uganda can be divided analytically into two distinct phases. Following independence, ideological modernization was regarded as an important task but not necessarily the first priority. With the transfer of constitutional power from the imperial authority to an indigenous elite, social cleavages became bases of intractable opposition. Steering away from what it regarded as a divisive course and toward a safer alternative, the regime's initial approach to ideology was pragmatic and gradualistic. The new leaders wanted to test their options in a period when the pressing task was to consolidate power. The consolidation of power is indispensable to the introduction of an ideology of modernization; for new ideologies unleash disruptive forces of change as well as opening new avenues for success. Conversely, ideological modernization is a means whereby leaders in developing countries seek to generate and manage power.

During the first phase (1962–1969), aspirations concerning socialist construction were articulated but limited in the main to broad hints at the rhetorical level; a frontal assault with an ideology of modernization would clearly have been abortive. The dominant pattern was that government pronouncements would be made, to be followed by extreme caution or even vacillation in nonverbal behavior and frequent assurances to cushion the impact of an intended course of action. In this period, greater militance could be displayed in foreign affairs than in domestic affairs; continental pan-Africanism, antineocolonialism, and neutralism and nonalignment were more remote and less threatening than ideological themes bearing on domestic matters affecting entrenched interests in Uganda.

Searching for yet another method that might succeed in promoting solidarity among Ugandans, Obote turned to a more concrete ideology of modernization and sought to move his country to the left. The attempt to modernize gives rise ultimately to the need to fit beliefs and values to changes in the political system. After an initial period of restraint, attention normally turns to the increasingly apparent inbalance between normative values and the sociopolitical environment. By 1966—some would say 1969—Obote appeared to have triumphed over the centrifugal forces of local nationalism. Uganda seemed to be succeeding where others had failed. Feeling more secure in his political position, Obote set out to advance an explicit ideology. The second phase (1969–1971) was a period of ideological assertion, during which, the president intended, particular ideological themes should be Ugandanized. The Move to the Left was an attempt to hasten the rate of change by building socialism.

The Western literature suggests that the latent beliefs of mass publics are largely determined by the forensic belief systems of the elites; the elites represent the source and dominant concentration of ideology, and the masses approve or disapprove of what the elites propagate. Examination of Uganda's experience validates this proposition but demonstrates that analysis of innovation and diffusion must be more specific. The links are not quite as direct as scholars imply; a number of other factors must be taken into account. Analysis of ideological innovation and diffusion in Uganda indicates some of the critical questions that should be asked: Under what conditions do the masses accept or reject elite belief systems? What tactics and what strategy are conducive to the innovation and diffusion of ideology? How can an alliance of strongly motivated groups be created behind a new ideology? What structures are most readily utilized? How, if at all, do leaders compensate for the dislocations caused by the introduction of an ideology of modernization?

The importance for ideological diffusion of formal technological apparatus—for example, parties or the media—is much emphasized in the literature. In order to analyze the prospects for ideological diffusion in Africa, however, one must take a historical step backwards and consider the intensity of the struggle against foreign domination. The political infrastructure for ideological diffusion is frequently developed in the course of sustained struggle against alien intrusion. Further comparative inquiry might well show that there is a positive correlation between the intensity of resistance to foreign control and the capacity to diffuse ideology in a post-colonial setting.

Whereas the scholarly literature stresses the importance of concrete institutions as agents of diffusion, a study of Uganda suggests, first, that political style—the amount of enthusiasm displayed by local opinion leaders and agents at the middle levels—is a vital factor in ideological diffusion; and, second, that the structural relationships in and between the processes of innovation and diffusion is of importance. In large part, diffusion of Uganda's ideology was primarily a matter of discussion and speech-making by ministers, party officials, and civil servants. Since the party was not effective, the logical alternative would have been the bureaucracy. The predominant group in the party had the most to lose from socialism; those whose occupational interests were consonant with socialist objectives constituted only a small minority. Unfortunately for Obote, the attitudes and behavior of high-level officials in the civil service contributed to the failure to marshal support for the new ideological initiatives. Their proclivity toward modernizing norms and the favoritism they had experienced under colonialism had left the Baganda—the ethnic group most hostile to the president—overrepresented in the public services. Increasingly, Nilotic northerners became identified as the source of ideological innovation, while Bantu southerners occupied the technical positions for ideological diffusion. The upshot was a fundamental structural imbalance in and between the processes of innovation and diffusion.

When the positions through which diffusion should take place are in the hands of those who are either unenthusiastic about or antagonistic toward proposed innovations, there is little likelihood that the broader process of ideological modernization will succeed. Similarly, when social cleavages divide the sources of innovation and the agents of diffusion, the probability that the proposed innovations will take hold is low. The reverse, however, is not true; if key positions of diffusion are in the hands of those who are intent on the success of the proposed innovations, it does not follow that the innovations will take root. Nor is it the case that when the sources of innovation and the agents of diffusion are consonant, the probability that the proposed innovations will succeed is necessarily high. The proper political style (of which there are many culturally specific varieties) and consistency in and between the processes of innovation and diffusion are necessary but not sufficient conditions for successful ideological modernization.

A final lesson to be learned from the Ugandan experience seems obvious but has nevertheless been ignored in many developing countries. If leaders in the Third World pursue modernizing ideologies, they also introduce discontinuities among the agents of socialization. At the time Obote heralded the creation of a "socialist revolutionary society," Uganda's schools were still staffed to a considerable extent by expatriate teachers with no professed commitment to socialism. Largely because they had been trained by expatriates, the local staff was imbued with Western values. Text books conveyed norms that contradicted the official ideology. While Obote and his cohorts spoke in visionary terms of the "new political culture," radio and television continued to broadcast foreign programs, many of which transmitted the values of advanced, capitalist societies. If discontinuities among the agents of socialization are to be reduced or avoided, much foresight, an acute sense of timing, and sharp anticipation are required in launching the transition to a new social system. Moreover, if a modernizing ideology is to become operative and move a society toward new attitudes and patterns of behavior, the level of sophistication of the instruments used for ideological innovation and diffusion must be appropriate to the particular society. Obote's ideological tracts— elaborate manifestoes, wordy documents—might have suited an industrial, literate society; they were incapable of generating support in a country whose peoples are largely illiterate and do not share a working language.

Ideology and Political Violence

Broadly speaking, the difficulties encountered in Uganda are paralleled in many other parts of the world. There are innumerable differences among Uganda's peoples, relative to class, ethnicity, religion, and language, that have become politicized. The potential for political violence in Uganda has crystallized around such distinctions as mass-elite, citizen-noncitizen, Baganda-non-Baganda, monarchy-federal/unitary, Christian-Moslem, Catholic-Protestant, and English language-African languages. Never in the country's history has the cleavage pattern worked to produce overlapping identities or multiple loyalties capable of mediating group conflict. Instead of providing bases for countervailing centers of power, cleavages have meant polarities. The lines of cleavage intersect in shifting patterns; a vast number of reinforcing combinations are possible. The result is fluidity, in which intrigue, cabal, maneuvering, and ruthlessness flourish. Such is the context in which the major underlying social and political factors operating at the time of the Move to the Left must be considered.

By 1969, viable political institutions were totally lacking. The party had atrophied and was regarded as unreliable by its president. The senior posts in the bureaucracy were occupied, in the main, by the group with the most to lose from Obote's initiatives. Interethnic antagonism was rife, and the rivalries of the not-too-distant past were deeply embedded in the consciousness of Uganda's citizens. Economic stagnation is an ineluctable problem in any low income country affected by fluctuations in the prices of primary products and, hence, in the world market; but the obstacles to employment faced by the younger generation, the corruption and nepotism of the elites, and the siphoning-off of scarce resources into prestige projects had exacerbated Uganda's economic problems by the time of the major attempt to restructure the social system. The severity of the basic problems and the tenacious grip of tradition limited the scope for devising a formula that would make fundamental social changes acceptable; at the same time, the very difficulty of devising such a formula created among Uganda's leaders a new sense of urgency about arriving at a solution.

When Obote responded, his solution was to set forth a blueprint for transforming the sociopolitical environment. The myth of the "new political culture" was intended to create solidarity on the basis of what was presented as the logic of the independence movement and postcolonial efforts to establish political control. But the intractability of cleavages, and the sociopolitical climate at the time of the Move to the Left, were limiting factors for Uganda's leaders; with a malfunctioning party, educational institutions that were suffused with Western values, and myriad cultural traditions giving rise to mutual hostility, the president found few options open to him. The political constraints under which leadership was operating can be broadly catalogued as the pressures of local nationalism versus modern nationalism, royalism versus progressivism, and neotraditionalism versus pan-Africanism. In terms of financial and political capital, resources were indeed scarce. Obote sought, above all, a device that would bridge the immense gaps between elites and masses and among mutually opposed ethnic groups.

The multicentered power structure of the immediate postindependence era proved incapable of withstanding the centrifugal forces of local nationalism. Finding that building power from the bottom up was not the answer, Obote opted for a strategy of penetration from the top down. Though not malevolent in intent, Obote's maneuvers were designed to eliminate autonomous centers of power. The rationale implicit in the aggrandizement of power was that decentralization could more logically be undertaken after a period of central institutional growth. The initial steps would be to destroy any ambiguity in the lines of authority from the center and to imbue local personnel with the official ideology. The practical application of this strategy involved the storming of the kabaka's palace by the national army, the renewal of emergency regulations in Buganda every six months, preventive detention to stifle opposition groups, and the postponement of national elections. Uganda's constitutional progression was from a neofederal structure reinforcing pluralism to abolition of monarchies, the vesting of power in an executive presidency, and a unitary state. A new party constitution was adopted to bring the UPC into line with the government through greater centralization. Following the dismantling of the parliamentary alliance between the UPC and the KY, Uganda became a de facto one-party state, and opposition parties were ultimately banned.

With the introduction of the Move to the Left, the regime responded to the need to wed ideology and political organization by issuing official documents, though relatively few concrete measures resulted. The weaknesses of the general strategy pursued since 1962 were already beginning to show themselves. The problem was the overcentralization of what little power existed. Because of excessive centralization, political organizations lacked roots. The party, in particular, was notable for its failure to widen the base of government support. Throughout Obote's tenure of office, the UPC was, it is fair to say, his Achilles heel. After interparty schism was eliminated by banning the UPC's rivals, intraparty strife reflected the maneuvering of opposition groups against the president from within. Not only the party suffered from the excessive centralization. Having alienated potential sources of support, particularly trade unions and students, Obote turned on the middle class and well-to-do. Privileged groups faced the threat of deprivation—loss of sinecures as well as diminished status, influence, and prestige—which ultimately heightened the disposition of one such group to intervene. And, workers and peasants were chagrined by the continued elitism when the government was preaching austerity.

The problem for ruling elites is that, as they attempt to transform a society, development programs alienate or even undercut their bases of political support. When they persist in pursuing their development goals, their perseverance adds to the alienation of support groups. Conversely, when they try to retain their bases of political power and to survive in positions of leadership, ruling elites limit their ability to pursue development goals. It follows that a fairly considerable initial reserve of support is necessary if a regime is to pay the political costs of development without undue strain or economic failure. In Uganda, as Obote tried to come to grips with this problem, the dilemma presented itself as exclusion versus participation: If the number of people sharing political responsibility is increased, oppositional tendencies are likely to be reduced. But can institutional growth proceed when historically antagonistic groups are suddenly asked to share the prerogatives of decision-making? Can consensus be reached? Or does a rapid expansion of political power politicize social cleavages? Obote opted for exclusion. The sinews of autonomous centers of power were severed. Yet there remained an overriding contradiction between two fundamental goals: political survival, which, in the short run at least, is linked to stability; and transition to a new social system, which invites instability. That is, Obote could choose between stabilizing policies that would sustain the status quo, and a new development program launched at the expense of stability. He was caught between maintaining Uganda's ongoing course, which legitimized his continued rule, and pursuing a program of mobilization that threatened to exacerbate social divisions. In other words, the immediate strain was between legitimacy and mobilization. From a long-run perspective, however, it seems likely that if the government had opted for the status quo, growth would have been blocked; then stability would have been undermined either way.

Paradoxically, Obote's strategy was to deal with existing conflict by inducing another form of conflict. His approach was to attempt to shift the basis of social antagonism onto the plane of ideological preference. In the search for a means to create the tolerance and confidence that would make differences acceptable, the regime calculated that a modernizing ideology would redefine the boundaries of political conflict and realign social cleavages. The assumption was that economic distinctions and primordial loyalties could be defused by orienting beliefs and values to a cause stressing more universal aspirations and de-emphasizing parochial sentiment.

Obote was correct: conflict does have integrative potential, and cooperation and consensus can be forged by inducing conflict. But the introduction of an ideology of modernization also promotes class consciousness and other group loyalties. Obote failed to realize that social ills are neither solved nor settled by presenting them as politically undesirable under the banner of ideology. Not only did Obote's scheme prove impossible to implement, but in addition it lacked certain fundamental political dimensions. If economic and communal groups perform major social roles and exercise consonant power, they must either be allowed to partake in the transformation of their society or be expected to resist in every way possible. An ideology of modernization can be used to encourage people to think about redefining group memberships and political loyalties, but it may also accentuate deeply rooted antagonisms. The attempt to introduce an ideology of modernization may well have the unanticipated result of activating political conflict. As well as transforming class antagonisms and communal identities, new ideologies can also politicize them.

This mix of highly politicized cleavages, a destabilizing sociopolitical environment, constraints on leadership, and the deleterious impact of government strategies forms the matrix of generalized social grievance. Such conditions precluded socialism in Uganda and created a propitious atmosphere for military intervention.

Ideological Stress and Socialist Transformation

The impact of the Obote strategy suggests that analysis must not be restricted to the functions ideology may perform but extended to take account of the dysfunctions or stress ideology places upon fragile political systems. In Uganda, increasing rhetoric about a socialist revolutionary society unaccompanied by a sufficient degree of visible structural change only compounded the existing predisposition to social distrust. An expanding gap between word and deed aggravated a climate of cynicism and skepticism. Policies that have the net effect of encouraging cynicism and skepticism are particularly dangerous among peoples whose history has been marked by a high propensity to political violence. On the one hand, a measure of ambiguity is a desideratum of successful ideological modernization. If ideology is too explicit, its activist programs and prescriptions are difficult to fulfill. A modernizing ideology must be general enough to encompass diverse interests; moreover, if it is to be viable, a degree of elasticity is not just permissible but desirable —as the modernizing ideology is implemented, practitioners can be expected to disagree over concrete policies and implications. On the other hand, if ideology is so diffuse that imprecision in statement becomes the norm, its practitioners are given little direction regarding implementation. In the case of ideological imprecision, the gap between verbal assertions and nonverbal behavior can escalate and add stress to an already fragmented political system.

The Obote pattern shows that this escalatory process may be influenced by the directions taken by ideological modernization in neighboring states. To the extent that the demonstration effect of Tanzania's ideology was a significant factor, it worked against Obote. He devised an ideology which, in good part, was transplanted from another national context. The Move to the Left proved to be inappropriate for social structure in Uganda, unsuited to the historical setting, and misconceived in its application. In Uganda, ideology was an escape from praxis. The lesson is that attempts by low income countries to copy outside models are unlikely to serve their interests. To introduce a modernizing ideology successfully, new socioeconomic formations must be created. If new norms are to take hold, it is essential to change the base of social and economic interests. Prevailing concentrations of wealth and privilege need to be challenged.

In Uganda, one of the major difficulties was inadequate concern for the institutional consequences of suddenly imposing an ideology of modernization. Some of the proposals introduced under the Move to the Left were a surprise to many of Obote's own colleagues in the cabinet. The Nakivubo Pronouncements, for example, were not subject to debate prior to the decision to nationalize eighty-four major firms and industries, and the document's provisions took effect immediately, from the time of the president's speech. By comparison, though the official ideology in Tanzania has yet to deal fully with certain issues, the merit of ujamaa is its consistency. With each step, Nyerere tried to anticipate the ways in which new norms could be attached to political institutions. The "Arusha Declaration," for example, gave tangible meaning to government policies of the previous years. In releasing it in 1967, Nyerere sought the propitious moment. The announcement had been expected since 1963, when the national executive committee of TANU called for the establishment of a commission to make recommendations on socialism. The president waited to establish the instruments for implementation; but he was also wary of the dangers of delay. He remarked once that if another eighteen months had been allowed to elapse, it would have been impossible to assault the various citadels of privilege. Thus, Tanzania's ideology was different from Uganda's in the extent of its indigenous contribution, its better timing, in the thought given to planning for the impact of values, and, particularly, in its credibility, in terms of the relationship between rhetoric and reality.

While the Ugandan president was by no means a mere puppet of his close friend in Tanzania, he did allow personal loyalties to play a major role in decision-making. The evidence suggests that Obote at times took the lead, but for the most part he was much more an ideological bedfellow, offering reinforcement and confirmation in response to Nyerere's moves in Tanzania. He adopted many policies that were identical to Nyerere's but were neither grounded in common political and material interests nor attuned to a shared social structure.

Obote also found that the introduction of an ideology of modernization gives rise to stress by jeopardizing entrenched interests. The impact of regime-induced attempts to promote socialism is disruptive for those in dominant class positions and for others holding traditionally rooted values. For many Ugandans, Obote's socialism reflected not ideological commitment but his desire to suppress the power of the Baganda and was, thus, little more than tribalism. Paradoxically, Obote, the man who spoke out more strongly than any of his countrymen against tribal politics, came to be identified with ethnic parochialism. Certainly his contribution to forging unity in this highly fragmented African state was by no means inconsiderable; the harsh measures of 1966, even if illegal, were necessary to maintain an entity that had been artificially created by colonialism. Ultimately, however, the unity proved to be insufficient to withstand the pressures engendered by potentially threatened interests. The army, having, unlike the Baganda, a near monopoly of the means of coercion, was provoked into removing the source of its concern. And with his overthrow, Milton Obote joined that very special, rapidly expanding club of deposed African leaders.

A modernizing ideology, then, challenges. But if ideology is a challenger, ideological modernization is also a gamble. With the introduction of an ideology of modernization, the stakes are raised. As a regime encourages its citizens to think in terms of ultimate goals and objectives, ideology becomes the agent of success but must also bear the stigma if failure occurs. Yet to ignore the normative dimensions of social change is also chancey. A regime that neglects change at the normative level runs the risk of suffering from the steady grip of tradition, under which conservative orientations frustrate achievement of development goals. Given the gap between beliefs and values on the one hand and a rapidly changing sociopolitical environment on the other, there is a compelling need to fill the void and realign elements of the political process. In this regard, modernizing ideologies are potentially valuable.

For Obote, however, ideology did not prove a valuable resource. He lost on the gamble. And his experience demonstrates the point (which, obvious though it may seem, has been overlooked in Ghana and a host of other countries): you can't have socialism without socialists. Uganda's political commander mapped the battle plan; with no lieutenants or foot soldiers to engage in combat, however, the strategy of attack was flawed from the outset. If Obote was a genuine socialist—and his personal inclinations as well as his early childhood training in Lango seem to suggest that he was—the fundamental error was to launch a premature and miscalculated program of socialist construction. To change the metaphor, Obote was handicapped from the beginning in that he fielded a team with too few players and with those who played lacking commitment; his team was routed, and its captain paid the penalty of suspension. At this point, however, the analogy breaks down. To transform a society is not to engage in sport. The rules are not recorded, there are no referees, and the personal and social costs of competition are prohibitive. Moreover, damage to the social fabric is not easily repaired. Incidents of political violence are often cumulative, for each act of violence can increase the probability that such acts will recur.

But what of culpability? Is Obote to be blamed for malfeasance and misfeasance in Uganda? Clearly no one man is to blame for the intractability of Uganda's seemingly interminable problems. The self-serving African bourgeoisie, those members of the Asian community who sought to subvert the Move to the Left, and foreign enterprise and its attempts to perpetuate Uganda's role in a relationship of dependency have all played a part. Given the commanding position of external market forces in the Ugandan economy and the collaboration of local agents with those forces, the question is, why was Obote not removed by the imperial system before Amin's coup of January 1971? The answer is that the hegemonic powers had little to fear from the Move to the Left. Despite all the fanfare about economic nationalism, Obote faced formidable, if not overriding, constraints in his attempt to threaten fundamentally the dominant concentrations of wealth and power. The Ugandan experience confirms that legal decolonization is not tantamount to effective decolonization. As is indicated by the success with which the multinational corporations bargained around Obote's nationalization measures, "independence" does not necessarily usher in autonomous, self-defined patterns of development. Rather, except in unusual circumstances, structures of dependency remain operative and even extend themselves.

But to advance a purely economic interpretation would be an error. Merely to posit a series of economic givens is not only unduly deterministic but also neglects the possibility of the intervention of a political will. If politics is the art of the possible, the task of leadership is to rise to challenges. Too little time has elapsed to tell how history will judge Obote. Perhaps his record is not yet complete. Even if he does not return to power, history's judgment of him may be influenced by events still to take place. The readings of political barometers change both retrospectively and well beyond the lifetimes of particular politicians. The successes and failures of deposed statesmen do not change with time, but the climate in which they are being judged does.

The harshest criticism Obote will have to stand up to is that he pre-empted socialism in Uganda. By launching a program of socialist construction that was inept and misguided, he may have vitiated chances for effecting socialism in Uganda in the future. But this charge begs other questions: Is it possible to impose socialism from above? Or must revolutionary movements spread from a peasant base and eventually seize power? The evidence from Vietnam, China, and Cuba suggests that revolutionary socialism builds on the support of the masses. Although it may be premature to draw any final conclusion, the experience of Tanzania indicates, too, that under favorable conditions, a properly planned program for the introduction of socialism can be launched from above. It would be comforting if a general theory of transition to socialism could be erected on the basis of this study; unfortunately, the Ugandan experience is not conclusive. It is safe to say, nevertheless, that Uganda's unsuccessful attempt at socialist construction in no way invalidates the viability of the socialist course for the Third World. Some observers would argue that the failure of socialism in Uganda confirms the "Mboya line." This argument holds that socialism emphasizes the distribution of wealth rather than its creation; and the view that gained currency in some quarters of Uganda during the Move to the Left was that the effect of socialism would be merely to spread poverty equitably, not to increase the productive capacity of a society.

The evidence does not support this argument, which in any case is more theoretical than real. Socialism, to the extent it is practiced in Tanzania, is capable of generating wealth in low income areas and does tolerate acceptable levels of social differentiation where productive capacity is well established. The ruling elite in Tanzania has pursued a villagization scheme for promoting wealth in poor, rural areas. While tolerating vested interests in the countryside— the cotton regions of Sukumaland and the coffee belt—Nyerere sought to implement a series of carefully calculated measures designed to reduce social stratification and correct distributive inequities. In terms of Tanzanian socialism, this is not a contradiction. Socialist construction does not necessarily involve the doctrinaire approach its detractors would have us believe. In the final analysis, the unsuccessful attempt to achieve socialism in Uganda does not provide confirmation for the case against socialism in Africa. Rather, it should serve as a warning of the difficulties, obstacles, and ambiguities encountered by socializing societies.

A number of related issues merit further attention. It is difficult to study the role of political ideology over a short period. The result is that in modern political science social time is either largely ignored or left to the historian. In Uganda, because Obote's initiatives failed, the relationship between this ideology and social time can only be a matter of speculation. When Obote was overthrown, were other major documents forthcoming? Was a new phase planned? At what point? And to what end? As we know, a new phase was initiated, but not by the civilians who launched the Move to the Left. Thus the fate of Obote's program, had it been allowed to proceed as planned, can never be known. Would Obote's ideology of modernization have succeeded eventually if he had not been deposed by the military? Given Obote's relatively brief tenure of office, are the judgments advanced in this book premature or unfair? Can one generalize about what time span is adequate for modernizing ideologies to take root? If an ideology is successfully diffused, under what conditions and at what stages are new innovations necessary? When and how should ideology be redefined and reinaugurated in the process of modernization?

These issues give rise to a series of more fundamental questions about social change, revolution, and power. Can ideology provide redeeming structural change in a society, such as Uganda, bedeviled by social cleavage and lack of political control? How can ideology be used to ease traditional attitudes in such a way as not to become a threat to existing sources of support for the regime? Once under way, can ideology be used to prevent the deradicalization of revolutionary movements? If so, when a regime consolidates power, is ideology a viable agent to sustain revolutionary fervor? If, as Fanon suggested, revolution endures only through continued struggle, what is the relationship of ideology to that struggle?

The politics of transition to new social systems clearly need more rigorous analysis. The concept of ideology can play a valuable explanatory role in the study of transition. As a concept, however, it requires further refinement and modification to explain complex political phenomena.

Uganda's Future

Writing in early 1975, for publication many months later, one is bound to be outdistanced by events. Inevitably, analysis of the recent past becomes quickly outdated. Hence it is useful to speculate about Uganda's future. But when scholars shift from empirical analysis to social forecasting, they move to uncertain terrain. Given the speed with which civilian and military governments in Africa rise and fall, attempting to predict the course of events in any one country may well be impertinent. Yet the endeavor is worthwhile, for forecasts are based on projected trends and relevant comparisons.

Uganda's major problems will continue to be ethnic strife, economic and class cleavages, dependency on world market mechanisms, and civil-military relations. It can be predicted with assurance that ethnicity will continue to be a source of bitter conflict in a society as tradition-oriented as Uganda. Since the Baganda are disproportionately numerous among the technically skilled, they fill a majority of the high-level positions in the country's civil service and are overrepresented in the professions. While the military distributes patronage to its own clientele, the economic interests of the Baganda point to continuing prerogatives that cause other groups to feel a sense of deprivation. According to the 1970 *Statistical Abstract,* cash wages and payments in kind going to employees of private industry and the public services are four times as high in Kampala as in any other town. And the disparity between Kampala and immediate environs and the rural areas is, of course, much greater. The number of square kilometers of land registered in the names of individual Africans (rather than the public), too, is much higher in Buganda than in any other region. Production of coffee, by far the most lucrative export commodity, is primarily centered in Buganda—196,000 of 228,000 hectares of robusta. Buganda has benefited from such ecological factors as fertile land and generous rainfall as well as from the uneven development encouraged by colonialism. And the private ownership and management of the coffee industry leads to major concentrations of wealth in Buganda. Most of the coffee growers are small landholders, who employ an unspecified but presumably large number of casual or part-time laborers. In 1969 (the most recent year for which data for all the items discussed here are available), despite coffee's position as the chief foreign exchange earner— Shs. 779,929,000, or 53.5 percent of total foreign exchange earnings—the coffee curing industry provided only 1.1 percent of the monetary and nonmonetary income going to African employees in the formal sector. Even if most of Uganda's coffee is processed abroad and marketed overseas, a labor intensive industry such as coffee processing could provide additional employment and earnings and thereby reduce the income disparities among Ugandans.

Calculations based on data in the *Statistical Abstract* indicate that the value of coffee sales by growers in 1969 totaled Shs. 468,000,000 and that monetary and nonmonetary earnings received by Africans and non-African employees in the formal sector amounted to Shs. 12,648,000; private processing firms and middlemen, government, and cooperatives retained a balance of Shs. 319,281,000 (the value of coffee exports less the amount received by growers and by employees of coffee processing firms), a sum representing 39.9 percent of the revenue from Uganda's chief export. Moreover, unsold and government-owned coffee stocks are held over from year to year because of international marketing quotas; and in 1971, at the end of Uganda's second five-year development plan, coffee stocks amounted to more than half of annual sales. Data on non-Africans' monetary and nonmonetary earnings are available only for 1969; but if the percentage of total monetary and nonmonetary earnings in the coffee curing industry going to non-Africans is assumed to have been the same in 1965– 1968 as in 1969, then the percentage of the value of Uganda's coffee exports going to purchasing agents, private processing firms, government, and cooperatives was 49.3 in 1965, 53.3 in 1966, 53.4 in 1967, and 62.1 in 1968.

While northerners have been dominant in government, their investments have tended to be centered in Buganda rather than in their home districts. Moreover, government and cooperative funds are used to benefit disproportionately the larger landholders and others who control the productive wealth. Although the cooperatives were designed to remove middle profit takers, cooperative officers frequently short weigh and fail to pay fully illiterate smallholders and growers. Hence, it seems fair to conclude that a commodity that has accounted for 52.6 percent of the country's exports over a five-year period, and has returned 51.6 percent of those earnings, over the same period, to dominant socioeconomic groups, has also contributed to a highly inequitable distribution of income.

Economic interests are not necessarily the same as class interests, however. Despite the severity of economic distinctions in Uganda, the major social groups are not cohesive. To speak of class solidarity would be incorrect. One test of class solidarity is whether transracial alliances based on class exist, and to what extent they have solidified. Throughout Uganda's history, such alliances have been the exception and not the rule. Class interests within Uganda have rarely coalesced across racial lines, tending rather to be competitive. Members of the African bourgeoisie (or aspirants thereto) received little support from their Asian counterparts, or vice versa. Links among members of a particular economic stratum have generally been unable to develop to the point of bridging racial and ethnic divisions. The present situation can be characterized more accurately as one of incipient class formation than as one of active class struggle. As the complexity of Uganda's society increases, however, class antagonisms will grow and present what is likely to be an even more divisive situation than before.

From a long-run perspective, stratification in the international system is as important as, and ineluctably related to, internal stratification. In terms of wealth and power in the world arena, Uganda is near the bottom rung of the ladder. As is indicated by the maneuvers of the foreign firms that evaded the Move to the Left, dependency relations represent an enduring obstacle for Ugandans attempting to establish genuine control over their own affairs. The most perilous aspect at the international level, for all parties concerned, is the correspondence between economic and racial stratification, which provides the structure of privilege and deprivation.

If Uganda is to deal with these problems effectively, civilianization is a necessary first step. The military simply has too many liabilities to rule efficiently. The army has a long history of hostile relations with major ethnic groups. The soldiers lack those skills of bargaining and compromise in which politicians are trained. Recruitment to the military is regionally based, and senior-level officers are from select ethnic groups.

Political power does not create institutional unity within the armed forces; political and ethnic rivalries are only aggravated. Faced with a shrinking power base, Amin sought to militarize the state. Initially he relied on northerners within the army; however, he alienated one group after another. Having purged the Acholi, Langi, and various Western Nilotic groups, his support was largely reduced to his own Kakwa and the Nubians. (The Kakwa represent less than one percent of Uganda's population; the small Nubian community is composed of Arabic-speaking blacks who fought for the British in the nineteenth century and settled in Uganda.) Amin attempted to rule by coupling growing Islamic hegemony and favoritism for the Nubians with the use of black mercenaries—southern Sudanese Anyanya fighters and Zairian rebel exiles.

The credibility of the officers, particularly in terms of cosmetic pretensions to populism, has been undermined by their vast accumulation of wealth and their increasing reliance on terrorism. Seizing power by force inevitably raises questions of legitimacy, and civilians press for a return to the barracks. Though such a change will not answer all the problems of modernization, the military must seek a means of disengagement from politics. And the logical way to begin is by forming a party that would expand the base of participation, provide a forum for debate, and build unambiguous lines of authority for institutional growth. But the military can be expected to pursue such a course of action only if and when it is consistent with their class and corporate interests.

If the soldiers refuse to withdraw from politics voluntarily, how can they be removed as a dysfunctional element? A mass uprising is the most decisive means of breaking the military's hold. In exceptional cases, student riots, labor strikes, and peasant rebellions have led to the overthrow of the armed forces (for example, Sudan's Abboud government in 1964); even under such unusual circumstances, however, the military usually retains a major role in political life. Only full-scale revolution has the mobilizing impact to allow citizens to compete with the armed forces. In a revolutionary situation, the military's vital resource—its monopoly of coercion—is appropriated by large numbers of citizens. Yet while this may be the most effective way to end predatory militarism, in few societies is revolution imminent. In the absence of a mass uprising against Uganda's military regime, the most likely source of change is the officer corps itself. There is little hope that the first military regime will be a Roman-style junta, that is, a short-term military government in the interregnum between two civilian governments. In all likelihood, General Amin will be displaced in a second-stage military coup. For Ugandan citizens, this may mean more of the same or even something worse than the violence and intimidation perpetrated by the Amin regime. Intensified military upheaval would lead only to more internecine warfare, a succession of coups, and institutionalized instability.

This bleak, yet I believe patently warranted, outlook stems from my view that the root causes of Uganda's problems are systemic, not idiosyncratic. To regard Idi Amin-style leadership as an aberration, a curiosity, or a deviation from the norm is an error. To be sure, Uganda under Amin suggests a highly personalized style of politics. But the tendency to stress the idiosyncratic element underemphasizes persistent patterns of Ugandan politics. The excessive use of force, loss of life, and disregard for human rights are enduring features of the colonial legacy, not the creation of a malevolent regime. The expulsion of the Asians, for example, represented the response of the forces of economic nationalism to the racial caste society established by imperial expansion. Interethnic grievances predated the European intrusion; but the postcolonial structure of conflict was largely the result of the metropole's divide-and-rule policy of ethnic recruitment to the armed forces and civil service. The swing from a political elite to the technocrats of violence reflects the difficulty of finding lasting solutions to the multiplicity of problems facing low income countries.

Under an oppressive military regime, Uganda's official ideology developed into an ambiguous and highly manipulative form of black nationalism. Primarily a rationalizing device, this ideology has been an inadequate façade for numerous policy contradictions. Paradoxically, the populous awaits a mass-based system of normative values rooted in local tradition and capable of serving as an effective mobilizing force for the transition to a new political and economic order. Yet local traditions are fiercely competitive; mobilization may erode a regime's base of political support; and economic interests are linked to or supported by external elements. Neither the politician who authored the "Common Man's Charter" nor a soldier-president of peasant origins could resolve this dilemma. Uganda's common man, staunch in his ability to persevere, may well have to weather political storms more tempestuous than hitherto.

The Common Man's Charter

First Steps for Uganda to Move to the Left

1. We the members of the Annual Delegates' Conference of the Uganda People's Congress, assembled on this Eighteenth Day of December, 1969, in an Emergency Meeting in Kampala, being the body charged under the Constitution of the Uganda People's Congress with the responsibility "to lay down the broad basic policy of the Party" and being conscious of our responsibility and of the fact that the Government of the Republic of Uganda, District Administrations and Urban Authorities are currently run by our Party and on policies and programmes adopted by our Party, and recognising our responsibility to the people of Uganda as a whole and to the association of Uganda, Tanzania and Kenya in the East African Community and to Uganda's membership of the Organisation of African Unity, do hereby adopt this Charter for the realisation of the real meaning of Independence, namely, that the resources of the country, material and human, be exploited for the benefit of all the people of Uganda in accordance with the principles of Socialism.

2. We hereby commit ourselves to create in Uganda conditions of full security, justice, equality, liberty and welfare for all sons and daughters of the Republic of Uganda, and for the realisation of those goals we have adopted the Move to the Left Strategy herein laid as initial steps.

3. We subscribe fully to Uganda always being a Republic and have adopted this Charter so that the implementation of this Strategy prevents effectively any one person or group of persons from being masters of all or a section of the people of Uganda, and ensures that all citizens of Uganda become truly masters of their own destiny.

4. We reject, both in theory and in practice, that Uganda as a whole or any part of it should be the domain of any person, of feudalism, of capitalism, of vested interests of one kind or another, of foreign influence or of foreigners. We further reject exploitation of material and human resources for the benefit of a few.

5. We reject, both in theory and practice, isolationism in regard to

one part of Uganda towards another, or in regard to Uganda as a whole to the East African Community in particular, and Africa in general.

6. Recognising that the roots of the U.P.C. have always been in the people right from its formation, and realising that the Party has always commanded us that whatever is done in Uganda must be done for the benefit of all, we hereby reaffirm our acceptance of the aims and objectives of the U.P.C. which we set out below in full:—

"(i) To build the Republic of Uganda as one country with one people, one Parliament and one Government.

(ii) To defend the Independence and Sovereignty of Uganda and maintain peace and tranquillity, and to preserve the Republican Constitution of Uganda.

(iii) To organise the Party to enable the people to participate in framing the destiny of our country.

(iv) To fight relentlessly against Poverty, Ignorance, Disease, Colonialism, Neo-Colonialism, Imperialism and Apartheid.

(v) To plan Uganda's Economic Development in such a way that the Government, through Parastatal Bodies, the Co-operative Movements, Private Companies, Individuals in Industry, Commerce and Agriculture, will effectively contribute to increased production to raise the standard of living in the country.

(vi) To protect, without discrimination based on race, colour, sect or religion, every person lawfully living in Uganda and enable him to enjoy the fundamental rights and freedom of the individual, that is to say,

(a) Life, Liberty, Security of the person and Protection of the Law.

(b) Freedom of conscience, of expression and association.

(c) Protection of Privacy of his home, property and from deprivation of property without compensation.

(vii) To ensure that no citizen of Uganda will enjoy any special privilege, status or title by virtue of birth, descent or heredity.

(viii) To ensure that in the enjoyment of the rights and freedoms, no person shall be allowed to prejudice the right and freedoms of others and the interests of the State.

(ix) To support organisations, whether international or otherwise, whose aims, objects and aspirations are consistent with those of the Party.

(x) To do such other things that are necessary for the achievement of the aims, objects and aspirations of the Party".

7. Republicanism in Uganda, just like the political Independence of

Uganda, is now a reality, but the demand and struggle for Uhuru has no end. This is part of life and part of the inalienable right of man. It is also the cornerstone of progress and of the liberty of the individual, the basis of his prosperity and the hallmark of his full and effective participation in the affairs of his country. October 9th, 1962, therefore, was the beginning of a much greater struggle of many dimensions along the road to the goal of full Uhuru. During the last seven years the U.P.C., by action and exhortation, has shown to the people of Uganda that it is wrong and deceitful to treat and regard the 9th October, 1962, as the end of the road; or the day on which the people of Uganda as a whole reached a stage in their development when all that remained was to divide the spoils on the principle of the survival of the fittest; or that the well-to-do, the educated and the feudal lords must and should be allowed to keep what they have, and get more if they can, without let or hindrance.

8. The Party has always made it clear to the people that the only acceptable and practical meaning of October 9th, 1962, is that the people of Uganda must move away from the ways and mental attitudes of the colonial past, move away from the hold of tribal and other forms of factionalism and the power of vested interests, and accept that the problems of poverty, development and nation-building can and must be tackled on the basis of one Country and one People. The Strategy laid down in this Charter aims at strengthening the fundamental objective of the Party. We do not believe that any citizen of Uganda, once free of the mental attitudes of the colonial past, freed of the hold of tribal and other forms of factionalism, and free of the power of vested interests, will find himself or herself at a disadvantage. On the contrary, it is our firm belief that such a citizen will gain that part of his/her freedom which has so far been in the hands of others, and which enabled those others to exploit for their own benefits not only the wealth of the country, but also the energy of our people, thereby arresting the mental development of our people.

9. Less than ten years ago the most prominent and explosive political issues which faced the people of Uganda had in reality, and in practical terms, nothing to do with the people as such. The issues were "The form of government suitable for an independent Uganda" and "Who was to be the Head of State on the achievement of Independence?" These issues were made to appear as of national importance, not because when solutions were found they would advance the lot of the common man, but because the feudalists, on account of their hold on the people, saw Independence as a threat to their then privileged positions and sought to make these positions synonymous with the interests

of the common man. It cannot be denied that the then privileged positions of the feudalists were a barrier to the full and effective participation of the common man in the Government of Independent Uganda.
The feudalists wanted to continue to rule as they used to before the
coming of the British and they did not want the common man to have
a say in the shaping of the destiny of an independent Uganda. That situation, however, is no longer with us. Uganda is now a Republic. We
hold it as the inalienable right of the people that they must be masters
of their own destiny and not servants of this or that man; that they
must, as citizens of an Independent Republic, express their views as
freely as possible within the laws of their country, made, not in separate Parliaments, but in one Parliament in which the people as a whole
have an equal say through their representatives.

10. The Republican status, therefore, has taken Uganda further towards the goal of full Uhuru. It must not be accepted, however, that
our new status by itself is sufficient, or that it has removed exploitation
and has brought full Uhuru. We realise that it is, by itself, an advance
towards the goal of full Uhuru, but because we are also convinced that
more has yet to be done, this Charter has been adopted, and its Strategy is, in our view, a logical development from the fact that we have
been moving away from the hold of feudal power since 1966. For so
long as that feudal power was a factor in the politics and the economy
of Uganda, it could not be disregarded. Thus the reason for this Charter. It must also be noted that in a society in which feudalism is an important and major political and economic factor, that society cannot
escape being Rightist in its internal and external policies. With the removal of the feudal factor from our political and economic life, we
need to do two things. First, we must not allow the previous position of
the feudalists to be filled by neo-feudalists. Secondly, we must move
away from circumstances which may give birth to neo-feudalism or
generate feudalistic mentality.

11. The Move to the Left is the creation of a new political culture
and a new way of life, whereby the people of Uganda as a whole—
their welfare and their voice in the National Government and in other
local authorities—are paramount. It is, therefore, both anti-feudalism
and anti-capitalism.

12. In 1968, the U.P.C. Delegates' Conference passed the following
resolution on the important matter of nation-building:—

"NOTE with deep satisfaction the liquidation of anti-national and
feudal forces, and the introduction of the Republican Constitution.

THANK the leaders of the Party and the Government on initiating
the revolution for economic, social and political justice.

RECOGNISE that the most important task confronting the Party and the Government today is that of nation-building.

RESOLVE that its entire human and material resources be committed in that task of nation-building.

DIRECT that the National Council of the Party do examine ways and means for active involvement of all institutions, State and private, in joint endeavour with the Party to achieve and serve a nation united and one".

13. We have no doubt whatsoever about the high priority which must be given to nation-building, and we are fully aware that there may be many people in this country who are either uninformed or misguided, who have not yet come to appreciate the importance of nation-building. We, therefore, consider it our responsibility to inform the uninformed, and to guide the misguided. It is also our responsibility to enlighten the people about the necessity of all the institutions in this country and the people as a whole being actively involved in the joint endeavour to serve the Nation.

14. When the U.P.C. proposes a policy or programme on behalf and for the benefit of the people of Uganda, the meaning of the phrase "people of Uganda" is always clear and definite. It is, One People under One Government in One Country. Accordingly, over the seven years of Independence the Party has indicated more than sufficiently that to belong to a clan, a tribe, a linguistic group, a region or a religion, is neither an advantage nor a disadvantage to any citizen of Uganda. The fact of being a citizen of Uganda, however, is a decided advantage which gives him fundamental rights and freedoms, and affords him full opportunity to exercise his social duties and obligations to his clan, tribe, region or religion, save as forbidden by laws passed by Parliament. These laws, as it is clearly stated in Principle 6 of the U.P.C. Aims and Objects, and in the Republican Constitution, are desirable so as to enable all citizens to enjoy their fundamental rights and freedoms without infringing upon the rights and freedoms of any other citizens to do the same.

15. In seven years of Independence we have experienced that the mass of our people are law-abiding citizens, who believe in the security of their families, stable conditions around their homes and throughout Uganda; who appreciate the need for expanding economic and social services, and who are desirous to work hard to improve their conditions of living and participate fully in the political control of governmental institutions. This experience is in contrast to another, namely, the desire of foreign powers and institutions to choose leaders for us, to influence the policies of the Government of Uganda to the benefit of foreign interests, and to use the sons and daughters of Uganda to advance these

interests. In our experience we have not found a single instance where foreign interests have sought to use the masses of the people to serve the interests of foreigners. We have, however, had abundant instances where the well-to-do, the educated and the feudal elements have been bought to serve the interests of foreigners. This kind of corruption of the intentions and frustration of the wishes of the people may be tolerated in countries where nationhood has been firmly established, illiteracy is almost unknown and other factional issues do not play any important part in elections or in formulation of Government policies. Uganda has not yet reached that stage of development; but even when we eventually reach that stage we will not tolerate, on principle, the corruption of the intentions and the frustration of the wishes of the people.

16. One of the most important considerations facing the people of Uganda, in the view of the U.P.C., is the future of the youth. We have only to look at the figures of all the young men and women in the Universities, in the Secondary Schools, in other institutes of learning and in the Primary Schools, to speak nothing of those who are at home, to realise that these are citizens of Uganda who are being prepared to shoulder responsibilities of consolidating further the political independence we now have, and to open more and more avenues which will lead the people of Uganda to real, economic and social independence.

17. If, here in Uganda, we adopt the policy of developing our country and preparing our youth within the confines of tribal governments, tribal parliaments and traditions, and as tools of sectionalism and factionalism of any kind, we would neither be making a contribution to the African Revolution, nor would we be giving these young people what is within our power to give them—that is, the broadening of their horizon to look at the whole of Uganda and not just a part of it as the centre and platform of their operations. It is our duty and responsibility to accept these young people irrespective of the corner of Uganda which may be their birthplace. The whole of Uganda is their inheritance and we must not deny either all of them or a majority of them or even a minority of them, that heritage. They are growing in a different world—a world very different from the world in which those who faced the British when they first imposed colonial rule in Uganda lived. Young people are growing in a world which is becoming smaller and smaller, and for us to make that world even smaller by inducing them, directly or indirectly, to become the exponents of tribal Herrenvolk principles, religious bigotry and fanaticism and feudalistic selfishness, and capitalistic rapacities would be to do a disservice that Africa will never forget, and a disservice that will certainly reduce the mental ca-

pacities of our young men and women. Uganda cannot afford to be so heartless to her youth.

18. It is not only the youth whom we must think about. Those who are grown up are equally important. Even the old and the infirm are important. The tribal confines and security are no longer strong enough to give them the requirements of modern times, or to protect their lives and property or to give that important recognition of human dignity and citizenship of a sovereign State.

19. We reiterate the fact that the struggle for Independence was not a one-tribe struggle, nor was it a struggle confined to people professing one religion. The colonial power heard voices from all corners of Uganda. The struggle, however, was not that different parts of Uganda should return to the days of tribal quarrels, disunity and wars, but to move to the new era wherein all people of Uganda are one and the country is one, and to regain our dignity as human beings.

20. We recognise that ours is a society in transition. We want to bring out our considered assessment of the present situation as the starting point for our adoption of the Move to the Left Strategy set out in this Charter. Uganda is a country which is already independent politically. It is that status that makes it the responsibility of the people of Uganda to shape their destiny. Before the 9th of October, 1962, the people of Uganda did not have that responsibility or power. The sixty-nine years of colonial rule, during which an alien way of life was not only planted but also took root, resulted in the phenomenon of developing our human and material resources to bear the imprint of this factor in our society. What was planted in Uganda during the era of British protectorate appeared in the eyes and minds of our people as the final word in perfection regarding the development of our material resources and human relationship. Consequently, both before and after Independence, our people have been living in a society in which an alien way of life has been embedded. The result has been that most of our people do not look in to the country for ideas to make life better in Uganda, but always look elsewhere to import ideas which may be perfectly suitable in some other society but certainly unfitting in a society like ours. The more we pursue that course, the more we artificially organise our society, our material resources and human relationship, and the more we perpetuate a foreign way of life in our country.

21. We cannot afford to build two nations within the territorial boundaries of Uganda: one rich, educated, African in appearance but mentally foreign, and the other, which constitutes the majority of the population, poor and illiterate. We do not consider that all aspects of the African traditional life are acceptable as socialistic. We do not, for

instance, accept that belonging to a tribe should make a citizen a tool to be exploited by and used for the benefit of tribal leaders. Similarly, we do not accept that feudalism, though not inherently something peculiar to Africa or to Uganda, is a way of life which must not be disturbed because it has been in practice for centuries. With this background, we are convinced that Uganda has to choose between two alternatives. We either perpetuate what we inherited, in which case we will build on a most irrational system of production and distribution of wealth based on alien methods, or we adopt a programme of action based on the realities of our country. The choice adopted in this Charter is the latter. We must move away from the ways of the past to the avenues of reality, and reject travelling along a road where the signpost reads: "Right of admittance is belief in the survival of the fittest". To us, every citizen of Uganda must survive and we are convinced that Uganda has to move to the Left as a unit. Conditions must be created to enable the fruits of Independence to reach each and every citizen without some citizens enjoying privileged positions or living on the sweat of their fellow citizens.

22. The emergence and growth of a priviledged group in our society, together with the open possibilities of the group assuming the powers of the feudal elements, are not matters of theory and cannot be disregarded with a wave of the hand. Nor should the same be looked at from a doctrinaire approach. It is for this reason that in this Charter we do not intend to play with words, even if those words have meanings, such as "capitalism" or "Communism". We are convinced that from the standpoint of our history, not only our educational system inherited from pre-Independence days, but also the attitudes to modern commerce and industry and the position of a person in authority, in or outside Government, are creating a gap between the well-to-do on the one hand and the mass of the people on the other. As the years go by, this gap will become wider and wider. The Move to the Left Strategy of this Charter aims at bridging the gap and arresting this development.

23. We identify two circumstances in which the emergence of a privileged class can find comfort and growth. First, there is our education system which aims at producing citizens whose attitude to the uneducated and to their way of life leads them to think of themselves as the masters and the uneducated as their servants. Secondly, the opportunities for self-employment in modern commerce and industry and to gain employment in Government and in other sectors of the economy are mainly open to the educated few; but instead of these educated few doing everything possible within their powers for the less educated, a tendency is developing where whoever is in business or in Government

looks to his immediate family and not to the country as a whole in opening these opportunities. The existence of these circumstances could lead to actual situations of corruption, nepotism and abuse of responsibility. It is unrealistic for anyone to believe that the answer to such situations lies in the strict application of the laws. Much as the laws might assist in preventing such crimes being committed against the nation, it is our view that the answer lies in tackling the roots of the problem, namely, to generate a new attitude to life and to wealth, and new attitudes in exercising responsibilities. Our country is fortunate in that these problems have not taken deep roots and the crimes which they generate are universally condemned by the society. If we do not take initial effective measures to change the course of events at this stage of our history, it may be too late to avoid violence in future years. It is because we are convinced that this is the right moment to reorientate our course that we have adopted the measures set out in the Move to the Left Strategy of this Charter.

24. The ordinary citizen of Uganda associates economic development of this country with a rise in his own private real income. This income may accrue to him from self-employment, *i.e.,* farming, fishing, cattle-keeping, or paid employment. What is of crucial importance to the ordinary citizen is that Government should provide him with certain social services free and that his income should rise faster than the cost of living, so that he can afford more goods and services for his own use. But there are also three other major dimensions of economic development which must concern our Government. These are: the distribution of the national income, the structure of the economy and the creation of institutions conducive to further development and consistent with the Socialist Strategy outlined in this Charter.

25. Let us begin with the examination of the distribution of income in our country. It is obvious that for development to take place, there should be a rise in the average income per head (*per capita* income). This can only occur if the rate of growth of national income exceeds the rate of population growth. For this reason our Government must always place great emphasis on the fast rate of growth of the economy and the national income. Indeed, increased production and wealth is one of the three major goals of the current Plan ("Work for Progress") 1966–71. We are fully convinced that this emphasis is not misplaced, since raising the standard of living of the Common Man in Uganda must be the major aim of our Government. It is possible, however, for the overall rate of growth to rise without affecting large masses of the population. This is a danger that we must guard against. We must not, either because of inertia, corruption, or academic love for the principle

of the theory of free enterprise, fail to take bold corrective measures against this danger.

26. There is also the danger that economic development could be unevenly distributed as between regions of the country. The fact is that there is no automatic mechanism within our economic system to ensure an equitable distribution of the national income among persons, groups of persons or regions. We need only to stretch our eyes not the distant future but to the years immediately ahead of us, taking into account the fact of our present expanding economy, to recognise that if no new strategy is adopted now, inequalities in the distribution of income will change dramatically the status of millions of our people, and might result in our having two nations—one fabulously rich and living on the sweat of the other, and the other living in abject poverty—both living in one country. In such a situation, political power will be in the hands of the rich and the maximum the Government will do for the poor will be paternalism, where the lot of the masses will be not only to serve the well-to-do, but to be thankful on their knees when opportunity arises to eat the crumbs from the high table.

27. The nature of our economy today is such that the resources are not allocated by a central authority. The reality of the situation is that allocation of resources in Uganda today is directly proportionate to the distribution of income. The practical fact which emerges from this can be illustrated in this way. If 5 per cent of the population receive, say, 50 per cent of the national income among them, this small minority possesses the power to command at least half of the productive resources of the country. With so much wealth at their disposal, their consumption habits will affect the whole economy. As it happens, these habits will be characterised by the consumption of luxurious goods not produced in the country but imported from outside, or produced in the country at extremely high cost. If the goods have to be imported, then the bulk of the population must produce for export in order to pay for the import of such luxurious goods. Our argument for a change to make it impossible for such a situation to develop as a feature of Uganda is that the consumption habits of the very rich not only impinge directly on the disposal of one of the very important resources of the country, namely, foreign exchange, but also constitute a negation of the real meaning of our Independence. The crucial point here is that inequitable distribution of income leads directly to non-development of resources which could cater for the consumption needs of the poor, since the masses cannot afford to pay for the goods which would be produced, and instead the economy becomes dependent on exports of primary commodities in order to pay for imports of luxurious goods

for the rich. The end result is a constant problem of unfavourable balance of payments and external debts, and a neglect of the welfare of the Common Man.

28. We must examine the argument in another way. A redistribution of income which puts more purchasing power in the hands of the Common Man, who constitutes the greatest proportion of the population, would give an impetus to the development of local industries. This is because the needs of the masses are unlikely to be of the luxurious type. As the mass of the people of Uganda begin to acquire higher and higher incomes, they would in all probability acquire more and more of the goods produced in their country; but to open the door only to the rich to buy at high prices any quantity of imported goods and locally produced goods at high costs, which put them beyond the means of the Common Man, is to disregard the existence of the mass of the population or to acknowledge their servitude to the rich.

29. The heart of the Move to the Left can be simply stated. It is both political and economic. It is the basic belief of the Uganda People's Congress that political power must be vested in the majority of the people and not the minority. It is also the fundamental belief of the Uganda People's Congress that economic power should be vested in the majority and not in the minority, as is the case at present. It is, therefore, our firm resolution that political and economic power must be vested in the majority.

30. The structure of Uganda's economy is characterised by: an excessive dependence on agriculture as a source of income, employment and foreign exchange; a heavy dependence on exports based on two major export crops; heavy dependence on imports, particularly of manufactured products; and the limited participation of Ugandans in the modern industrial and commercial sectors of the economy. It has therefore been the policy of the Party to diversify the economy to make it less dependent on foreign trade, to promote the participation of citizens in all sectors of the economy, and the Move to the Left is intended to intensify these efforts through collective ownership, viz. Co-operatives and State enterprises.

31. Economic development demands, among other things, capital (money). We recognise that a country cannot depend upon capital from outside because this, apart from being unpredictable, is subject to variation by various factors and has always got strings attached to it. We are convinced from experience that this country is capable of generating sufficient capital out of the savings of all the citizens. We therefore propose that a suitable scheme where savings of the citizens can be

effectively tapped and correctly channelled into further economic development should be introduced.

32. To this effect we propose that the system be based on the present basis of calculation upon which wage-earners pay contributions of a fraction of their earnings into the Social Security Fund. The basis of the calculation of that part of the income of the wage-earners that goes into contributions to the National Social Security Scheme should apply proportionately to the income earned by all other persons, either by way of salary or other method of determinable income. With the exception of the wage-earner who is already required by law to make contribution to the National Social Security Scheme, all other persons will either pay direct or have it deducted and paid into an approved scheme.

33. The present banking institutions cater mainly for the needs of commerce and industry. It is not possible for the peasants, who constitute the majority of our population, to advance their lot through financial assistance in the form of loans from these commercial banks. Even if they were to do so, they would spend a substantial part of, if not, their entire income, in paying back these loans. It is, therefore, imperative that a new banking system, to be known as the Co-operative Bank, be established to cater solely for the peasants who are members of the Co-operative Unions. The policy of such a Bank should include a provision to the effect that the Co-operative Union of the person applying for a loan from the Bank gives a guarantee and takes over administration of the repayment of the loan, and that the loan in the majority of cases should be given in relation to what the applicant is already doing.

34. We reiterate the fact that there can be no investment unless somebody first makes a corresponding saving. This applies equally to local and overseas investment.

35. With regard to local investment, we have now proposed a scheme for compulsory saving in a number of schemes, and the establishment of Co-operative Banks.

36. With regard to foreign investment, we fully realise that foreign investors want guarantees, and we consider that the Foreign Investment (Protection) Act covers this adequately and generously. Much as we appreciate the need to attract foreign investment, we are fully convinced that the economic future of this country depends on local capital formation and local savings and investment.

37. In future we would wish to see foreign investments coming into Uganda under the Foreign Investment (Protection) Act engaging in priority projects and not projects decided solely on the basis of profit-

ability. Similarly, local investments should be controlled in such a way that they are made in priority projects determined by the needs of the economic development of the country.

38. In our Move to the Left Strategy, we affirm that the guiding economic principle will be that the means of production and distribution must be in the hands of the people as a whole. The fulfilment of this principle may involve nationalisation of the enterprises privately owned.

39. The issue of nationalisation has already been determined and therefore it is a settled matter. It was in the 1962 Constitution, as it is in the Republican Constitution of 1967. Therefore no citizen or person in private enterprise should entertain the idea that the Government of Uganda cannot, whenever it is desirable in the interests of the people, nationalise any or all privately-owned enterprises, mailo and freehold land and all productive assets or property, at any time, for the benefit of the people. The Party, therefore, directs the Government to work along these lines.

40. In this Charter, we lay emphasis first on the people being given massive education in operating and establishing institutions controlled, not by individuals, but by the people collectively. This massive education should aim at reorientating the attitudes of the people towards co-operation in the management of economic institutions, and away from individual and private enrichment. We therefore direct the Government to give education to the people to acquire new attitudes in the management of our economy where collective exploitation of our resources to the benefit of all will take the place of individual and private enterprise aimed at enriching a few.

41. We must move in accordance with the principles of democracy. That is the way that brings human progress. Ideas must be generated and sifted, and citizens—educated or not—must be able to think for themselves, learn to work together, and to participate in the processes of governing themselves.

42. The Move to the Left involves government by discussion. This Charter and the principles enunciated herein should be widely disseminated through mass media of communication, and discussed by study groups and individuals all over the country.

43. Principles are a good thing but they are no substitute for hard work. The success of the Charter demands full commitment of leaders to its realisation, acceptance by the mass of the population, and hard work by all.

44. The adoption of the Charter provides an opportunity to the Common Man for the realisation of the full fruits of his labour and of social justice.

Bibliography

PRIMARY SOURCES

Government of Uganda

Adoko, Akena. *Uganda Crisis.* Kampala: African Publishers, 1968.

Amin, Idi. *Speech by His Excellency the President of the Republic of Uganda General Idi Amin Dada at the Commonwealth Heads of State and Government Meeting Held at Ottawa, August, 1973.* Entebbe: Government Printer, 1973.

———. *Speeches by His Excellency the President Idi Amin Dada.* Entebbe: Government Printer, 1972.

Bank of Uganda Quarterly Bulletin, III, No. 1 (December 1970).

The Birth of the Second Republic. Entebbe: Government Printer, 1971.

Budget Speech Delivered at Uganda International Conference Centre, Kampala, on Wednesday, 12th Day of June, 1974 by the Minister of State for Finance, Hon. M. S. Kiingi. Entebbe: Government Printer, 1974.

Commission of Inquiry into the Missing Americans Messrs. Stroh and Siedle Held at the Conference Room, Parliament House, Kampala. Entebbe: Government Printer, 1972.

Embassy of the Republic of Uganda, Washington, D.C. *Uganda Newsletter,* IV, No. 8 (August 1972).

Facts about Uganda. Entebbe: Government Printer, 1968.

Industrial Charter: Sessional Paper No. 1 of 1964. Entebbe: Government Printer, 1964.

Ministry of Economic Affairs, Statistics Branch. *Uganda Census 1959: The African Population.* Entebbe: Government Printer, 1963.

Ministry of Foreign Affairs. *Uganda Quarterly Bulletin,* I, No. 1 (January 1974).

Obote, Milton A. "Address to African Summit Conference." Addis Ababa, May 1963. Mimeographed.

———. *The Common Man's Charter with Appendices.* Entebbe: Government Printer, 1970.

———. "Election of the President of the Republic: Report to the Delegates Conference." Mbale, December 18, 1970. Mimeographed.

———. "The Footsteps of Uganda's Revolution," *East Africa Journal,* V, No. 10 (October 1968), 7–13.

———. "His Excellency the President's Speech from the Chair to the Na-

tional Assembly on the 4th November, 1963." Kampala, 1963. Mimeo-
graphed.
———. "Memorandum by the President of the UPC, Dr. A. Milton Obote, to
the Delegates Conference to Be Held at Mbale on 28th August, 1970."
Kampala: Uganda Peoples Congress Headquarters, August 21, 1970.
———. *Myths and Realities: A Letter to a London Friend*. Kampala: African
Publishers, November 16, 1968.
———. "Policy Proposals for Uganda's Educational Needs," *Mawazo*, II, No.
2 (December 1969), 3–9.
———. "Speech Delivered to the Annual Conference of the Uganda Educa-
tion Association August 14, 1963." Jinja, 1963. Mimeographed.
*The Public Accounts of the Republic of Uganda for the Year Ended 30th
June, 1969*. Entebbe: Government Printer, 1970.
*The Report of the Committee on Africanisation of Commerce and Industry
in Uganda*. Entebbe: Government Printer, 1968.
Report of the Visitation Committee to Makerere University College. En-
tebbe: Government Printer, 1970.
1970 Statistical Abstract. Entebbe: Government Printer, 1970.
1971 Statistical Abstract. Entebbe: Government Printer, 1971.
Uganda Peoples Congress. *Policy Statement*. Kampala: Uganda Peoples
Congress, 1962.
Uganda: The Second Year of the Second Republic. Entebbe: Government
Printer, 1973.
Uganda's Third Five Year Plan 1971/2–1975/6. Entebbe: Government
Printer, 1972.

International Organizations

"Addendum to Open Letter to General Idi Amin." Supplement to *Violations
of Human Rights and the Rule of Law in Uganda*. Geneva: International
Commission of Jurists, June 1974.
"Open Letter to General Idi Amin from Wanume Kibedi, Former Uganda
Foreign Minister (1971–1973), Dated June 21, 1974." Supplement to
Violations of Human Rights and the Rule of Law in Uganda. Geneva:
International Commission of Jurists, June 1974.
Organization of African Unity. *Basic Documents of the Organization of
African Unity*. Addis Ababa: Secretariat of the Organization of African
Unity, n.d.
United Nations, Department of Economic and Social Affairs. *Multinational
Corporations in World Development*. ST/ECA/190. New York: United
Nations, 1973.
Violations of Human Rights and the Rule of Law in Uganda. Geneva: In-
ternational Commission of Jurists, May 1974.

Newspapers and Periodicals
Africa, London
The African Recorder, New Delhi

Africa Research Bulletin, Exeter, Devon (Political, Cultural and Social Series; Economic, Financial and Technical Series)
The Daily Nation, Nairobi
The Economist, London
The Financial Times, London
Inside East Africa, Nairobi
The Los Angeles Times
The New York Times
The Observer, London
The People, Kampala
The Quarterly Economic Review, London
The Reporter, Nairobi
The Standard, Dar es Salaam
The Star, Johannesburg
The Sunday Nation, Nairobi
The Sunday Post, Nairobi
The Times, London
The Uganda Argus, Kampala
The Voice of Uganda, Kampala

SECONDARY SOURCES

Books and Monographs

Amin, Samir. *Accumulation on a World Scale: A Critique of the Theory of Underdevelopment.* New York: Monthly Review Press, 1974.

Andemicael, Berhanykun. *Peaceful Settlement among African States: Roles of the United Nations and the Organization of African Unity.* New York: United Nations Institute for Training and Research, 1972.

Apter, David E., ed. *Ideology and Discontent.* New York: The Free Press, 1964.

———. *The Political Kingdom in Uganda: A Study in Bureaucratic Nationalism.* Princeton: Princeton University Press, 1961.

Ashford, Douglas. *Ideology and Participation.* Beverly Hills: Sage Publications, 1973.

Barnett, Homer G. *Innovation: The Basis of Cultural Change.* New York: McGraw Hill, 1953.

Beattie, John. *The Nyoro State.* Oxford: Clarendon Press, 1971.

Bienen, Henry. *Tanzania: Party Transformation and Economic Development.* Princeton: Princeton University Press, 1967.

Booth, Richard. *The Armed Forces of African States, 1970.* London: Institute for Strategic Studies, 1970.

Brett, E. A. *Colonialism and Underdevelopment in East Africa: The Politics of Economic Change, 1919–1939.* New York: NOK Publishers, 1973.

Carter, Gwendolen M., ed. *National Unity and Regionalism in Eight African States.* Ithaca: Cornell University Press, 1966.

——, ed. *Politics in Africa: Seven Cases.* New York: Harcourt, Brace, and World, 1966.

Cliffe, Lionel, and John S. Saul, ed. *Socialism in Tanzania: An Interdisciplinary Reader.* 2 vols. Dar es Salaam: East African Publishing House, 1972.

Driberg, Jack Herbert. *The Lango: A Nilotic Tribe of Uganda.* London: T. F. Unwin, 1923.

Dumont, René. *False Start in Africa,* trans. Phyllis Nauts Ott. Worcester: Ebenezer Bayles, 1966.

Durkheim, Emile. *Les formes élémentaires de la vie religieuse.* Paris: Aclan, 1912.

Easton, David. *A Systems Analysis of Political Life.* New York: John Wiley, 1965.

[Elliott, Charles.] *Employment and Income Distribution in Uganda.* Norwich: University of East Anglia Development Studies Discussion Paper, n.d.

Erikson, Erik H. *Young Man Luther: A Study in Psychoanalysis and History.* New York: Norton, 1962.

Evans, David R. *Teachers as Agents of National Development: A Case Study of Uganda.* New York: Praeger, 1971.

Falk, Richard A. *Legal Order in a Violent World.* Princeton: Princeton University Press, 1968.

Fanon, Frantz. *Toward the African Revolution.* New York: Monthly Review Press, 1967.

First, Ruth. *The Barrel of a Gun: Political Power in Africa and the Coup D'Etat.* London: Penguin Press, 1970.

Fitch, Bob, and Mary Oppenheimer. *Ghana: End of an Illusion.* New York: Monthly Review Press, 1966.

Franck, Thomas M. *East African Unity through Law.* New Haven: Yale University Press, 1964.

Frey, Frederick W. *The Turkish Political Elite.* Cambridge, Mass.: M.I.T. Press, 1965.

Fromm, Erich. *Escape From Freedom.* New York: Holt, Rinehart, and Winston, 1960.

Geertz, Clifford, ed. *Old Societies and New States: The Quest for Modernity in Asia and Africa.* New York: The Free Press, 1963.

Gerth, H. H., and C. Wright Mills. *From Max Weber: Essays in Sociology.* New York: Oxford University Press, 1946.

Ghai, Dharam P., ed. *Portrait of a Minority: Asians in East Africa.* Nairobi: Oxford University Press, 1970.

Goldthorpe, J. E. *An African Elite: Makerere Students 1922–1960.* London: Oxford University Press, 1965.

——, and F. B. Wilson. *Tribal Maps of East Africa and Zanzibar.* Kampala: East Africa Institute of Social Research, 1960.

Grundy, Kenneth W. *Conflicting Images of the Military in Africa.* Nairobi: East African Publishing House, 1968.

——. *Guerrilla Struggle in Africa: An Analysis and Preview.* New York: Grossman Publishers, 1971.

Haas, Ernst B. *Beyond the Nation-State: Functionalism and International Organization.* Stanford: Stanford University Press, 1964.

——. *The Uniting of Europe: Political, Social, and Economic Forces 1950–1957.* Stanford: Stanford University Press, 1958.

Hanreider, William F. *Comparative Foreign Policy: Theoretical Essays.* New York: David McKay, 1971.

Hoffer, Eric. *The True Believer: Thoughts on the Nature of Mass Movements.* New York: New American Library, 1951.

Huntington, Samuel P., ed. *Changing Patterns of Military Politics.* New York: The Free Press, 1962.

——. *Political Order in Changing Societies.* New Haven: Yale University Press, 1968.

Hyden, Goran. *Political Development in Rural Tanzania: TANU Yajenga Nchi.* Nairobi: East African Publishing House, 1969.

Ibingira, Grace S. K. *The Forging of an African Nation: The Political and Constitutional Evolution of Uganda from Colonial Rule to Independence, 1894–1962.* New York: Viking Press, 1972.

Johnson, John J., ed. *The Role of the Military in Underdeveloped Countries.* Princeton: Princeton University Press, 1962.

Kabwegyere, Tarsis B. *The Politics of State Formation: The Nature and Effects of Colonialism in Uganda.* Nairobi: East African Literature Bureau, 1974.

Kiwanuka, Semakula. *A History of Buganda: From the Foundation of the Kingdom to 1900.* New York: Africana Publishing Company, 1972.

Ladefoged, Peter, *et al. Language in Uganda.* London: Oxford University Press, 1972.

Lane, Robert. *Political Ideology: Why the American Common Man Believes What He Does.* New York: The Free Press, 1962.

Lasswell, Harold, and Abraham Kaplan. *Power and Society: A Framework for Political Inquiry.* London: Routledge and Kegan Paul, 1952.

Lauterpacht, H. *Recognition in International Law.* Cambridge: Cambridge University Press, 1947.

Legum, Colin, ed. *Africa Contemporary Record: Annual Survey and Documents 1972–1973.* Vol. V. London: Rex Collings, 1973.

——. *Africa Contemporary Record: Annual Survey and Documents 1973–1974.* Vol. VI. London: Rex Collings, 1974.

——. *Pan-Africanism: A Short Political Guide.* London: Paul Mall Press, 1965.

Lerner, Daniel. *The Passing of Traditional Society: Modernizing the Middle East.* New York: The Free Press, 1958.

Lewis, William H., ed. *French-Speaking Africa: The Search for Identity.* New York: Walker and Company, 1965.

Leys, Colin. *Politicians and Policy: An Essay on Politics in Acholi, Uganda 1962–65.* Nairobi: East African Publishing House, 1967.

290 BIBLIOGRAPHY

290290

———, ed. *Politics and Change in Developing Countries: Studies in the Theory and Practice of Development.* London: Cambridge University Press, 1969.

Lieuwen, Edwin. *Arms and Politics in Latin America.* New York: Praeger, 1961.

Listowel, Judith. *Amin.* Dublin: Irish University Press, 1973.

Lofchie, Michael, ed. *The State of the Nations: Constraints on Development in Independent Africa.* Berkeley: University of California Press, 1971.

Low, Donald Anthony. *Buganda in Modern History.* Berkeley: University of California Press, 1971.

———. *Political Parties in Uganda, 1949–1962.* London: University of London, 1962.

Luttwak, Edward. *Coup D'Etat: A Practical Handbook.* Harmondsworth: Penguin Books, 1968.

McKay, Vernon, ed. *African Diplomacy: Studies in the Determinants of Foreign Policy.* New York: Praeger, 1966.

Mannheim, Karl. *Ideology and Utopia: An Introduction to the Sociology of Knowledge.* London: Routledge and Kegan Paul, 1954.

Martin, David. *General Amin.* London: Faber and Faber, 1974.

Marx, Karl. *A Contribution to the Critique of Political Economy.* Chicago: C. H. Kerr, 1904.

———. *Karl Marx: Selected Works.* Vol. II. New York: International Publishers, 1936.

———, and Friedrich Engels. *The German Ideology.* New York: International Publishers, 1947.

Mazrui, Ali A. *Cultural Engineering and Nation-Building in East Africa.* Evanston: Northwestern University Press, 1972.

———. *On Heroes and Uhuru-Worship: Essays on Independent Africa.* London: Longmans, Green, 1967.

Merton, Robert K. *Social Theory and Social Structure.* New York: The Free Press, 1968.

Morrison, Donald George, *et al.,* ed. *Black Africa: A Comparative Handbook.* New York: The Free Press, 1972.

Mutesa, Sir Edward. *Desecration of My Kingdom.* London: Constable, 1967.

Nyakatura, J. W. *Anatomy of an African Kingdom: A History of Bunyoro-Kitara,* trans. Teopista Muganwa, ed. Godfrey N. Uzoigwe. New York: Doubleday, 1973.

Nye, Joseph. *Pan-Africanism and East African Integration.* Cambridge, Mass: Harvard University Press, 1965.

Nyerere, Julius. *Freedom and Socialism: Uhuru na Ujamaa.* Dar es Salaam: Oxford University Press, 1968.

———. *Freedom and Unity: Uhuru na Umoja.* Dar es Salaam: Oxford University Press, 1967.

Obed, Arieh. *The Bayudaya: A Community of African Jews in Uganda.* Tel Aviv: Occasional Paper, The Shiloah Center for Middle Eastern and African Studies, Tel Aviv University, 1973.

Ogot, B. A., and J. A. Kiernan, ed. *Zamani: A Survey of East African History*. Nairobi: East African Publishing House, 1968.

Olorunsola, Victor A., ed. *The Politics of Cultural Sub-Nationalism*. Garden City: Doubleday, 1972.

Parsons, Talcott. *Structure and Process in Modern Societies*. Glencoe: The Free Press, 1960.

Passin, H., and K. A. B. Jones-Quartey, ed. *Africa: The Dynamics of Change*. Ibadan: Ibadan University Press, 1963.

P'Bitek, Okot. *African Religions in Western Scholarship*. Nairobi: East African Publishing House, 1972.

Plato. *The Republic*, trans. H. D. P. Lee. London: Penguin Books, 1955.

Przeworski, Adam, and Henry Teune. *The Logic of Comparative Social Inquiry*. New York: John Wiley, 1970.

Pye, Lucian W., ed. *Communications and Political Development*. Princeton: Princeton University Press, 1963.

Rogers, Everett M. *Diffusion of Innovations*. New York: The Free Press, 1962.

Rosenau, James N., ed. *International Aspects of Civil Strife*. Princeton: Princeton University Press, 1964.

——, ed. *Linkage Politics: Essays on the Convergence of National and International Systems*. New York: The Free Press, 1969.

Rotberg, Robert I., and Ali A. Mazrui, ed. *Protest and Power in Black Africa*. New York: Oxford University Press, 1970.

The Silent Class Struggle: Tanzanian Studies No. 2. Dar es Salaam: Tanzanian Publishing House, 1973.

Skurnik, W. A. E., ed. *African Political Thought: Lumumba, Nkrumah and Touré*. Vol. V, Nos. 3 and 4. Denver: University of Denver Monograph Series in World Affairs, 1967–1968.

Sorel, Georges. *Reflections on Violence*. Reprint ed., New York: P. Smith, 1941.

Tandon, Yashpal, ed. *Technical Assistance Administration in East Africa*. Stockholm: Dag Hammarskjold Foundation, 1973.

Tawney, R. H. *Religion and the Rise of Capitalism*. New York: New American Library, 1958.

Thomas, Ann Wynen, and A. J. Thomas, Jr. *Non-Intervention: The Law and Its Import on the Americas*. Dallas: Southern Methodist University Press, 1956.

Uzoigwe, Godfrey N. *Revolution and Revolt in Bunyoro-Kitara: Two Studies*. Part 2. London: Longmans, 1970.

Veliz, Claudio, ed. *The Politics of Conformity in Latin America*. London: Oxford University Press, 1967.

Ward, Robert E., and Dankwart A. Rustow, ed. *Political Modernization in Japan and Turkey*. Princeton: Princeton University Press, 1964.

Waxman, Chaim, ed. *The End of Ideology Debate*. New York: Simon and Shuster, 1969.

Weber, Max. *The Protestant Ethic and the Spirit of Capitalism.* London: G. Allen and Unwin, 1948.
——. *The Theory of Social and Economic Organization,* trans. and ed. A. M. Henderson and Talcott Parsons. New York: The Free Press, 1966.
Weeks, Sheldon. *Divergence in Educational Development: The Case of Kenya and Uganda.* New York: Teachers College Press, 1967.
Wellbourn, F. B. *Religion and Politics in Uganda, 1952–1962.* Nairobi: East African Publishing House, 1965.
Whiteley, W. H., ed. *Language Use and Social Change: Multilingualism with Special Reference to Eastern Africa.* London: Oxford University Press, 1971.
Woronoff, Jon. *West African Wager: Houphouet versus Nkrumah.* Metuchen, N.J.: Scarecrow Press, 1972.
Zartman, I. William. *International Relations in the New Africa.* Englewood Cliffs: Prentice Hall, 1969.
Zolberg, Aristide R. *Creating Political Order: The Party States of West Africa.* Chicago: Rand McNally, 1966.

Articles

Ali Picho. "Ideological Commitment and the Judiciary," *Transition,* VII(v), No. 36 (1968), 47–49.
Andrezejewski, Stanislav. "Are Ideas Social Forces?" *American Sociological Review,* XIV, No. 6 (December 1949), 758–64.
Berg, Elliott J. "Socialism and Economic Development in Tropical Africa," *Quarterly Journal of Economics,* LXXVIII, No. 4 (November 1964), 549–73.
Binder, Leonard. "National Integration and Political Development," *American Political Science Review,* LVIII, No. 3 (September 1964), 622–31.
Bonnafé, Pierre, and Michel Carty. "Les idéologies politiques des pays en voie de développement," *Revue Française de Science Politique,* XII, No. 2 (June 1962), 417–25.
Boutros-Ghali, Boutros. "The Addis Ababa Charter," *International Conciliation,* No. 54 (Janaury 1964), pp. 1–62.
"The Brushfire in East Africa," *Africa Report,* IX, No. 2 (February 1964), 21–25.
Cohen, D. L., and J. Parson. "The Uganda Peoples Congress Branch and Constituency Elections of 1970," *Journal of Commonwealth Political Studies,* XI, No. 1 (March 1973), 46–66.
Elliott, J. C. Howard. "The Uganda Budget 1971–72: An Economic Evaluation," *The Uganda Economic Journal,* I, No. 1 (December 1971), 7–30.
Emmanuel, Arghiri. "White Settler Colonialism and the Myth of Investment Imperialism," *New Left Review,* No. 73 (May–June 1972), pp. 35–57.
Engholm, G. F., and Ali A. Mazrui. "Violent Constitutionalism in Uganda," *Government and Opposition,* II, No. 4 (July–October 1967), 585–99.

Feit, Edward. "Pen, Sword, and People: Military Regimes in the Formation of Political Institutions," *World Politics*, XXV, No. 2 (January 1973), 251–73.

Gershenberg, Irving. "Banking in Uganda Since Independence," *Economic Development and Cultural Change*, XX, No. 3 (April 1972), 504–23.

———. "A Further Comment on the Uganda Coup," *Journal of Modern African Studies*, X, No. 4 (December 1972), 638–39.

———. "Slouching Towards Socialism: Obote's Uganda," *African Studies Review*, XV, No. 1 (April 1972), 79–95.

Gingyera-Pincywa, A. G. G. "Prospects for a One-Party System in Uganda," *East Africa Journal*, V, No. 10 (October 1968), 15–23.

Greene, Fred. "Toward Understanding Military Coups," *Africa Report*, XI, No. 6 (February 1966), 10, 11, 14.

Grundy, Kenneth W. "Recent Contributions to the Study of African Political Thought," *World Politics*, XVII, No. 4 (July 1966), 674–89.

Gupta, Anirudha. "The Asians in East Africa: Problems and Prospects," *International Studies*, X, No. 3 (January 1969), 270–302.

Gutteridge, William. "Why Does an African Army Take Power?" *Africa Report*, XV, No. 7 (October 1970), 18–21.

Huntington, Samuel P. "Political Development and Political Decay," *World Politics*, XVII, No. 3 (April 1965), 386–430.

Jacob, Abel. "Israel's Military Aid to Africa, 1960–66," *Journal of Modern African Studies*, IX, No. 2 (August 1971), 165–87.

Kapil, Ravi L. "On the Conflict Potential of Inherited Boundaries in Africa," *World Politics*, XVIII, No. 4 (July 1966), 656–73.

Keohane, Robert O. and Joseph S. Nye, Jr., ed. "Transnational Relations and World Politics," *International Organization*, XXV, No. 3 (Summer 1971).

Kiwanuka, M. S. M. "Nationality and Nationalism in Africa: The Uganda Case," *Canadian Journal of African Studies*, IV, No. 2 (Spring 1970), 229–47.

Klinghoffer, Arthur Jay. "Israel in Africa: The Strategy of Aid," *Africa Report*, XVII, No. 4 (April 1972), 12–14.

Leys, Colin. "Present Relations between the States of East Africa," *International Journal*, XX, No. 4 (Autumn 1965), 510–23.

Lipjhart, Arend. "Comparative Politics and the Comparative Method," *American Political Science Review*, LX, No. 3 (September 1971), 682–93.

Lofchie, Michael. "Uganda Coup: Class Action by the Military," *Journal of Modern African Studies*, X, No. 1 (May 1972), 19–35.

Lowenstein, Karl. "The Role of Ideologies in Political Change," *International Social Science Bulletin*, V, No. 1 (1953), 51–74.

MacRae, Donald. "Nkrumahism: Past and Future of an Ideology," *Government and Opposition*, I, No. 4 (December 1966), 535–45.

Mayanja, Abu. Letter to the Editor, *Transition*, VII(vi), No. 37 (1968), 14, 15.

Mazrui, Ali A. "Anti-Militarism and Political Militancy in Tanzania," *Journal of Conflict Resolution*, XII, No. 3 (September 1968), 269–84.

——. "Leadership in Africa: Obote of Uganda," *International Journal*, XXV, No. 3 (Summer 1970), 538–64.

——. "The Lumpen Proletariat and the Lumpen Militariat: African Soldiers as a New Middle Class," *Political Studies*, XXI, No. 1 (March 1973), 1–12.

Mittelman, James H. "The Development of Post-Colonial African Regionalism and the Formation of the OAU," *Kroniek Van Afrika*, XI, No. 2 (June 1971), 83–105.

——. "The Roots of Ethnic Conflict," *Journal of International Affairs*, XXVII, No. 1 (Spring 1973), 133–37.

Mujaju, Akiiki B. "The Demise of the UPCYL and the Rise of NUYO in Uganda," *African Review*, III, No. 2 (June 1973), 291–307.

Mullins, Willard A. "On the Concept of Ideology in Political Science," *American Political Science Review*, LXVI, No. 2 (June 1972), 498–510.

Needler, Martin C. "The Political Development of Mexico," *American Political Science Review*, LV, No. 2 (June 1961), 308–12.

Nelson, Daniel. "Newspapers in Uganda," *Transition*, VIII(iv), No. 35 (February–March 1968), 29–33.

Nkrumah, Kwame. "African Socialism Revisited," *African Forum*, I, No. 3 (Winter 1966), 3–9.

Nordlinger, Eric A. "Soldiers in Mufti: The Impact of Military Rule upon Economic and Social Change in Non-Western States," *American Political Science Review*, LXIV, No. 4 (December 1970), 1131–48.

Oberschall, Anthony. "Communications, Information and Aspirations in Rural Uganda," *Journal of Asian and African Studies*, IV, No. 1 (January 1969) 30–50.

——. "Rising Expectations and Political Turmoil," *Journal of Development Studies*, VI, No. 1 (October 1969), 5–22.

Patel, Dhiru. "Radio and Television in Uganda," *Vidura*, VIII, No. 2 (May 1971), 185–89.

Pratt, R. C. "Nationalism in Uganda," *Political Studies*, IX, No. 2 (June 1961), 157–78.

Proctor, J. H., Jr. "The Effort to Federate East Africa: A Post-Mortem," *Political Quarterly*, XXXVII, No. 1 (January–March 1966), 46–69.

Pye, Lucian W. "The Concept of Political Development," *Annals of the American Academy of Political and Social Science*, CCCLVIII (March 1965), 1–13.

Ryan, Selwyn D. "Electoral Engineering in Uganda," *Mawazo*, II, No. 4 (December 1970), 3–12.

——. "Economic Nationalism and Socialism in Uganda," *Journal of Commonwealth Political Studies*, X, No. 2 (July 1973), 140–58.

Sartori, Giovanni. "Politics, Ideology, and Belief Systems," *American Political Science Review*, LXIII, No. 2 (June 1969), 398–411.

Scott, William. "Empirical Assessment of Values and Ideologies," *American Sociological Review*, XXIV, No. 3 (June 1959), 299–310.

Tandon, Yashpal. "Military Coups and Inter-African Diplomacy," *Africa Quarterly*, VI, No. 4 (January–March 1967), 278–84.

Tribe, Michael. "Uganda 1971: An Economic Background," *Mawazo*, III, No. 1 (June 1971), 15–25.

"The Uganda Army: Nexus of Power," *Africa Report*, XI, No. 9 (December 1966), 37–39.

Uzoigwe, Godfrey N. "Kabalega and the Making of a New Kitara," *Tarikh*, III, No. 2 (1970), 5–22.

———. "Political Development in Uganda," *Conch Review of Books*, I, No. 2 (June 1973), 34–43.

Wallerstein, Immanuel. "African Unity Reassessed," *Africa Report*, XI, No. 4 (April 1966), 41–46.

Wasserman, Gary. "The Research of Politics; The Politics of Research," *East Africa Journal*, VII, No. 11 (November 1970), 12–14.

Young, M. Crawford. "The Obote Revolution," *Africa Report*, XI, No. 6 (June 1966), 8–14.

Young, Oran R. "Intervention and International Systems," *Journal of International Affairs*, XXII, No. 2 (1968), 177–87.

Zartman, I. William. "Africa as a Subordinate State System in International Relations," *International Organization*, XIII, No. 3 (Summer 1967), 545–64.

Unpublished Materials

Barnes, Samuel. "Ideology and the Organization of Conflict: On the Relationship between Political Thought and Behavior." Paper presented to the annual meeting of the American Political Science Association, Washington, D.C., September 1965. Mimeographed.

Kiwanuka, S. M. "The Politics of Destruction and the Organization of African Unity." Lecture delivered at Makerere University, Kampala, March 8, 1971.

Mittelman, James Howard. "Ideological Modernization: An Approach to the Study of African Political Systems." Unpublished Ph.D. dissertation, Cornell University, 1971.

Mujaju, Akiiki B. "The Uganda Presidential Debate Reexamined." Revised version of a paper presented to the Universities of East Africa Social Science Conference, Dar es Salaam, December 1970. Mimeographed.

Ryan, Selwyn D. "Economic Nationalism in Uganda and Ghana." Revised version of a paper delivered to the annual meeting of the Canadian Association of African Studies, Quebec City, February 1970. Mimeographed.

Schultheis, Michael J. "Economics and Economic Research in Uganda during the Amin Period." Paper presented to the annual meeting of the African Studies Association, Chicago, November 1974. Mimeographed.

Tandon, Yashpal. "East African Attitudes to Foreign Aid." Paper presented to the Universities of East Africa Social Science Conference, Dar es Salaam, December 1970. Mimeographed.

——, and A. G. G. Gingyera-Pincywa. "Uganda-Sudan Relations and Uganda-Congo Relations, 1962–66: A Comparative Examination." Paper presented to the University of East Africa Social Science Conference, Nairobi, December 1966. Mimeographed.

Willetts, Peter. "The Proposals for a New Ugandan Electoral System." Department of Political Science and Public Administration, Makerere University, Kampala, 1970. Mimeographed.

Zaidi, Juliet H. "The Asian Community in East Africa: Its Geographical Distribution and Economic and Social Characteristics." Unpublished M.A. thesis, University of Denver, 1967.

Index